PURCHASING
IN THE
21ST CENTURY

PURCHASING IN THE 21ST CENTURY

A Guide to State-of-the-Art Techniques and Strategies

Second Edition

JOHN E. SCHORR

John Wiley & Sons, Inc.
New York • Chichester • Weinheim • Brisbane • Singapore • Toronto

Copyright © 1998 by John E. Schorr. All rights reserved.

Published by John Wiley & Sons, Inc.

Published simultaneously in Canada.

This publication is designed to provide accurate and authoritative information in regard to the subject matter covered. It is sold with the understanding that the publisher is not engaged in rendering legal, accounting, or other professional services. If legal advice or other expert assistance is required, the services of a competent professional person should be sought.

Library of Congress Cataloging-in-Publication Data:

Schorr, John E.
    Purchasing in the 21st century: a guide to state-of-the-art
techniques and strategies / John E. Schorr.—2nd ed.
      p. cm.
    Includes bibliographical references and index.
    ISBN 0-471-24094-X (cloth: alk. paper)
    1. Industrial procurement. 2. Just-in-time systems.
    3. Manufacturing resource planning. I. Title.
HD39.5.S364   1998
658.7'2—dc21   97-49412

Printed in the United States of America.

10 9 8 7 6 5 4 3 2 1

This book is dedicated to Edna,
my loving wife of 33 years.
Without her support and encouragement,
this book would not have been completed.

Contents

Preface

This revision includes two new concepts that are being implemented in purchasing departments around the country today. They are Supply Chain Management and Vendor Managed Inventory. Both of these will be employed by purchasing professionals in the 21st century as a way to improve performance and reduce costs.

This book contains practical, how-to information about implementing supplier scheduling and carrying out purchasing in a Manufacturing Resource Planning (MRP II), Just-in-Time (JIT), and Total Quality Control (TQC) environment. It not only provides insights into the basic tools available to the purchasing professional, but focuses on the importance of developing valid schedules and continually improving purchasing performance using MRP II/JIT/TQC.

The Introduction sets the tone for purchasing as we move into the 21st century. Chapter 1 explores the benefits of using supplier scheduling, MRP II, JIT, and TQC. Chapter 2 covers what Supply Chain Management is and how it works. Chapters 3 and 12 discuss what is required of both sides, the supplier and the buyer, in a partnership environment. Chapter 4 describes the basics of supplier scheduling under MRP II, while Chapter 5 explains how the JIT/TQC process applies to purchasing.

After explaining the need for valid schedules and the JIT/TQC concept, the balance of the book covers the specific tools and techniques used to improve performance. Chapter 6 covers the organization needed for supplier scheduling, while Chapter 7 covers the need for supplier quality assurance. Chapter 8 discusses the difference between single-sourcing and sole-sourcing, as well as the reasons for reducing the supplier base. Chapter 9 discusses the need to synchronize with your suppliers' production schedules. It also includes techniques to reduce the freight costs on purchased components in a JIT environment when the buyer is getting smaller, more frequent shipments.

Chapter 10 describes the need for partnerships with suppliers and suggests a set of golden rules. This chapter also covers the use of Electronic Data Interchange (EDI) and the Internet in purchasing. Chapter 11 covers Vendor Managed Inventory and the use of standard ANSI transactions when EDI is employed. Chapter 13 covers special situations, such as buying commodities in short supply and maintenance requirements.

Performance measurements and management information necessary to continuously improve performance, the implementation of supplier scheduling and MRP II/JIT/TQC in purchasing, and supplier education are covered in Chapters 14 and 15. Chapter 16 reinforces the need to create a spark, ignite change, and use the one-less-at-a-time JIT approach.

Introduction

My career in purchasing began in 1965, when I accepted my first job as a junior buyer for a large company. I was responsible for buying several of the items used in the company's Manufacturing Department. During my first week on the job, I was directed to read the Purchasing Policy and Procedures Manual and learn "how to buy." I quickly realized, though, that the buyers around me were not going by the book. The manual did not explain how to expedite, yet expediting seemed to be the normal way of doing business. So for the rest of the 1960s, I learned that the informal system really ran the company. We used "Red Tags" to move the hot orders through the plant and we expedited all day long. When we ordered items, we always were required to buy an economic lot size although the unstated rules said, "Always have some on order and never run out of anything." Not surprisingly, we felt we were understaffed and management just didn't understand our problems.

Then the 1970s came along and I got my first exposure to the use of computers in purchasing. The computer, plus a Materials Requirements Planning (MRP) system, changed my life. The computer always seemed to "screw up" and the inventory on the computer was never right. The company started talking about a formal system, but I still spent most of the day expediting. While the environment changed, the only thing that seemed formalized to me was the shortage list. I don't remember having a shortage list in the 1960s; the planner would bring the traveling requisition or cardex card to me and I would check the status of the part. The computer, which was used for inventory planning, gave us the formal shortage list.

The 1980s saw offshore competitors taking large segments of our markets and causing severe profit pressures. All of a sudden, purchasing professionals had a new set of terms to deal with. These included

Manufacturing Resource Planning, Just-in-Time, Total Quality Control, Electronic Data Interchange, closed-loop systems, performance measurement, and accountability.

And as we entered the 1990s, yet another new set of terms began to appear: Continuous Improvement, Supplier Partnerships, Customer/ Supplier Linkages, and Benchmarking, to name a few. As we close out the 1990s, improved information systems and computer hardware are allowing companies to do Supply Chain Management and Vendor Managed Inventory, and to communicate via the Internet.

Despite the dramatic changes that purchasing has undergone in the more than 30 years since I entered the profession, the typical buyer is still buried in paperwork and caught up in expediting, is still using outmoded systems, and still has little opportunity to do the job better.

This book is designed to help the purchasing professional spearhead an effort for getting out from under the inefficiencies of the informal system and for realizing maximum benefit from the formal tools available today. A 1988 Oliver Wight survey of more than a thousand companies showed how large these benefits can be in purchasing. Those companies that had a Class A MRP II/JIT/TQC system enjoyed an average 96 percent on-time and a *13 percent* annual cost reduction in purchasing! Imagine what a 13 percent purchased cost reduction would do for your company. Helping you achieve such a reduction is what this book is all about.

Chapter One

Purchasing's New Leadership Role

THE HEAT IS ON

Purchasing professionals in companies that lack Manufacturing Resource Planning (MRP II), Just-in-Time (JIT), and Total Quality Control (TQC) may question the value of such tools. They typically ask, "How will they help me do a better job of buying?" The answer is very simple: The tools give them the time and information they need to focus on things that actually save their company money.

Today, because of competitive pressures from the Pacific Rim, manufacturing companies are learning to produce more product with fewer people. In other words, companies are doing more and more purchasing and adding less value internally. This has caused the ratio of purchased dollars to direct labor dollars in the typical manufacturing company to change from a three-to-one ratio in the mid-1980s to a four-to-one ratio in the early 1990s. In other words, for every one dollar spent on direct labor, the company is spending four dollars on direct purchased material. Most companies have a staff of skilled engineers who develop better methods in manufacturing and continue to reduce the labor content. As they succeed, their efforts will drive up the ratio to five to one or six to one by the 21st century. As the direct labor content continues to decline, purchasing professionals will come under greater pressure to find ways of cutting the costs of direct purchased materials.

The traditional way for Purchasing to reduce costs is to buy in larger order quantities. Not only are the prices associated with larger quantities lower, but often so are the freight costs and paperwork costs. But that is exactly the opposite of what the buyer is asked to do in a Just-in-Time environment; one of the goals of Just-in-Time is to drive the inventory down dramatically. Therefore, the buyer will be expected to bring in a high percentage of the items in smaller lot sizes, more frequently delivered. Instead of bringing in items on a monthly basis, weekly receipts will be expected. And in companies used to weekly receipts, daily receipts will be requested. The buyer, therefore, will not only be expected to lower the costs, but he or she will have to do so with smaller lot sizes.

As the company becomes more involved with Just-in-Time and Total Quality Control and starts bringing in items when they are needed, buyers will be under tremendous pressure to get defect-free, quality goods from their suppliers. The reasoning is simple: With little or no inventory on hand, the production line will have to shut down if incoming parts are rejected.

Also, to respond better to the ever-changing needs of customers, Purchasing will be requested to negotiate shorter, more stable lead times with their suppliers. With little or no inventory on the items, the suppliers will have to be able to respond quicker to changes in the marketplace.

Finally, receiving smaller, more frequent deliveries from suppliers increases the pressure to manage freight costs. Unless the buyer is able to effectively control inbound freight costs, the smaller lot sizes could drive up transportation costs and offset any savings associated with the inventory reduction. The buyer will therefore be expected to find creative ways to lower the freight rates.

To recap, the heat will be on Purchasing to reduce costs and increase flexibility while getting smaller lot sizes, more frequent shipments, defect-free quality, shorter, more stable lead times, and less inventory.

The problem buyers experience in the traditional setting is that they are too busy expediting and scaling mountains of paperwork to do an effective job. Even if they could find the time, they typically don't have all the information they need to negotiate the best deal for their company. The net result is that significant opportunities for savings are missed, which in turn means that companies aren't as competitive as they might be and purchasing people find themselves under constant pressure to reduce costs. The good news, though, is that all the tools necessary for creating and taking advantage of cost-saving opportunities, with the MRP II and JIT/TQC plans, are available today.

MRP II is a tried and proven planning and scheduling tool. It provides a rack-and-pinion connection between high-level and detail plans, so that as the business plans change to meet the demands of the marketplace, the detail plans can be changed and executed as well. MRP II closely integrates the purchasing function to all parts of the business, which means that the purchasing professional can provide suppliers with solid schedules of the company's requirements.

JIT is not a tool for minimizing inventory or delivering parts when they're needed, as is commonly believed; rather, it is a methodology that leads to continual improvement by eliminating waste in Manufacturing, Purchasing, and all other departments within the company. As we'll see throughout this book, JIT coupled with TQC has enormous impact on the purchasing process, because it drastically reduces the number of suppliers a company deals with, eliminates a great deal of paperwork, and drives the continuous improvement process toward shorter, more stable lead times, more frequent deliveries, better quality, on-time delivery, and lower costs.

TQC—Total Quality Control—is the flip side of Just-in-Time. TQC is a collection of tools for eliminating defects from design engineering through delivery of the finished product. While JIT is a methodology for eliminating waste and uncovering problems, TQC is a set of tools for solving those problems and making continual improvements. Like JIT, TQC has major implications for the purchasing professional, such as source assurance of quality, which reduces paperwork, simplifies communication, and makes it possible to eliminate the need for separate inspections of incoming materials.

The following chapters will describe each tool in greater detail. First, though, let's imagine what life would be like if your company adopted the winning combination of MRP II and JIT/TQC.

PARADISE FOUND

To appreciate the way things could be in your company, we'll first review the traditional way Purchasing interacts with the rest of the company and its outside suppliers:

Round and Round the Merry-Go-Round

1. The material planner determines the need to buy more materials.

2. Next, the planner sends the buyer a written requisition for the materials to be purchased.

3. Upon receipt of the requisition, the buyer prepares a purchase order (PO) and shoots it off to the appropriate supplier.

4. If the supplier company can fill the order, it sends back an acknowledgment. If not, it typically suggests alternative quantities or delivery dates.

5. If the supplier acknowledges that the order can be filled, the transaction proceeds along a normal course. If the supplier company has proposed an alternative, the buyer has to check with the planner and/or the engineer to see if the alternative fits in with the production schedule. If not, the buyer might then have to recontact the supplier and work out a compromise. Even after a compromise is found, changes in production schedules may alter the requirements for the purchased material. In that case, the planner must again contact the buyer, who must again contact the supplier, and the merry-go-round continues.

The Major Drawbacks

Many purchasing veterans will tell you that the traditional way of buying materials is fraught with problems, the main ones being a lack of valid schedules, poor communication, too much paperwork, too much wasted time and energy, conflicting directions, and teamwork problems. Let's take a closer look at each of these major problem areas.

The first major problem area is the lack of valid schedules. The dates that Purchasing gets on the requisitions are not need dates—when the company needs the first piece for production—but rather replenishment dates—when the company would like to have more product in inventory. Because the company experiences many changes in the schedules due to inaccurate forecasts, customer changes, scrap and rework, engineering changes, new equipment, equipment breakdowns, and so forth, it may want to carry safety stock. For example, the company might choose to have one or two months' supply of purchase material inventory on hand at all times to buffer against production schedule changes. Purchasing in these companies might be charged with buying material to maintain an inventory level, not to support a particular production schedule. If the due date on the requisition is from four to eight weeks before the need date, the buyer knows that the material is being ordered to maintain the safety stock, and so does the supplier. (The situation becomes evident if there are purchase orders two or three weeks past due and the company hasn't run out of the material yet.) As a result, if a problem occurs at the supplier's plant, the buyer typically has no way of knowing exactly when the items are really needed.

The second problem area is communication. The traditional method of purchasing requires intensive communication within the company and between the company and its suppliers. Communication is also extremely inefficient, because no one has the "big picture." Only the planner knows what the company needs, and only the supplier's people know what their company can deliver. The buyer functions as an intermediary, relaying information between the two. Unfortunately, information conveyed in this manner is always subject to miscommunication and misinterpretation. And once the communication is out of sync, the result may be inaction, with the attendant lost time, or a decision by default, which may not turn out to be a very good decision at all. In addition, every buyer has, at one time or another, wasted a fair amount of time and energy just playing telephone tag with the supplier's personnel in trying to relay information.

The third major problem area is paperwork. The merry-go-round between the company and supplier runs on paper. And lots of it. Purchasing Departments spend thousands of hours just processing requisitions, reviewing and signing POs, matching up acknowledgments with POs, generating change orders, matching change orders with original orders, and carrying out other paper-intensive tasks.

The fourth major problem area is wasted time and energy. As we stated earlier, the dates on purchase orders aren't valid. In fact, the dates often change before the shipment is due. The buyer has some orders due in two weeks that are now being asked for ASAP. The buyer also has some orders that are two weeks past due and no one is asking for them. As a result, buyers must spend much of their time expediting all orders just to keep the production line running. Otherwise, people and equipment would be sitting idle while they waited for material to arrive. And yet, expediting is also an extremely inefficient way of doing business; it not only leads to higher costs and diminished customer service, but it also diminishes the overall quality of life in the workplace. Typical purchasing personnel, when asked if they would like to be hired or fired based on being 95 percent on-time to the dates they get on the requisitions, say, "No way."

One other major problem area needs to be mentioned: the conflicting directions that the buyer receives from management. The buyer's job description cites controlling costs and cost reductions as a major responsibility, but all the hidden messages buyers receive paint quite another picture. Every time buyers save a dollar, they get an "Attaboy" or

"Attagirl." Every time buyers are short material and cause a production line to go down, they get a "Dummy." It takes 863 "Attaboys" to equal one "Dummy," so the buyer quickly learns to work to the shortage list first and tend to cost reduction second.

Unfortunately, when management sends the auditors into Purchasing to determine how well Purchasing is performing, they spend their time seeing if all the pieces of paper were handled correctly and had the correct approvals, not discovering how well the department performed in the areas of cost reduction, delivery, and quality. So the buyer now learns that keeping the production lines running is the first priority, handling all the paperwork correctly is the second priority, and doing cost reduction is the third priority—if time is available.

Next, management gets concerned about the inventory being too high and has a discussion with the Inventory Control Department about reducing inventory levels. As a result, Inventory Control reduces the order quantities on the requisitions it sends to Purchasing. This just makes it all the more difficult for Purchasing to control costs. The buyer goes to Inventory Control and requests an increase in the order quantity and is told, "No, we need to control inventory levels." The buyer's job description may say cost reduction, but the hidden messages say something else.

Therefore, the typical buyer's day looks like the pie chart in Figure 1.1. As you can see, most of the day is spent expediting, doing paperwork, and attending meetings, leaving very little time to spend money well.

Other Drawbacks

In addition to the problems cited above with the flow of information and conflicting directions, the traditional approach to purchasing carries with it several subtle, but nevertheless serious, drawbacks.

The traditional approach perpetuates long lead times. Long lead times are a company's natural enemies. They're bad for a company because they cause it to appear less flexible; they make it difficult to phase in new product; they tie up cash in inventories; and they subject the production process to changes and disruptions because they force people to commit further into the future and guess more about what the company will need.

Lead times quoted by suppliers can often expand into the hazy future. Unfortunately, with the traditional way of purchasing materials, you're at the mercy of the suppliers' current business level or backlog. Since suppliers typically have little forward-planning information other than

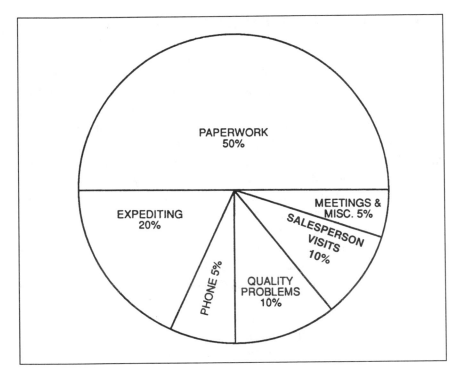

Figure 1.1 Traditional Buyer's Day.

the current customer orders, they often place new incoming orders at the end of the line.

The traditional approach also perpetuates teamwork and accountability problems. As mentioned earlier, purchasing people are caught between a rock and a hard place. On the one hand, management directs them to order in very small quantities to keep the inventories down. On the other hand, the suppliers require large order quantities before they will give attractive price breaks. The net result is a tug-of-war between Purchasing and Production Control, so that the two departments compete against each other rather than the real competitors down the street and across the ocean.

Because of all of the above-mentioned problems, the traditional way of doing purchasing is replete with waste and opportunities for errors. And when people have to deal with a system that they can't trust, they're generally not eager to put their jobs and careers on the line. In other words, they won't assume accountability for their decisions and actions. And without accountability, no system can operate effectively.

Operating under the MRP II/JIT/TQC Umbrella

In contrast to the traditional approach, consider what life is like when a company operates with MRP II/JIT/TQC tools. Companies such as Xerox and Black & Decker have long-term supplier contracts that give them a stable price over the life of the contract but allow the company to buy only the quantity needed to support their current production schedule. The schedules both the buyer and suppliers work to are valid and represent the real need dates for the material. Routinely—at least weekly—schedules of the company's requirements are transmitted to the suppliers, ideally electronically. The suppliers produce in sync with the company's own internal production facilities. They frequently make deliveries to a company once a week, once a day, or several times a day, depending on the nature of the company's business. The suppliers assure the quality of the parts, so as a result, there's no need for incoming inspections, and parts can be delivered by the supplier directly to the point-of-use at the buyer's company. Because this cycle repeats itself routinely, like clockwork, the buyer now finds the time to do what his or her job description states—getting the materials on time, in specification, at the lowest total cost for all the items purchased.

The company's customers are also tied into the MRP II network in a supply pipeline arrangement that allows everyone—the customer, the production facility, and the supplier—to synchronize production schedules, to produce only what is needed when it is needed, and to eliminate excess inventories, poor communication, and excess costs.

The typical buyer's day is now dramatically different from that represented by the pie chart shown in Figure 1.1. As Figure 1.2 shows, fully 50 percent of the buyer's time is now spent on value analysis, negotiations, and supplier selection. Thirty-five percent of the time is spent gaining a better understanding of the requirements of each part and how it is used, as well as a better understanding of how those requirements can be met in shorter lead times, smaller lot sizes, and at the lowest possible cost. Only 15 percent of the buyer's time is spent expediting, doing paperwork, and holding follow-up meetings, but the expediting occurs before the item hits the shortage list. Because the buyer has a clear picture of future requirements and the MRP system nets the on-hand and the on-order quantities against inventories, the buyer can see potential shortages in advance. This gives the buyer the opportunity to prevent the shortage from occurring in the first place.

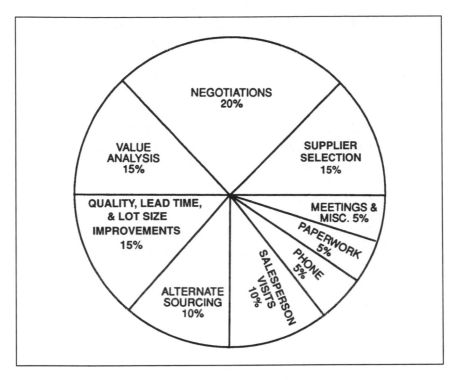

Figure 1.2 Buyer's Day Using MRP II/JIT/TQC.

The Major Benefits

The MRP II/JIT/TQC umbrella offers many advantages over the traditional merry-go-round approaches. The two biggest advantages are in the areas of valid schedules and cost reduction/value analysis. As mentioned in the Introduction, the Class A users of MRP II/JIT/TQC reported on average 96 percent on-time and a 13 percent cost reduction in a 1988 Oliver Wight survey. In a company that has six dollars in purchasing for every dollar in direct labor, that 13 percent savings is equivalent to the entire direct labor cost for the year. And a dollar saved in purchasing goes directly to the bottom line of a company's balance sheet.

Of the many benefits of doing purchasing in the style described in this book, here are the key ones that any company will appreciate. To begin with, your supplier can deliver the right material at just the right time, on a routine basis. The supplier's shipping schedules and internal production schedules will also be in sync, so both of you are producing at the same rates. In addition, you can bring in quantities that exactly match production requirements without being penalized for buying in small quantities.

Next, you deal with fewer suppliers, which means that you develop long-term "partnerships" rather than short-term adversarial relationships. When the supplier ships the material, you will be so confident of its quality that it can go straight to the production floor. Purchased-material inventories can be dramatically cut, while actually improving service to manufacturing. You can also operate with supplier lead times of a few days or weeks rather than many months.

Then there's the issue of teamwork. People can finally work together as a team and legitimately be held accountable for doing their jobs. Purchasing professionals will have the time to do the really important parts of their jobs, too: sourcing, negotiating, contracting, cost reduction, value analysis, supplier certification, and other actions that help drive down the cost of purchased materials.

Finally, long-term partnerships with carriers enable them to make more frequent deliveries to you without charging premium freight charges.

SUPPLY CHAIN MANAGEMENT

A new business philosophy has developed in the 1990s that, if implemented correctly, will allow the buyer another tool. That philosophy is Supply Chain Management. Using MRP II/JIT/TQC allows a company to internally balance its supply and demand, generate valid plans that people are willing to be accountable for, and then execute those plans flawlessly. The emphasis of MRP II/JIT/TQC tends to be internal—how to plan and execute inside the company better. Although you may use techniques such as Demand Management to better understand your customer needs, and techniques such as Supplier Scheduling to share your purchased requirements with suppliers, the reason you do so is so you can perform more efficiently inside your own company. It is very important to have control over your own environment before working with customers and suppliers to manage the supply chain.

Supply Chain Management, on the other hand, has an outward focus. How do you integrate planning and balance supply and demand across the entire supply chain? That includes my customers and my suppliers. It could include my customers' customer and my suppliers' supplier. Supply Chain Management can be defined as a process that links concurrent business processes and core competencies along the entire supply chain so as to maximize the performance of each member of the supply chain. This should generate significant improvements in customer service, delivery performance, lead time reduction, time to market on new products, reduced costs, inventory reduction, and improved communication across the entire supply chain.

BECOME A CATALYST FOR CHANGE

If the benefits of operating in an MRP II/JIT/TQC environment sound like a wish list, be assured that they are being realized at this very moment by companies throughout the world, very possibly by your own competitors. If your company is not at present using MRP II/JIT/TQC to its full potential, your mandate as a purchasing professional is to act as a catalyst and demonstrate the invaluable contribution these programs can make to the company's bottom line. No doubt you'll encounter resistance; after all, the concept of shrinking the supplier base runs counter to traditional wisdom, especially in purchasing, and the idea of weekly—let alone daily—deliveries sends shivers up the spines of many manufacturing veterans.

The fact is, you can adopt MRP II and JIT/TQC without tearing your company apart, by making gradual changes to the way you do business at present. Today's best manufacturing companies all operate with MRP II and JIT/TQC, but they didn't simply incorporate the tools overnight. For instance, when Xerox reduced its supplier base from more than three thousand to less than three hundred, it did so gradually, over a period of several years. No successful company unplugs the old tools on Friday and powers up the new ones on Monday morning.

Consider starting to work on MRP II immediately; if your company isn't currently operating under MRP II, spearhead an effort to get it in place—you'll see the positive effects on purchasing in less than a year. You can also begin some JIT activities once your MRP II efforts are under way. Perhaps you can consolidate your supplier base, spreading your volume over fewer suppliers. Then start more frequent deliveries, maybe shifting from once a month to once a week. Once you've gotten accustomed to this way of doing business, you can begin working with your best suppliers to improve quality so that eventually you're able to eliminate inspection of incoming materials. Continue gradually until you accomplish your full range of goals and achieve purchasing excellence at your company.

As you implement the new tools of the trade, you'll be taking a major step toward reducing the four dollars your company is spending on purchased materials for each dollar it spends on direct labor. And in today's highly competitive manufacturing arena, every cent counts.

SUMMARY

- In traditional settings, schedules are not valid and dates are constantly changing. Buyers are typically not willing to be held accountable for on-time deliveries against the dates they get on requisitions.

- Because of competitive pressures, companies are spending an increasing amount of money on direct purchases relative to labor. The financial incentives for reducing the cost of purchased materials are significant.

- In traditional settings, communication merry-go-rounds waste valuable time and energy.

- In a traditional environment, buyers are put in a double bind: "Save money, but don't short us on materials."

- In an MRP II/JIT/TQC environment, most problems that exist in a traditional purchasing environment simply disappear as communication improves dramatically, valid schedules replace best guesses, waste is eliminated, and the company seeks a course of continual improvement.

- Supply Chain Management will provide the buyer with improved, more timely information by integrating and linking the planning processes across all the members of the supply chain.

Chapter Two

Supply Chain Management

HISTORICAL PERSPECTIVE

In the 1960s, Material Requirements Planning was first introduced. Sometimes called MRP I or little MRP, it facilitated the job of planning raw materials and components. A company would input the forecasts and customer orders for its products, run those against a bill of material that defined how many of each component was used in the product, and calculate the total requirements for each raw material and component. Those requirements were then netted against the current inventory and little MRP calculated how many of each component you had to purchase or build to support the production schedules. Lead time offsets were used to calculate when purchased components needed to be ordered (see Figure 2.1).

Companies quickly realized that if you had all the components and raw materials, but did not have the capacity required, you still could not execute the production schedules. So the term Closed Loop MRP came about in the early 1970s (see Figure 2.2). The master schedule was a statement of what was going to be produced. It took the management policy, as expressed in the production plan, and broke it down to the detailed level. Detail capacity planning defined the capacity required by each work center to execute the plan. Dispatch Lists and Supplier Schedules were developed to schedule both the inside and outside requirements. Closed Loop MRP allowed companies to develop a valid manufacturing operating system.

Closed Loop MRP was strictly manufacturing- and purchasing-oriented. It lacked a top management perspective, a customer perspective,

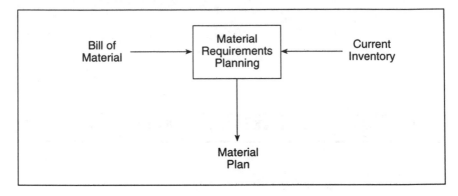

Figure 2.1   Little MRP (MRP I).

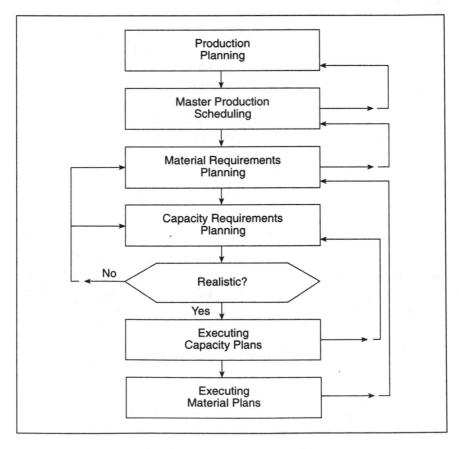

Figure 2.2   Closed Loop MRP.

and a financial perspective. As a result, the term Manufacturing Resource Planning or MRP II developed in 1978 to encompass these areas as well. Top management strategy and planning was included through Business Planning and Sales and Operations Planning. Sales and Marketing gave the system a customer focus through Demand Management. Because the system had a total company view and valid data, Finance was able to use the system to do Financial Planning, and simulation capabilities were developed to do what-if planning. Because all the functions of the company now used the system, MRP II became a company operating system (see Figure 2.3). During the 1980s, a series of industry-specific enhancements were added to broaden the applicability of

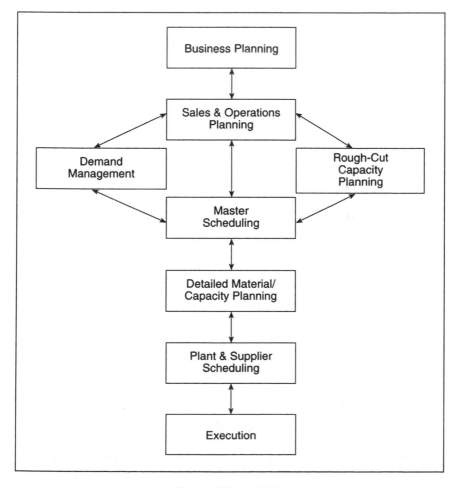

Figure 2.3 MRP II.

MRP II to all companies. These enhancements included lot trace, repetitive manufacturing, by-products and coproducts in the chemical industry, aerospace and defense requirements, and others.

In the late 1980s, the term Enterprise Resource Planning (ERP) started to appear. Basically MRP II plus logistics planning, ERP systems started to support truck fleet management, both outbound and inbound transportation planning, and warehouse management and planning. Some of the very large ERP systems tended to support a more global approach to MRP II planning by readily facilitating multiple languages, currencies, facilities, and so on. Whether you use MRP II or ERP, the emphasis is still on one company and how to maximize the performance of that company or enterprise.

But the high bar keeps rising, and competing in today's highly competitive marketplace is getting more difficult every day. It used to be enough to manage marketing, sales, and production. Today it is as important to manage the flow of products to the marketplace and the flow of information throughout the supply chain. This started with the mass merchandisers, but is now spreading to every industry. The push to everyday low prices in the retail industry drove some of the original work in Supply Chain Management, but the push to remain competitive in the future is driving other industries to follow.

WHAT IS SUPPLY CHAIN MANAGEMENT?

Supply Chain Management integrates planning and balances supply and demand across the entire supply chain. It ties suppliers and customers together in one concurrent business process that is focused on the ultimate customer. By creating a seamless process, the supply chain is able to respond quickly to market opportunities, lower costs throughout the supply chain by eliminating duplicate functions, and quickly respond to market changes and opportunities.

In the traditional way of doing business, each company in the supply chain has different goals and measures of what is considered success. Companies do not readily share information with their customers and suppliers because they want to gain an advantage over their trading partners in order to be more profitable. Each company in the chain makes decisions about its business that are hidden from their customers and suppliers, thus causing disconnects in the supply chain and adding costs to their trading partners. Each company in the supply chain does sequential information processing that adds time at each step, causing the supply chain to be not as responsive to customer needs as it should be. All of these disconnects, redundancies, and hidden decisions add cost, not value, to the supply chain. The traditional approach's concentration on individual functions (see Figure 2.4) suboptimizes the supply chain results.

Your customer receives an order for product from its customer. Your customer gives its customer a promised ship date and then creates a master production schedule to plan the production of the product. Material and capacity are projected using material requirements planning and capacity planning. Additional raw materials and purchased components will be needed, so your customer generates a purchase order to your company to acquire the needed material. You receive the order and give a promised ship date. You then create a master production schedule, plan your material and capacity, and then order the needed purchased components from your suppliers. Your suppliers then follow the same process of planning and execution. Your suppliers then ship to you, you process the material, and you ship to your customer, who then processes and ships. Because this process is slow and not always responsive to customer needs, your customer will carry some finished goods on the shelf to be able to respond quicker to its own customers. Because there is a lead time involved in acquiring raw materials from you, your customer will probably carry some of your raw materials in stock in case it needs more in less than your lead time. You, wanting to be a good supplier, will also carry some of your finished raw materials in stock in case your customer wants more in less than stated lead time, and some of the raw materials you purchase to make your customer's product to be able to respond more quickly. Your supplier and supplier's supplier also carry just-in-case inventory that adds cost at every level of the supply chain.

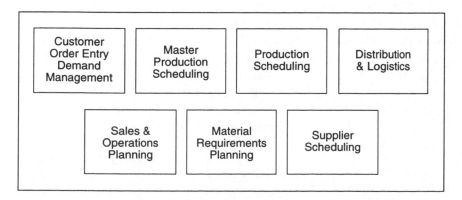

Figure 2.4 The Traditional Approach—No Linkage.

Your customer generates a forecast of future sales and develops a Sales and Operations Plan to support that sales forecast. Your customer does not share that forecast with you, and you probably have not asked for the information anyway. You generate your own internal forecast of what you think your customer is going to purchase based on historical sales data, and develop a Sales and Operations Plan to support your sales forecast. You do not share your plans with your suppliers, so they develop forecasts of what they think you are going to need in the future. What are the chances these forecasts will be the same? Zero.

The result is that all are operating with different sets of numbers, different plans, different priorities, different goals, sequential processes, disconnects, and firewalls between each company, and these add only costs, not value. The adversarial relationships and poor service levels created put us at a competitive disadvantage in the marketplace.

SUPPLY CHAIN INTEGRATION

Supply Chain Management integrates planning and balances supply and demand across the supply chain (see Figure 2.5). In Supply Chain Management, information is considered an asset and is readily shared with all members of the supply chain. In effect, you can consider the supply chain an information conduit. Your customer develops a sales forecast and shares that with all members of the supply chain. You do not individually develop your own forecast—you consider the forecast for the ultimate customer to be better and more reliable than your own forecast developed with only part of the market channel information. You substitute information for inventory buffers and reduce just-in-case inventory from the pipeline. You all work as a multifunctional, multicompany team to reduce costs, reduce redundant activities, and streamline business processes so they are concurrent and seamless. Working as a team to develop new products so that all the latest supplier technology is incorporated into the product, you are able to get new products to market quickly. Your systems are linked and you are able to process information in both directions, so you can ensure that the supply chain has adequate capacity to capitalize on all new market opportunities. The supply chain becomes, in effect, a virtual company that allows you to develop a competitive advantage in the marketplace. Greater customer value can be delivered more quickly and at a lower cost by flowing the information in a timely manner to every member of the supply chain and then quickly pulling the production of the product to the marketplace by synchronizing all of the activities of manufacturing and logistics.

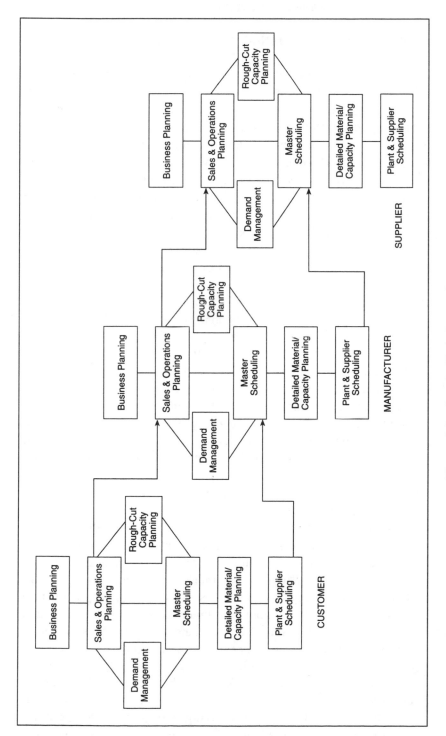

Figure 2.5 Supply Chain Integration.

19

WHY IS SUPPLY CHAIN MANAGEMENT CRITICAL?

Supply Chain Management is critical if companies are to be competitive in the future. Customer expectations are constantly increasing. Customers are looking for the highest product quality possible, suppliers who are responsive to their needs, the lowest total delivered cost, and outstanding service. In terms of delivery, they expect day of or even hour of delivery performance, not just week of delivery performance. They expect delivery to their request date, not your promise date. They want to expand relationships and have you take on more of the planning and inventory responsibilities. They want delivery to point-of-use on the plant floor with defect-free product.

The competition in the future will be supply chain to supply chain, not company to company. Supply chains exist, regardless of whether we plan them. Most supply chains are very complex and have a lot of disconnects. These disconnects add costs and make competing more difficult. Also, the move in most companies today is to downsize their supplier base. If you are not part of a supply chain, it may be more difficult for you to grow the business in the future.

Reengineering has accelerated downsizing in many companies. Downsizing means fewer people to do the same amount of work. By setting up supply chain partnerships and eliminating duplicate activities, you can reduce the workload of all the members of the supply chain. Why have someone develop a forecast at each company when the end customer forecast can be shared? Why have the supplier's quality control department check an item and then your incoming inspection department duplicate the quality check? Certify your supplier's quality and eliminate the duplicate process.

Cross-functional and cross-company teams can add product and service combinations that add more value. By including customers and suppliers in the new product development team, you can be sure you are developing products that fit your customer's needs while taking advantage of your supplier's core competencies. Why develop a specification for a component that the supplier encounters difficulty in making and then modify the specification at a later date to allow the supplier to make the part to specification and hopefully at a lower cost?

Supply Chain Management helps develop a true understanding and valuing of the idea of partnerships. A partnership is a true win-win relationship in which all of the partners benefit. Too often these relationships are "us against them." Any cost savings we can squeeze out of our suppliers we keep and any advantage we can develop with our customers we keep. The push is to maximize the bottom line at the expense of suppliers and customers. But we cannot figure out why they do not want to work with us and share information with us. In a true partnership, all the partners sit down and discuss ways to reduce costs throughout the supply chain and then share those savings with all partners. The partnership becomes a true win-win because all share in the risks and the rewards.

Technology today lowers the barriers to Supply Chain Management. A few years ago, it would have been impossible to link companies and effectively share data. The hardware and software to support Supply Chain Management either was not available or was not designed to support such an effort. Today, the software is available and the cost of computing capacity is constantly decreasing. Timely and efficient information processing allows companies to effectively compete in a global economy. Tools such as electronic data interchange (EDI), point of sale (POS), electronic funds transfer (EFT), efficient consumer response (ECR), distribution requirements planning (DRP), and bar coding simplify and speed information processing. More and more companies are starting to use the Internet to share information and conduct business.

As more companies benchmark their processes against world-class manufacturers, they realize their need to improve, and this forces a critical self-examination of current practices. One of the results of benchmarking is that more companies are outsourcing. Manufacturers are now specializing their operations to gain a competitive advantage. A manufacturer that limits its processes to injection molding can make that operation very efficient and purchase plant equipment to maximize its specific processes. The final manufacturer then becomes an assembler of the components from several highly specialized manufacturers, and wants those parts delivered in a Just-in-Time (JIT) time frame. The final manufacturer must be able to plan production and manage suppliers and deliveries throughout the world in a tightly integrated supply chain.

Supply Chain Management allows a company to better service its customers with faster response times and to do it at a lower total delivered cost. Not having Supply Chain Management in place will make it difficult for a company to effectively compete in the future.

EXAMPLES OF SUPPLY CHAINS

Often, companies see Supply Chain Management as nothing more than a different way to work with suppliers. Some have a Supply

Chain Management philosophy in place, but include only the key suppliers in the program and rarely customers or multiple layers of suppliers. Two examples demonstrate how these supply chains work. The first is an engine manufacturer, the second a large equipment manufacturer.

Before striking up the partnership shown in Figure 2.6, the engine manufacturer had to forecast how many trucks the truck manufacturer would build, and which engine models would be needed. This forecast was always incorrect in terms of quantity, timing, or mix. The errors caused the engine manufacturer to constantly change its schedules, which in turn became a headache for all the suppliers. The engine manufacturer approached the truck manufacturer and suggested that overall service and delivery could improve if everyone worked more closely together as a team.

Specifically, the engine maker suggested that the truck manufacturer install an MRP II system in order to get better control over its schedules and then share the planned orders for engines with the engine manufacturer. The truck manufacturer agreed, installed an MRP II system, and then began sharing a supplier schedule showing the next 26 weeks' schedule by engine model. The engine manufacturer responded by putting together a build schedule (that is, master-scheduled those planned orders in their own MRP II system) to support the truck manufacturer.

Next, the engine manufacturer approached all its suppliers and suggested that they also install MRP II. Several suppliers either already had MRP II or agreed to install it. The engine manufacturer then began shar-

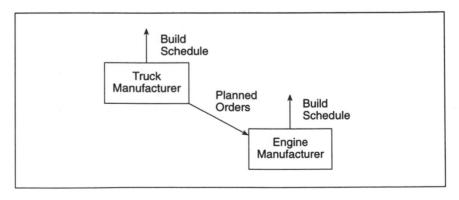

Figure 2.6   One-Level Supply Chain.

ing a supplier schedule showing the next 26 weeks by item number needed to support the truck engine schedule. This supplier schedule was based on the truck manufacturer's plan broken down into the items each supplier produced. The suppliers then put together a build schedule to support the engine schedule and ultimately the truck schedule. All three of these schedules (the truck, the engine, and the purchased items) were then tied together electronically. Now, whenever the truck manufacturer changes its schedule, all the suppliers see the changes on-line. Forecasting has been eliminated and everyone is working to support the truck manufacturer's schedule. Inventory has been reduced, productivity improved, and costs lowered at every level in the relationship. The suppliers and the engine manufacturer, in effect, synchronized their schedules to that of the truck manufacturer. (See Figure 2.7.)

At some companies, this supply pipeline concept is being used to schedule several layers down into the supplier network. One large equipment manufacturer, for example, had been purchasing a long-lead-time assembly from a supplier. The lead time was long because the equipment manufacturer's supplier had to purchase a machined forging used in the assembly that, in turn, had a lengthy lead time. The buyer persuaded all the parties to sit down together and work out an arrangement whereby the buyer would schedule all the levels in the supply pipeline, from the raw material to the assembly. The buyer now

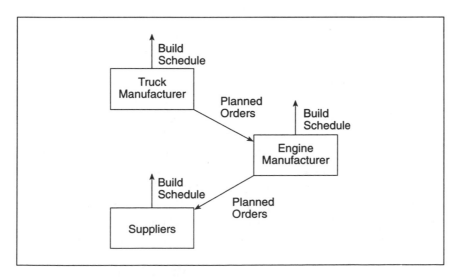

Figure 2.7 Two-Level Supply Chain.

schedules, with a supplier schedule, four layers down the pipeline. The layers include:

Supplier	Material
Steel mill.	Steel ingot.
Forging house.	Hammer forging.
Machine shop.	Machined forging.
Primary supplier.	Assembly.

This supply chain has allowed the buyer to reduce the lead time by 75 percent, reduce inventory in the pipeline, and reduce costs by 5 percent on the purchased assembly.

HOW TO START

Following are the 10 steps to develop a Supply Chain Management process in your company.

1. *Top Management Leadership.* Anytime you are going to take on a project of this magnitude that changes the way the company operates, you need to get top management to commit to lead the change. Supply Chain Management involves building trusting relationships with your customers and suppliers and openly and honestly sharing data and information about your business. Many management teams do not want to share forecasts, production schedules, costs, shortcomings, and so on with their suppliers and customers. Supply Chain Management involves sharing benefits equally with all the partners. Often, management teams want everything to go to their bottom line and are not really concerned about how the customers and suppliers are affected by changes in the supply chain. Supply Chain Management involves developing cross-functional and cross-company teams to solve problems in the entire chain, not just at one company. Some management teams are not willing to let their people work on problems outside their company unless they can see how solving those problems will benefit their own company directly. If top management does not understand what you are trying to accomplish and gives mixed signals, suppliers will see Supply Chain Management as one more attempt to push costs down onto the supplier, and this process will quickly disappear.

2. *Vision/Mission Statement.* Once you have top management leadership in place, you need to develop a clear vision/mission statement of what you are trying to accomplish. This vision/mission statement

should empower the entire organization to develop a Supply Chain Management strategy.

3. *Communication.* Communicate that vision/mission both inside and outside the organization so everyone understands what the company is trying to accomplish. If you want customers and both internal and external suppliers to agree to and align themselves with the vision, you need to clearly let them know what is expected of them.

4. *Preparation.* Get your own house in order first. Telling your customers and suppliers to do something you are not capable of doing will not work. Show them how it works. Develop integrated management processes to manage your entire business. Develop a Sales and Operations Planning process that creates one set of numbers to run the business, and make that plan visible to everyone in the company. Be sure that all management processes have a clear customer focus. Clearly define each department's roles and responsibilities in a Supply Chain Management environment, and be sure all individuals understand their individual roles. Conduct business following formalized policies and business rules. Openly share information and issues with all employees. Approve only valid plans that are achievable. Develop a silence in approval attitude among your employees so there is a commitment to meet the plan and to communicate early if the plan cannot be met. Develop an attitude where continuous improvement is the norm and the results are measured. When these are in place, you are ready to involve your customers and suppliers. If you do not openly share information and issues inside your own company, you will not share them with your supply chain partners. If your management processes do not have a clear customer focus, why would your customers want to be involved? You must get your own house in order first, and then your supply chain partners will know you are serious about integration with their planning and control systems.

5. *Identification.* Map out your entire supply chain. Identify who are the key suppliers and customers that need to be involved to dramatically improve the performance throughout the supply chain. Initially this would include your immediate suppliers and customers, but eventually would spread to your suppliers' suppliers and customers' customers.

6. *Benchmarking.* Benchmark yourself and your supply chain plans against the best supply chains in place today. By searching on the World Wide Web and the Internet using terms such as Supply Chain Manage-

ment and benchmarking, you can easily identify what leading edge companies are doing in this area today and their future plans.

7. *Teams.* Develop cross-functional and cross-company teams to identify opportunities for improvement. These teams should include—at a minimum—the areas of demand management, forecasting, order entry, master production scheduling, material planning, supplier management, production management, distribution/logistics, and performance measurement.

8. *Measurement.* Develop the performance measurements to be used throughout the supply chain so all supply partners will know what is expected and how performance is measured.

9. *Reinforcement.* Constantly reinforce the need to develop trusting relationships, valid partnerships, open and honest communication, and the sharing of benefits among all of the partners.

10. *Implementation.* Implement concurrent planning and execution technologies so that all of the resources of the supply chain are aligned to efficiently meet the needs of the ultimate customer quickly and profitably.

PURCHASING'S ROLE

The Purchasing Department has a critical role to play in Supply Chain Management because of its responsibility of linking the supplier into the supply chain. Purchasing is where the rubber meets the road in terms of making this relationship work effectively. In the past, Purchasing found as many suppliers for a part as possible and played one against the other to get the best price, then placed the purchase orders and hoped the supplier would perform. Often the chosen supplier did not, so the buyer had to spend time expediting and handling quality problems. The relationship with suppliers was often adversarial at best.

In Supply Chain Management, that relationship with the supplier needs to be cooperative and based on mutual trust. Purchasing needs to develop a true partnership relationship with suppliers if Supply Chain Management is to work. Supplier partnerships are covered in Chapter 10. Because of the close relationship needed with suppliers in Supply Chain Management, the supplier base is often reduced, and the supplier is the single source or major supplier of an item. Purchasing's role is to reduce the supplier base (covered in Chapter 8). Purchasing must also provide the suppliers with valid schedules and work with the suppliers to reduce lead times so the supply chain can respond to customer needs quickly and reliably. Supplier Scheduling and Just-in-Time are covered in Chapters 4 and 5. Because of the reduction in inventory throughout the supply chain, Purchasing must certify supplier quality to eliminate shortages due to poor supplier quality. Supplier Quality Assurance is covered in Chapter 7. To improve performance, Purchasing needs to establish performance measurements and work with suppliers to be sure the reasons for poor performance are eliminated. Chapter 14 addresses the area of performance measurement. A key to all of these areas is education. The buyer is going to need to explain to the supplier how Supply Chain Management and Supplier Scheduling are going to work; Chapter 15 addresses supplier education.

SUMMARY

- Supply Chain Management integrates planning and balances supply and demand across the entire supply chain.

- Supply Chain Management requires companies to look outside their own operations.

- Information is an asset and is shared readily with all members of the supply chain.

- Competition in the future will be supply chain to supply chain, not company to company.

- Supply chains exist regardless of whether we plan them.

- Purchasing has a critical role to play in Supply Chain Management.

Chapter Three

Profile of a Good Supplier

UNITED YOU STAND

As more and more companies are coming to realize the importance of win-win relationships with their suppliers, it's become popular to think of good suppliers as business partners. For companies to succeed with Just-in-Time and Total Quality Control programs, this kind of thinking is essential, because suppliers must consistently provide the highest possible level of service.

In legal terms, a partnership is a voluntary agreement between a number of individuals who decide to conduct business together. Partners are required to supply one another with accurate and complete information about anything that affects the working arrangement. A partnership also entails a commitment to use available resources to achieve the common objectives, as well as a joint sharing of risks and liabilities. The commitment to using these resources and the willingness to share in the risks means that the partnership entity will be an ongoing relationship that will endure bad times and thrive in good times.

The same holds for partnerships between companies and their suppliers. The relationship must be open and honest in terms of information; it must be based on a commitment to use available resources to achieve common objectives; and it must share the risks as well as the rewards. Finally, a partnership between company and supplier is a long-term proposition, intended to endure the inevitable highs and lows that all businesses encounter.

Let's say a supplier is willing to enter into a partnership arrangement, as described above. This partnership is a two-way street. Therefore, the buyer and the supplier must change the way they do business if the relationship is to be win-win and long-term. Chapter 12 covers the qualities a buyer needs to possess in order to be a suitable member of the team. The present chapter covers the qualities the supplier needs. Based on the collective experience of many thousands of companies, we can paint an ideal supplier profile based on 10 key criteria:

1. Delivery.

2. Quality and reliability.

3. Price.

4. Responsiveness.

5. Lead time.

6. Location.

7. Technical capabilities.

8. Research and development (R&D) investment plans.

9. Financial and business stability.

10. Supply Chain Management.

Each of these points is discussed in this chapter. We have developed a separate list of questions for evaluating your suppliers to help determine if they are capable of delivering the level of service and performance you should be looking for in each of the above 10 areas. Those questions appear in Appendix A.

DELIVERY

Just-in-Time Means on Time

In a JIT environment, material must be on hand when it is needed. There are two reasons for this. First, the inventory on all items is dramatically reduced, and if the supplier were to deliver late, the company would run the risk of running out of the material. Second, the items are often delivered by the supplier directly to the location where they are to be used. Typically, there is very little storage area for the parts in the production area, and if the items were delivered too early, say two weeks before they were needed, there would not be room to store them. Therefore, it is not unusual for JIT companies to require their suppliers to deliver product within a very tight window; the supplier can deliver a maximum of two days early, but never late.

This is very different from the traditional method (see Figure 3.1) in which material is delivered to the receiving area by the supplier, is then moved to a receiving inspection area where it is checked by quality control, and is then moved to a store or warehouse location. At a later date it is moved to the manufacturing floor, or to a remote location where reconditioning or remanufacturing operations are performed, or to a distribution center where it may be sold as a spare part.

None of these traditional steps add value to the product—they just add cost. By suppliers delivering material directly to where it is used in the manufacturing process (see Figure 3.2), you eliminate all of the waste incurred through the traditional method. You can do this because your supplier is certifying the quality and quantity of the delivered goods. A good supplier is one who delivers material just when it is needed, in the quantity needed, directly to the location where it is needed on the manufacturing floor or to remote distribution centers, and certifies the quality.

But what happens if the supplier can't make a particular delivery date? Ours is not an ideal world and unforeseen problems are bound to occur. In the event of a problem, a good supplier will be willing to notify the buyer as early as possible of the difficulty. Bad news is bad news—the sooner the buyer is informed, the sooner the company can develop alternative plans and reschedule accordingly.

Finally, delivery performance generally improves when it is monitored. Someone once said, "Anything that gets measured gets better." If we don't measure where we are and establish where we would like to get (98 percent on-time), it is very difficult to say whether performance is acceptable. (Chapter 14 covers how to measure supplier performance.) A good supplier will monitor its own delivery performance and

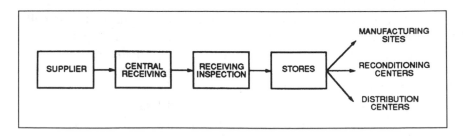

Figure 3.1 Traditional Delivery Method.

Figure 3.2 Just-in-Time (JIT) Delivery Method.

work with its customers to see how they can jointly remove the obstacles that prevent 100 percent on-time performance.

Short and Frequent Deliveries, Stable Lead Times

If you have Just-in-Time working at your company, suppliers must be willing and able to deliver in small quantities on a daily or weekly basis as specified on your schedules. This is a big change from the traditional Economic Order Quantity concept that recommends buying in larger quantities to get a price break, but it is essential to making JIT work. And as will be explained later in this book, smaller quantities don't have to translate into higher prices—they should be offset by the better planning information you're offering the supplier and the opportunity to become more efficient at manufacturing your items through methods such as repetitive flow processing.

To achieve the kind of delivery schedule you need, the supplier must be willing to commit to short lead times—days, maybe two or three weeks at the most. Equally important, the lead times must be stable. Since you're providing the supplier with your schedule, the supplier should plan capacity and raw material around your dates. This should stabilize the supplier's lead times into the future.

Delivery: Have It Your Way

A good supplier will not only deliver items according to your need date, but will also package the items according to your specification; if you want them packed in lots of 100, for example, that's how they should arrive. You might also provide the supplier with standardized baskets or tubs.

When you provide the supplier with standardized baskets and instructions on how to fill them with parts, you simplify your receiving process. For instance, if your instructions say to fill the basket to a certain mark on the side that indicates that the basket contains 95 items, then you'll know exactly what you're getting. Your receiving personnel verify that the 10 baskets received are all filled to the mark, so they know for certain that they have received 950 parts (10 baskets times 95 units per basket) and do not have to count the parts.

A related issue is how the items are delivered. Ideally, good suppliers (if local) should be agreeable to using their own truck if they have one. If not, they should be willing to use a vehicle or carrier that you designate. In addition, whether it's their own truck or a commercial carrier, good suppliers should make sure that the same driver makes the run each time, and that the delivery will be made to the point-of-use as specified above. The reason for using the same driver is that you will eliminate any confusion about where the material should be delivered, and avoid possible delays caused by items being dropped off at the wrong location.

Flexibility

The marketplace can change very quickly, and the best-laid plans and schedules may have to be changed at the last minute to seize opportunities or avert crises. You and your supplier need to understand and agree that change is the only constant in the world of business, and that flexibility is the key to survival. Good suppliers would be willing to review their processes and try to build in the flexibility you need.

A good example of this flexibility is the area of sand castings. Current lead times on sand castings run 10 to 14 weeks, but in actual practice, the supplier packs the sand around the core and pours the metal into the mold the week the product is shipped to the customer. Let's say that your company purchases four similar configurations and uses a total of 100 castings per week. Your company would like the supplier to reserve capacity for 100 molds per week (per the supplier schedule) and let the buyer choose one week before the delivery is required which configuration is to be put into the mold. This same logic holds if your company is buying plastic molded parts, chemicals, and so forth. The supplier who is able to build in this flexibility can more easily respond to customer and marketplace changes.

QUALITY AND RELIABILITY

Toward Zero Defects

Correct quality means that the good supplier ships materials according to your agreed-upon specification. The good supplier is in conformance to your requirements not only on the first delivery, but on each and every delivery for as long as the partnership lasts. That conformance includes not only the physical requirements of the specifications, but all the other requirements as well. Correct quality would also include correct quantity. When you order 100, the good supplier will ship 100—not 95 or 105. If each shipment is the exact amount you requested and the supplier's paperwork shows the correct quantity, you should not have to count the items when they arrive at your receiving dock. If the quality is correct every time, you should not have to inspect the items. If you don't have to count or inspect the items, the good supplier can deliver the items directly to the point-of-use on the manufacturing floor.

The buyer will want to certify that the supplier is capable of delivering the correct quality. The first step is to sit down with a representative from the supplier and discuss the specification. Next, the buyer will want to bring his or her quality-assurance people into the supplier's plant, walk them through the supplier's manufacturing process, and verify that the supplier can make the material to your specifications. Once the buyer's quality-assurance people verify that the supplier has the capability to produce the desired quality level (i.e., the equipment and the understanding), they will probably need to check only the first few shipments. If the materials meet the buyer's specifications, from that point on the supplier is accountable for shipping only good parts and the buyer should not have to inspect the parts when they arrive at the receiving docks. Good suppliers will welcome the buyer's audit, will want to be certified on quality, and will conform to the requirements of the buyer. Chapter 7 discusses supplier quality assurance.

Feedback

To help the supplier stay on target, the buyer should request that the supplier send the quality measurements for each lot the supplier produces. The measurements, which should be sent with each shipment, will reveal whether the supplier's quality is stable or a negative trend is forming. These measurements, all the key specification requirements requested by the buyer, are usually plotted on a control chart.

Figure 3.3 shows a control chart. The particular requirement being charted has a range of .88 to .92, and each "X" represents a test result of a lot of material. In Figure 3.3, the control chart indicates that the supplier is in danger of going out of range. If the supplier does not correct the cause that is allowing the particular test requirement to deteriorate, the next lot could be .93 and out of range. Maybe the tool isn't sharp anymore, or the process isn't being run correctly by the operator—it

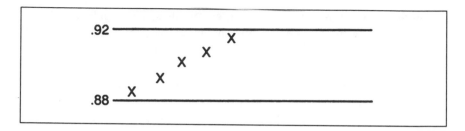

Figure 3.3 Control Chart—Trending Out of Range.

could be any one of a hundred different reasons. Figure 3.4 indicates that the supplier has corrected the problem and, likewise, the trend has been corrected. A good supplier is willing to chart the process to correct deviations in order to consistently deliver product that is acceptable within the tolerances established.

To ensure ongoing high quality, the good supplier should have a monitoring and measuring system in place. It is not unusual for companies to occasionally visit their suppliers and perform random spot checks to ensure that the supplier is following established procedures and, in fact, monitoring the process. A good supplier would welcome these random checks and not interpret them as a lack of trust, but rather as an essential element in a cooperative team effort to ensure good quality. A good supplier would also perform random checks of their own facility to assure that their quality-assurance process is indeed producing the desired results.

People will come to appreciate the value of feedback and regular communication between your quality-assurance people and the supplier's. When this two-way communication becomes a way of life, quality becomes a way of life. Highly visible quality programs promote this kind of thinking and are therefore an important criterion for selecting a good supplier.

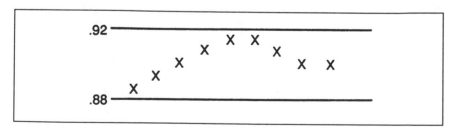

Figure 3.4 Control Chart—Trend Corrected.

Building Quality into the Product

Another important aspect of the good supplier's program is controlled design. Good suppliers should have documented policies and procedures that enable them to build in quality, not to wait and inspect the items after a production run is complete. For example, if the supplier has a run of a thousand parts, then inspects them *after* the last one is finished and finds that the first is bad, the odds are that the whole lot is bad and they will have to start over. In other words, the entire run is wasted, and everyone has lost time and money.

In contrast, if there is a process control in place, quality will be verified as they go along. If a problem is detected and cannot be immediately corrected, the operator will be authorized to turn off the machine. It's therefore important for the good supplier to have a policy in place that enables an operator to shut down the equipment and correct any problems that affect quality.

It is sometimes difficult for managers in manufacturing companies to accept this concept, because most of them are judged on their ability to get product out the door. Consequently, the idea of giving people line authority to turn off a machine might be tough to swallow. But the alternative—taking good raw material and good labor and making bad parts—makes no sense either.

Resistance to this concept dissolves when people understand that quality is something that must be built into the system, not checked for afterward. That starts in the beginning, with incoming material. If suppliers start off with substandard or defective material, they can only make substandard or defective products. The old computer acronym, GIGO—"garbage in, garbage out"—applies equally well to a manufacturing company. Good suppliers will have documented programs for building quality into the parts they produce.

Maintaining Top-Notch Service

Since ours is not an ideal world, problems will occur even in the best environments. Good suppliers will recognize the inevitability of problems and will have the equipment and capabilities in place so they can quickly recover from problems as they arise. Remember, in a JIT environment it is unacceptable to have defective purchase items or delays. JIT operates under the same principle as a series of dominoes: If your supplier is late, it could shut you down; if your supplier gives you defective material, it could also shut you down. You want to minimize the chance that your supplier(s) will initiate a negative chain reaction.

One way to minimize the likelihood of a negative chain reaction is to make sure that suppliers understand that surprises are not acceptable. That is, they cannot change any raw materials or their manufacturing process without telling you first, because the effects could be devastating.

This is well illustrated by the case of a manufacturer that had been purchasing the same ingredient used in processing vinyl for many years. All of a sudden, the vinyl manufacturing process wouldn't generate acceptable product. The reason? The supplier of the ingredient didn't tell the manufacturer that the supplier was using a new raw material. And the new material, it turned out, contained a trace element that caused the end process to go out of control. This sin of omission on the supplier's part cost the manufacturer a great deal of time and money (and almost caused the supplier the business). Had the supplier simply told the vinyl manufacturer of the change, the vinyl maker could have run a sample and quickly determined that the new compound wouldn't work.

A Teamwork Approach

A good supplier understands that quality programs and troubleshooting require teamwork, both within the supplier company and between that company and yours. It doesn't matter who's at fault; the focus must be on solving and eliminating the quality problem. The supplier must therefore adopt the attitude that there's no such thing as a problem— only an opportunity for improvement. Suppliers must firmly believe that as their people work together with your people as a team, they'll learn from mistakes and improve. Moreover, they'll be able to provide better service to their other customers, too, so the benefits will continue beyond their dealings with your company.

Full-Service Capabilities

You will want to find suppliers who have the ability to take an idea and then design, as well as manufacture, the necessary items. Some suppliers are excellent at designing quality items. They incorporate quality planning as a regular part of the design function, and design all items with an eye toward manufacturability. Unfortunately, their manufacturing processes may not be capable of producing quality parts at the level you desire.

The opposite situation may also exist. The supplier may not have the ability to design items for you or make suggestions as to how to design a part so it is more manufacturable. But given the proper tooling by the buyer, that supplier may be able to consistently produce good parts for you.

The most desirable supplier will be full-service, one who can take your idea and design a quality part that can be manufactured to the desired quality level. The good supplier should then have the ability to build the required tooling and test equipment to assure the quality of the part when it is produced. Finally, a good supplier should be able to use the tooling and manufacture defect-free parts that consistently conform to your specifications, comply with your delivery schedules, and at the same time maintain minimum costs. A full-service supplier who has all of the above capabilities can truly be an asset to your company as you develop new products and improve your current offering.

PRICE

Fairness for All

Traditionally, the buyer's job is to hammer the price down as low as possible. The supplier then accepts the lowest possible margin out of fear of losing the business, and tries to figure out how to cut corners and regain a profit. With Just-in-Time, such tactics are eliminated in favor of setting a fair price. It may not be as low as you would like or as high as the supplier would like. But a fair price is one that works for both parties. "Fair" means that the supplier can make a profit, but you can still remain competitive in the marketplace. In other words, a fair price represents a win-win, mutually beneficial situation.

To arrive at a fair price, a good supplier will reveal how its profit margins are established. If you understand the elements of the supplier's costs and pricing, you can actually help the supplier reduce costs by having your engineers assist in making those processes more effective. The reverse of this is also true: The supplier's engineers can assist you in the design of the item to lower the cost.

An office furniture manufacturer used a self-leveling glide on the bottom of certain desk models. The glide, purchased from an outside supplier, used to consist of nine separate parts. To reduce the complexity of the glide, the manufacturer sent a group of its engineers to the supplier's company to redesign the item. The engineers, working hand-in-hand with the supplier's engineers, found a way to cut out four parts. This reduced the unit cost of the glides from 25 cents to 12 cents. The supplier passed the lower cost on to the manufacturer while still retaining its desired profit margins, and further profited by applying what was learned in the process to other customers as well.

This example shows how you can perform value analysis that asks, "What makes it work?" (the primary function) and "What makes it expensive?" (the secondary function). If we can the eliminate the secondary function while maintaining the primary function, costs will be effectively reduced. Another way to look at it is, "How can we define the part better so it does what it's supposed to, but at a lower cost?"

In for the Long Haul

In addition to a willingness to accept a fair price, a good supplier will agree with the buyer to a long-term commitment, which means at least two, three, or four years. If you can tie the pricing over a long-term agreement, both of you will benefit. This should help ensure that you will get the same price over time regardless of the individual release quantities, because the supplier can plan raw material and capacity well into the future and take advantage of economical purchasing and manufacturing opportunities.

Another aspect of long-term commitment is the agreement to future price reductions. Over the term of the contract, you want to work together with your supplier to reduce costs so that at the end of the contract the purchased parts will be less expensive. At first blush, this defies common sense. After all, over the course of time, the supplier will experience increases in raw material or labor due to situations that may be beyond its control.

Increases in the cost of raw materials, though, don't have to translate into higher prices for finished goods. First, you want to work with a supplier who will inform you of price increases in raw materials as they occur. You can then work together to tackle the problem. Perhaps your people will suggest an alternative process that will still yield acceptable parts. Or, if the supplier's increase is substantial, you might authorize the supplier to make a substantial purchase of raw materials in advance to hold off the increase. While this may add to the supplier's cost in the short run, it may allow you to accept a very small increase in the price now and delay a substantial increase to later. If the supplier gives you advance notice of price increases, you have time to determine if alternate actions would be appropriate.

One company was notified by a paint supplier that a substantial price increase was about to go into effect due to an increase in the solvent cost. The supplier was willing to commit to more inventory but didn't have any place to store the materials. So the buyer paid the demurrage charges to let the solvents sit on a railcar, since the cost of doing so was actually less than the price increase. Now, that's a creative partnership arrangement!

RESPONSIVENESS

Who's in Charge Here?

Is there someone here in the supplier's Order Entry or Planning Department who's assigned to my account? Does that person know my items? Is there someone in Customer Service who can follow through with problems and complaints and get back to me very quickly? Is there a technical service representative assigned to my account? Where can I call that person if I have a problem? Who is the quality contact—can I call that person by name if I have a problem?

These are the kinds of questions that you'll want answered before doing business with a supplier. A good supplier will never dismiss the issue with "Call Customer Service if you have a problem." Instead, you'll be provided with an organizational chart with telephone numbers.

The supplier should also inform you of whether there are field and technical support people in your area who can quickly respond if you have a problem. It's vitally important that the supplier gives you an honest assessment of the skill level, strengths, and weaknesses of the individuals who might be servicing your account. The reason you want to know the skill level is that if you have a technical problem in an area in which the field support person is weak, that person may give you an incorrect answer or may have to call someone else to get the solution. You want to be able to talk directly to someone who will understand your problem and be able to give you a good solution. In short, when you call for help, you don't want to get the runaround. The attitude again must be, "Let's work together as a team."

LEAD TIME

Since lead times are one of the keys to competitiveness, your suppliers must be willing to discuss their true lead time situation: How long does it take them to get raw material? When do they set aside capacity? How long does it take them to actually make the item? In other words, what are the elements of the supplier's lead time?

You need to know how your supplier's own key suppliers are scheduled. This is important, because if one of your customers makes a special request, you must know whether your supplier can comply with it. If the supplier stocks the necessary items, you know you can make the changes quickly. But if the supplier requires three months to produce the necessary material, your special needs probably won't be met. In that case, you need to understand your supplier's—and hence your own—constraints.

Take fabric manufacturing as an example. The quoted lead time today is 10 weeks, which is made up of four weeks to order the yarn, four weeks to weave the "greige goods" (the undyed fabric), and two weeks for dyeing. If the supplier is willing to allow you to make color changes at the two-week window, it eliminates a constraint in responding to last-minute customer needs. In this example, the buyer buys the capacity to weave the fabric needed, authorizes the supplier to buy the necessary yarn, and specifies the color at the two-week window.

Another issue, and a key one in reducing and managing lead times, is the supplier's willingness to work with you as a partner. Are there technologies that you employ in your plant that the supplier doesn't (i.e., quick tool changeovers, cellular manufacturing, etc.)? Is the supplier willing to let your employees visit its facilities and assist in reducing lead times?

One small manufacturer of molded Plexiglas® sheets employed no engineers and, as a result, had a very inefficient plant layout and some very long tooling changeover times. Because of this, the supplier's manufacturing lead times on the sheets were 10 days. The buyer's company sent a group of engineers, tooling designers, and quality personnel to the supplier for a two-day visit. They suggested how the supplier could change the layout of the equipment on the plant floor, and how tooling changeover times could be reduced. As a result, the supplier was able to reduce the manufacturing time to *one* day!

How receptive are your suppliers to working on lead-time reduction? Good suppliers should be eager to reduce their lead time in any way they can.

LOCATION

An Open-Door Policy

A supplier who has multiple manufacturing locations and is honest regarding capabilities will reveal the capacity and other vital numbers of each location. Are all of the plants equally efficient? Do they all produce the same quality level? If not, do you have the right to choose which factory will be used to make your material?

If the supplier subcontracts, who are key subcontractors? Where are they located? Will the supplier help you talk with them so you can determine their strengths and weaknesses? This is important so you can be assured that quality will be maintained throughout the supplier's operation.

Part of the supplier's open-door policy involves revealing all of the other products manufactured for other companies. How is the supplier allocating resources to your product versus other products? You must be able to know that at a particular work center, your product will be a certain percentage of the workload. Let's say a supplier is 60 percent sold out, except for one drill press, which is used for your product, and that drill press happens to be 100 percent sold out. Another customer places an unusual order, which requires your drill press. If that order exceeds the capacity of your drill press, your order may suffer as a result. Good suppliers honestly explain how they allocate capacity among customers. That information is essential to knowing what kind of service you can expect over the long haul.

Finally, what is the overall quality level of the product that the supplier offers to other customers? If it is excellent, you can make an assumption that your products could be made just as well.

TECHNICAL CAPABILITIES

In Search of the Cutting Edge

When it comes to technology, suppliers come in two varieties: leaders and followers. Obviously, you want suppliers who are on the cutting edge of technology and are seeking better ways to manufacture their products. This will allow you to continuously improve your products in terms of quality and performance. If your suppliers are followers, they'll let someone else do the groundbreaking. Sure, the followers might offer slightly lower costs because they don't have to amortize the R&D and capital investments, but their products will never be cutting-edge—which means your products may never become cutting-edge, either.

Besides being on the cutting edge of technology, good suppliers have good track records for bringing in new products on time. This is important, because if they can introduce their own new products and new products for other customers on time, they can introduce your new purchase components on time, too.

A related issue is how well suppliers have documented their processes. Are the suppliers' successes hit-or-miss? Or are they part of a well-thought-out development strategy for bringing out new products and product improvements each year? If suppliers have such a strategy, chances are they have the resources to improve and enhance the products they make for you, too.

The same goes for product improvements. Do the suppliers' plans call for continual improvements in their product lines? Have they allocated money to improve your products? Are they continually upgrading and adding equipment? Do they have a sufficient number of people to support the improvement efforts? The supplier who can answer "yes" to all these questions is the kind of supplier you want on your team.

What about the supplier's history of success with new products and product improvements? The supplier should be willing to show you reliability data, problems and all. You also want to get a satisfactory answer about how problems have been handled in the past. What kind of process has been used to find solutions? Who was assigned to troubleshoot and correct the problems? These are important questions that a good supplier will readily answer. Finally, you want to see that TQC is a standard operating principle for the supplier's R&D team. If total quality is considered as early as the design phase, it will likely be built into the entire production process.

RESEARCH AND DEVELOPMENT (R&D) INVESTMENT PLANS

Funding Tomorrow

Good suppliers will have an R&D budget to improve old products and develop new ones. If they haven't set aside funds, then they aren't going to carry out any R&D activities. But R&D can also be a double-edged sword; after all, if a supplier is so wrapped up in its own or someone else's R&D efforts, will it have time for yours? You want a supplier who will be able to answer that question honestly.

Another important aspect of the R&D issue is whether the supplier is willing to participate in joint design programs. A good supplier will be willing to work with you in exploiting the creativity, technical expertise, and production knowledge that both firms bring to the party.

Finally, the kind of suppliers you want on your team will be responsive to your development needs. When you suggest a new project or joint effort, they'll be eager to sit down and discuss the details.

FINANCIAL AND BUSINESS STABILITY

Here Today . . . Here Tomorrow

Clearly, you want to trust your business only to a company that has the stability required to survive tough times. Why spend six months qualifying a supplier only to find out it's in Chapter 11 bankruptcy? This seems obvious, but it is too often overlooked. Even if a supplier doesn't slip into the abyss, a company that is teetering on the edge won't be able to provide the kind of quality and development services you need to be a world-class competitor.

In addition to checking the basics—Dun & Bradstreet rating, industrial average data, profitability for the past three years, return on equity, debt to equity, liquidity and solvency, and receivables turnover—you'll want to know whether the company is running on borrowed money or revenues from sales. You would also like to know if there is a high turnover in the management team or an expected change in ownership that could affect your long-term relationship. Good suppliers will provide all the necessary information you need to assess their financial and business strengths and weaknesses.

SUPPLY CHAIN MANAGEMENT

A Team Player

Good suppliers are customer-driven. They know their success is tied to how well they service their customers, and they are always looking for ways to improve that service. They want to be part of your team and not seen as an outsider. They are constantly trying to add value to the relationship and satisfy your expressed needs. Therefore, they would want to be part of a Supply Chain Management effort, because it would allow them to be part of a larger team and showcase their abilities to a wider audience. Good suppliers would want to openly share information and capabilities with all the members of the supply chain and share equally in the risks and rewards associated with the supply chain. They would realize that working in cross-functional and cross-company teams works to their advantage as well as to the advantage of other members of the supply team. By benchmarking their own processes against those of the supply chain team, good suppliers would be able to improve their service to all of their customers.

SUMMARY

- A good supplier will build quality into the product, aiming toward zero defect production. This requires a commitment to quality and a teamwork approach that entails feedback and the spirit of cooperation.

- Delivery performance is a key measure of a good supplier. Desirable delivery performance not only entails hitting a schedule, but involves a willingness to make short and frequent deliveries to point-of-use areas within your facility, as well as a willingness to package items according to your specifications.

- Good pricing means fair pricing; ultimately, the price may not be as low as you would like or as high as the supplier would like. But everyone wins with a fair price, because it buys you top-notch and sustained service and assures the supplier ongoing business.

- A good supplier will demonstrate responsiveness to your needs by ensuring that readily accessible people are in charge of servicing your account.

- Long lead times are the enemy of all businesses; a good supplier will work with you to reduce lead times as much as possible.

- It is vitally important to know a supplier's capabilities and work load at various locations. A good supplier willingly provides you with all necessary information regarding its locations.

- The best suppliers create the future rather than suffer through it. Look for suppliers on the cutting edge of technology.

- A cutting-edge company will reinvest some of its profits in R&D; you want a supplier who has a long-term view and is willing to spend for tomorrow.

- All suppliers must meet the stringent financial stability criteria you would use to evaluate potential new customers for credit.

- Good suppliers will welcome the opportunity to participate in Supply Chain Management efforts.

(See Appendix A for a list of questions that will help you identify good suppliers.)

Chapter Four

The Basics of Supplier Scheduling

One of the keys to effective purchasing is to have a valid schedule; that is, one that specifies what and when materials are needed. The typical buyer is swamped with past-due orders that no one needs, and at the same time is being asked to expedite in parts with a due date of next week. When asked whether he or she would like to be held accountable against the dates on the purchase orders and hired or fired based on 95 percent on-time to the dates on the requisitions, any sane buyer would answer, "No way!" Why? Because the dates aren't valid need dates; they are typically replenishment dates, two or three weeks before the parts are needed in production.

In this setting of invalid schedules, buyers are now being asked to bring in the material Just-in-Time. Unfortunately, it doesn't make sense to ask the supplier to ship more frequently, say weekly, to an invalid schedule. Why bring in parts more frequently just to see them sit on the shelf for several weeks before they're needed?

Despite the lack of valid schedules, buyers are also asked to participate in Total Quality Management (TQM) programs that move toward zero defects on all supplier items. The program is put in place and all the supplier education is completed. Quality is emphasized over and over. But because of invalid schedules, the buyer is asked to expedite the material in two weeks earlier than requested because it's needed this week. The supplier rushes the material through the system and is able to deliver it in two days, at which point it is rejected for poor quality. Since the materials are necessary for production, though, the rejection is waived and the defective materials are used. This, of course, gives a double message about quality. Formally, the company demands zero defects, but in reality it will accept something far less. Thus, without valid schedules, it is impossible to do a good job of either Just-in-Time or Total Quality Management.

BUSINESS AS USUAL REVISITED

The flaws of the traditional communication process between supplier and buyer were described previously. This chapter will revisit the traditional communication pattern, then describe a more effective means of carrying out purchasing: supplier scheduling. To recap the traditional flow of information, it begins when the planner requisitions the buyer. The buyer then sends a purchase order to the supplier's Sales Department, and the Sales Department communicates with the planner in the supplier's plant. This is summarized below:

```
        CUSTOMER                    SUPPLIER
PLANNER ─────────→ BUYER ────────→ SALES ─────────→ PLANNER
```

If a problem arises at the supplier's end and the supplier can't comply, the planner at the supplier's operation notifies the salesperson, who notifies the buyer at the customer company, who then notifies the planner. This reverse flow of information looks like this:

Now let's say that the revised promise dates aren't satisfactory and will seriously affect the production schedule. The planner so advises the buyer, and so on, as shown below:

This communication flow is not only inefficient, but it's also unnecessary. It's also the method most frequently used in American industry today. Why? Because it grew up that way. Back in the days of manual inventory systems, only the people posting the inventory records knew the requirements, and it didn't make sense to have the buyers also posting inventory records. The inventory clerks (planners) therefore sent requisitions to the buyers, who did the ordering.

THE SUPPLIER SCHEDULING CONCEPT

Letting Buyers Be Buyers

With computers and formal systems that work, it's no longer necessary to do purchasing the old way. Instead, it makes more sense to put the Manufacturing Resource Planning (MRP) planners in direct contact with the supplier. These people are called supplier schedulers, and they typically communicate directly with scheduling people at the supplier's plant. It is their job to take the valid schedules generated by MRP and work with suppliers to be sure those schedules are attainable. (Chapter 6 explains their roles in greater detail.)

With supplier scheduling, the buyers are freed from the ongoing pressure of expediting and paperwork, and as a result have the time to do the really important parts of their jobs: sourcing, negotiation, contracting, value analysis, and so forth. See Figure 4.1.

As you can see, the buyers buy from the suppliers and the supplier schedulers schedule the suppliers. In this environment, there is normally a business arrangement, called a supplier agreement, between the company and the supplier. This agreement, as a rule, is the result of efforts by the buyer (for the company) and the salesperson (for the supplier), as well as, possibly, their managers.

Customer	Supplier	Activities
Buyer	Salesman	Sourcing, negotiation, contracting, value analysis, QA, solving major problems
Supplier scheduler	Plant scheduler	Operating MRP, releasing, rescheduling, solving minor problems, capacity planning

Figure 4.1   Communications Using Supplier Scheduling.

The supplier scheduler enters the picture after the supplier agreement has been finalized. The supplier scheduler's job is to operate Material Requirements Planning and provide the suppliers with schedules within the context of the supplier agreement. When near-term requirements change, the supplier scheduler works with the supplier's people to implement the reschedule. When the supplier has a problem meeting the schedule, the supplier notifies the supplier scheduler, who can advise the supplier of the exact requirements and help develop an alternative plan.

Take the following example (from a Fortune 500 company) of a phone conversation between Jerry, the supplier scheduler, and Sid, Jerry's contact at the supplier's plant.

SID: Jerry, we've hit a problem running your order for Item #28184.

JERRY: Let's see. . . . That's for a thousand pieces due next Monday, right?

SID: Right. We're less than halfway through the run and the machine went down. It'll take about a week to fix, so I'm afraid we'll be late.

JERRY: Hold on. I'll check MRP II.

Jerry checks the MRP II display for Part #28184 (see Figure 4.2).
He notes the following:

1. There are requirements for 250 in Week 2 and 750 one week later.

2. The order ("scheduled receipt") for 1000 due in Week 2 was intended to cover both these requirements.

JERRY: Sid, how many good ones did you get before the problem happened?

SID: Three hundred fifty for sure, maybe four hundred.

JERRY: Fine, ship me those. When can you get the rest?

SID: In a week or less.

JERRY: Fine, no problem. By the way, Sid, how's the family?

Elapsed time for the conversation: 30 seconds. Contrast that with the traditional flow of information, which probably would have been mapped as follows:

Part #28184

		Weeks							
	1	2	3	4	5	6	7	8
Projected gross requirements			250	750					
Scheduled receipts			1000						
Projected avail. balance	0	0	750	0	0	0	0	0	0
Planned order release									

Figure 4.2   Sample MRP II Display.

Even in the unlikely event that all of these communication steps are executed successfully, the buyer has spent valuable time playing messenger, time that could have been spent saving the company money.

An End to Endless Paperwork

Question: With supplier scheduling in place, what happens to the need for written purchase requisitions? Answer: It goes away. Requisitions are the traditional common linkage between two people: the person operating the inventory replenishment system (the planner) and the person in direct contact with the supplier (the buyer). Those two functions are now combined into one person: the supplier scheduler. If the supplier scheduler were to generate a requisition, there would be no one to send it to. With supplier scheduling, purchase requisitions for production material are no longer needed. And as that need for requisitions vanishes, so do hundreds and hundreds of pieces of paperwork.

BENEFITS OF SUPPLIER SCHEDULING

Chapter 1 described the most significant benefits of supplier scheduling. The following summarizes the main ones:

• *Low inventories.* Manufacturers can get just the amount they need, just when they need it.

• *Low prices.* Buyers have negotiated pricing in advance, across the board. They've asked the supplier for the best price on the entire volume of business and no longer need to be concerned with the details of the traditional pricing structure on a given item for a specific order. Also, price breaks, in the traditional sense, are not as significant as before. Price breaks exist largely to enable the supplier to run a larger quantity at one time, in order to amortize the setup costs over a larger quantity.

The information and visibility contained within the supplier schedule gives the supplier a far better opportunity for cost reduction and efficiency, via techniques such as combining runs, sequencing runs to minimize changeover time, and so forth. It then becomes the buyer's job to ensure that the supplier passes on a good percentage of these savings. The supplier benefits, and so does the company.

• *Constant pricing.* Another result, in addition to lower prices, is constant pricing over a longer period of time. Price increases based on "price at time of shipment" are surprises that most buyers like to avoid. Since the supplier is authorized to acquire material out into the future with supplier scheduling, price increases based on rises in the supplier's material costs should be sharply reduced in the near term.

If the supplier's labor costs are scheduled to increase, the company may wish to authorize the supplier to run the entire schedule prior to the increase, but to ship the material as needed. Again, this gives the company constant pricing over the life of the schedule.

• *Shorter lead times.* Most of a supplier's lead time is often caused by backlog. And as the backlog increases, so do the quoted lead times. With supplier scheduling, however, quoted lead times aren't nearly as important. The supplier schedule extends out into the future, well beyond the supplier's quoted lead times. This is a win-win situation. The supplier has more and better information with which to plan, and the company is freed from issuing purchase orders for specific items in specific quantities far into the future.

With supplier scheduling, the most important supplier lead time is the finishing lead time. This is never more than the complete manufacturing time, and is almost always less than the quoted lead time. It represents the point of commitment to specific finished items. This finishing lead time, plus perhaps a week or so for the supplier's internal scheduling, establishes the firm zone on the supplier schedule (this is often referred to as the firm time fence).

In the example shown in Figure 4.3, this zone is the first four weeks. All quantities shown within that period are firm. The supplier scheduler resists making changes in this zone, and supplier concurrence is required prior to making a change. Thus the supplier is assured of stability in the schedule, and the company receives the benefits of shorter lead times.

The different items bought from this supplier are listed vertically on the left side of the chart. Time is expressed in weeks, horizontally. The first four weeks are shown individually; the next four weeks are grouped, as are the following eight weeks.

The quantities shown in the columns are the customer's requirements for the various items. Note the asterisks on the requirements in the first four weeks—they represent firm requirements. This four-week firm period reflects the supplier's finishing lead time plus an allowance for scheduling time. In this example, the supplier agreement (not shown) specifies a four-week firm horizon, which means:

1. The supplier is required to ship according to this schedule.

2. Inside the four-week window, the company cannot change the quantity or timing of these requirements without approval from the supplier.

Jones Company supplier schedule for: Smith, Inc.

Part # Week:	1	2	3	4	5-8	9-16
13579		100*			100	200
24680	20*	20*	20*	20*	80	160
42457	300*			200*	800	1600
77543			40*		40	

*Firm

Figure 4.3   Supplier Schedule with Firm Zone.

3. The supplier is authorized to produce any of these firmed-up requirements early and hold them in inventory until it's time to ship. The company is obligated to take them, but not sooner than the schedule specifies without authorization. The supplier is then able to group production runs to achieve internal efficiency. The company receives shipments in quantities that directly match the production requirements and, if the buyer chooses, on a Just-in-Time basis.

To take this example further, the supplier agreement might also specify that requirements in the second four-week period represent a commitment to cover the supplier for any material unique to that customer. In other words, the supplier is authorized to purchase special material for these requirements. If the company's requirements are eliminated for all items using a special or unique material, the company may have agreed to protect the supplier from being saddled with obsolete stock. This could be done, if necessary, by paying the supplier's restocking charge from its supplier or, in a worst-case scenario, directly reimbursing the supplier for the costs of the material.

The column furthest to the right, representing Weeks 9 to 16, contains information only, and does not reflect any company commitment. The information column is mainly to help the supplier plan resources (people, equipment, tooling, money, etc.).

As mentioned in the previous chapter, this is one of the characteristics of a good supplier—the willingness to work to shorter, stable lead times.

• *Reduced paperwork.* For the reasons described earlier, supplier scheduling greatly reduces the paperwork burden.

THE SUPPLIER SCHEDULE: CONTENT AND FORMAT

A purchase order is simply a contract with a schedule on it. This doesn't make a lot of sense, because schedules change frequently, every week or so, while contracts change infrequently, perhaps once a year. There's little reason to reissue a new contract every time the schedule changes. So why not separate the schedule from the contract? An increasing number of companies are, in fact, doing just that. They establish long-term supplier agreements and then issue schedules, typically once per week. In general, the buyer develops the supplier agreements, while the supplier scheduler takes care of the schedules. (See Figure 4.4.)

	Supplier agreement	Supplier schedule
What	Prices, terms, conditions, commitment periods, etc.	Which ones, how many, and when
Who	Buyer and salesperson (and/or their managers)	Supplier scheduler and designated person at the supplier's plant (ideally its master scheduler)
How often	Normally every year or two. Possibly open-ended.	About once per week

Figure 4.4   Development of Supplier Agreement and Schedule.

The dates and quantities shown on the supplier schedule are need dates. These dates are generated by the buyer's MRP system and are based on when the company needs the material to meet its production schedule. The quantities shown with an asterisk are scheduled receipts—they represent open orders. The supplier is authorized to produce and deliver those quantities in the appropriate weeks. The quantities to the right are planned orders; they're recommendations from the MRP system as to when the buyer will need additional quantities, and are provided to the supplier to give future visibility so the supplier can efficiently plan raw materials and capacities. An explanation of how those dates are generated is in Appendix D.

A more detailed example of a supplier schedule is shown in Figure 4.5. The schedule shows the following:

• The company's name, the supplier's name, the supplier number, the date, and the initials of the supplier scheduler and the buyer.

• The first six columns show weekly data, the seventh shows a four-week accumulation, and the eighth shows a 12-week accumulation. Thus, the supplier in this case is provided with 22 weeks of forward visibility. If necessary, more could be provided by merely increasing the number of weeks in the columns farthest to the right. The key is giving visibility to the supplier well beyond quoted lead times. A recent survey of companies using supplier scheduling indicated that 85 percent of the

Jones Company supplier schedule for: Smith, Inc. – week of 02/01/9X

Supplier #114

Supplier Scheduler: AB
Buyer: CD

Firm Zone: first 04 weeks Material Zone: next 06 weeks

------ Requirements ------
FFFFFFFFFFFFFFFFFFFFFFFFFFFFFFF MMMMMMMMMMMMMMMMMM

Item #	Description		Week 2/1 & previous	Week 2/8	Week 2/15	Week 2/22	Week 3/01	Week 3/08	Next 04 Wks	Next 12 Wks
13579	Plate	Qty:		100				100	100	300
		PO#:		B1146						
24680	Panel	Qty:	20	20	20	20	20	20	80	340
		PO#:	B1122	B1146	B1180	B1203				
42457	Tube	Qty:	300			200			1100	3500
		PO#:	B1122			B1203				
77543	Frame	Qty:			40		40			
		PO#:			B1180					

Figure 4.5 Supplier Schedule with Firm Zone and Material Zone.

companies gave their suppliers 12 or 13 weeks' visibility, 10 percent gave their suppliers 22 to 26 weeks' visibility, and 5 percent gave either a year's or some other number of weeks' visibility.

• The firm time fence is set at four weeks into the future. This is indicated in several ways:

1. It's spelled out in the header information.

2. The letter F, indicating firm, is shown above the dates for the first four weeks.

3. All required quantities in the first four weeks carry a purchase order number below them. In this example, the company has elected to retain PO numbers for administrative reasons, even though it has eliminated individual purchase order paperwork.

The issue of whether purchase orders are necessary can be an emotional one in some companies. While individual hard-copy purchase orders are not necessary, PO numbers may be needed for control purposes.

One method to accomplish this was demonstrated in Figure 4.5. Another would be to use the item number and due date. Thus, the first item would have a purchase order number of 13579-0208. A third alternative entails using the supplier number and due date. This would show all quantities in a given week under one number (e.g., 114-0208).

Companies not requiring purchase order numbers would probably print an asterisk next to the requirement to indicate that the order is firm, as shown earlier in Figure 4.3.

The Degree of Future Commitment

Questions sometimes arise regarding the degree of commitment to the suppliers involved in supplier scheduling. Does a company find itself making firm commitments further into the future with supplier scheduling than with conventional purchase orders? Or further than with blanket orders? Or further than with buying capacity?

In each of these cases, the answer is "no." Supplier scheduling, done properly, results in a reduced firm future commitment because it gives the supplier the future visibility necessary to plan the necessary resources to support the schedule. Here are the alternatives:

• Conventional purchase orders require commitments to specific items, quantities, and timing out through the supplier's total lead time. Of course, this includes the supplier's backlog time. Supplier Scheduling keys on the supplier's true manufacturing time and firms up only those orders within that period. Since these times are shorter, the commitment period is correspondingly smaller.

• Blanket orders typically require a commitment to the supplier for a specific quantity (or perhaps quantity range) of a specific item over an extended period of time into the future—often at a predetermined delivery schedule. In supplier scheduling, there is no long-term commitment to specific quantities and timing.

• Buying capacity usually means committing to the supplier for a given level of volume per time period over an extended period of time into the future. With supplier scheduling, there is normally no such firm commitment. There are situations, however, when good Supplier Scheduling requires capacity buying, and these will be discussed later in the book.

Why should the supplier see this as a win-win situation? At your company, would you rather forecast what all of your customers are going to buy, or receive from them a 13-week printout of what they needed? Of course you would like their actual schedules. Why would your suppliers be any different? The advantage to the suppliers is that you are giving them valid schedules into the future of what you intend to produce week-by-week. Based on that visibility, the suppliers are now able to better plan raw materials and capacity to hit your schedules. The suppliers no longer have to forecast what your actual week-by-week requirements are, because they can see them on the supplier schedule.

Multiple-Sourcing

Throughout this book, mention is made that the trend today is toward fewer suppliers and single-sourcing of components. (See Chapter 8.) There are still situations in which multiple-sourcing is important, however. For example, your volume requirements might be so great that you can't get all you need from one supplier. Similarly, there may be a geographical issue: You might have an East Coast and West Coast operation, both using local suppliers; why ship product 3,000 miles when the parts you need are 3 miles, 30 miles, or 300 miles away?

Another reason for multiple-sourcing is the government. For example, the FDA requires that pharmaceutical companies making new drugs identify all the sources for the active ingredients. Moreover, those sources—even backups—must make a certain number of batches per year, which means that for safety's sake you'll have to be dealing with multiple sources to satisfy the requirements. In some cases, the Department of Defense also requires multiple-sourcing to meet its regulations.

In an ideal world, you might be able to single-source. And JIT will always force you toward that goal. But the reality is that for one reason or another, most companies have to multiple-source in one way or another. Fortunately, supplier scheduling does not require single-sourcing, and most of the companies using it today are multiple-sourced in significant ways.

Good software for supplier scheduling makes multiple-sourcing more practical. With good software, the supplier scheduler is able to specify the percentage of an item's total requirements for Supplier A, Supplier B, and so on, and the supplier schedules reflect this split. (The supplier scheduler is typically not a decision maker in this matter of apportioning volume to various suppliers but executes decisions made by the buyer or the purchasing manager.) Some companies show the suppliers the total volume on the item as well as their share of it. This can serve as an incentive for each of them to do a better job and gain a greater share of the business.

WHY HELP THE SUPPLIER?

Sometimes people question why they should help their suppliers plan their capacity needs. Their attitude is: "It's not our problem." In fact, it is; if you don't provide the supplier with forecast information, the supplier will be forced to guess your future needs. The buyer will have to rely on the quality of the supplier's guess rather than on the quality of the planned orders in the MRP II system. In rising markets, customers often find themselves put on allocation when the supplier guessed wrong. The issue is not " to forecast or not to forecast," but merely "who forecasts."

Giving better information to suppliers enhances their ability to give customers what they need, when they need it. Many companies using supplier scheduling have found that high-quality information helps mediocre suppliers become good ones, and good ones become excellent. Their philosophy is: "Let's help them to help us. Their problems are our problems."

ENHANCEMENTS TO THE SUPPLIER SCHEDULE—
CAPACITY PLANNING

Figure 4.6 is an example of a supplier schedule enhanced by additional capacity planning information. A "capacity unit of measure (Cap u/m)" has been added to the right of the item description, for use when a customer is buying a variety of different items from a supplier. Let's assume that these items consume varying amounts of capacity in the supplier plant. In this situation, the supplier can't merely add up the requirements in pieces for a given period and get a meaningful measure of workload.

The capacity unit of measure translates piece part requirements into capacity requirements meaningful to the supplier. In Figure 4.6, for example, Part #13579 has a capacity value of 2.5. Therefore, the 100-piece requirement in the week of 2/8 translates to a capacity requirement of 250 for that week.

The other items require different amounts of capacity, the units of measure for which are shown. As with the first item, these are used to translate piece part requirements into supplier capacity terms. For example, the 20-piece requirement for Part #24680 in the current week and beyond is shown as 200 units of supplier capacity. Similar calculations are shown for the other items.

The resulting capacity requirements are totaled and shown at the bottom of the schedule. For columns containing more than one week, a weekly average is shown. (This information points out a potential problem with this supplier that will be discussed shortly.)

How does the company obtain these capacity units of measure? By asking the suppliers—they know where their bottleneck operations are and the capacity terms in which they think of them. Further, given the necessary education and training about MRP II and Supplier Scheduling, they will usually be more than glad to provide them. Some typical examples of suppliers' capacity units of measure are shown in Figure 4.7.

Some suppliers have required this type of translation into their own internal unit of measure for a long time. One example is sheet metal. Often the purchasing company's unit of measure is square feet. The bills of material are expressed that way, and the material is inventoried and issued in square feet. The supplier's unit of measure is pounds, however, and the supplier wants the information in that manner. This translation can be awkward, particularly in Purchasing and Receiving.

The capacity unit of measure on the supplier schedule can ease this situation. In the sheet metal example, the "Qty" row would show square

Jones Company supplier schedule for: Smith, Inc. – week of 02/01/9X

Supplier #114

Supplier Scheduler: AB
Buyer: CD

Firm zone: first 04 weeks   Material zone: next 06 weeks

------ Requirements ------
FFFFFFFFFFFFFFFFFFFFFFFFFFFFFFF MMMMMMMMMMMMMMMM

Item #	Descr.	Cap. u/m		Week 2/1 & previous	Week 2/8	Week 2/15	Week 2/22	Week 3/01	Week 3/08	Next 04 Wks	Next 12 Wks
13579	Plate	2.5	Qty.:		100				100	100	300
			P.O.#:		B1146						
			Cap.:		250				250	250	750
24680	Panel	10.0	Qty.:	20	20	20	20	20	20	80	340
			P.O.#:	B1122	B1146	B1180	B1203				
			Cap.:	200	200	200	200	200	200	800	3400
42457	Tube	1.0	Qty.:	300			200			1100	3500
			P.O.#:	B1122			B1203				
			Cap.:	300			200			1100	3500
77543	Frame	3.0	Qty.:			40		40			
			P.O.#:			B1180					
			Cap.:			120		120			
Total capacity requirements:				500	450	320	400	320	450	2150	7650
Weekly average:										538	638

Figure 4.6 Supplier Schedule with Capacity Planning.

59

Commodity	Supplier Unit of measure	Customer Unit of measure
Castings	Each	Molds, trees
Forgings	Each	Hammer strokes
Sheet metal	Square feet	Pounds
Cartons	Each	Square feet
Liquids	Pints, quarts, gallons	Liters

Figure 4.7   Examples of Supplier Capacity Units of Measure.

feet (the company's unit of measure) while the "Cap" row would show pounds (the supplier's unit of measure).

This display of information is also useful when future requirements are changing. The farthest right column of requirements, headed "Next 12 Wks," shows an average weekly requirement of 638 units per week (in capacity terms). This is substantially in excess of the customer's requirements now and in the recent past. It's also substantially in excess of the supplier's current level of output, which is closely matching current requirements. Again, this type of information should raise a flag to the buyer, the supplier scheduler, and the supplier personnel. Obvious questions arise:

1. Given the supplier's current situation, can it supply the customer at this higher level of volume easily?

2. If not, what changes can be made to enable the plant to do so?

3. Is the supplier willing and able to make these changes?

4. If not, can the company off-load some of this volume to another supplier?

Seeing these kinds of potential problems ahead of time can make a big difference. It can enable buyers and their suppliers to anticipate problems, rather than being forced to routinely react to them. If the buyer can communicate all of the future requirements to the supplier via the supplier schedule, and the supplier can in turn communicate all of the capabilities and limitations of the equipment used to produce the parts, then the two can work out all of the potential problems in the future before they become disasters in the present. In doing so, both sides can look forward to a long, mutually satisfactory relationship.

ENHANCEMENTS TO THE SUPPLIER SCHEDULE— INPUT/OUTPUT CONTROL

In an MRP II system, one of the key elements is feedback, or tracking performance to the plan. For the "inside factory"—one's own shop—the technique used to track capacity performance to plan is called input/output control. Standard hours of actual output for each work center are compared to its planned output. (The same is true for input to each work center, to ensure that the work is actually there.) Deviations of actual performance to plan are calculated. When the cumulative deviation exceeds a predetermined tolerance limit, corrective action is taken.

A similar approach can be taken for the "outside factories," that is, a company's suppliers. Figure 4.8 shows an example of a supplier schedule with supplier performance information added.

The performance information is shown at the bottom, in the area labeled "Performance summary." In this example, prior weeks' requirements are expressed in capacity terms—"Capacity units required"—as are receipts, so an "apples-to-apples" comparison can be made. The cumulative deviation line represents the running comparison of actual to plan. A cumulative deviation that increases beyond a predetermined tolerance limit would be a signal to the buyer, supplier scheduler, and supplier personnel that corrective action must be taken.

The last line shows deliveries missed by the supplier. This highlights supplier performance to specific deliveries, as opposed to performance to the overall plan.

The information in the two columns farthest to the right on the bottom of Figure 4.8 indicates that the supplier's volume performance year-to-date is very good, over 99 percent. But the supplier has missed 10 percent of the planned deliveries, which would normally be considered unacceptable.

Consider the similarities between information for the inside factory (the company's plant) and the outside factory (suppliers' plants):

1. With MRP II, companies can give their plant realistic, valid, attainable schedules of what to produce and when. They can do the same thing for their suppliers.

2. With MRP II, companies can do capacity requirements planning for their own plants. They can also do it for their suppliers.

3. With MRP II, companies can track input/output performance for their own plants. They can also do it for their suppliers.

Jones Company supplier schedule for: Smith, Inc. – week of 02/01/9X Supplier #114

Supplier Scheduler: AB
Buyer: CD

Firm Zone: first 04 weeks   Material Zone: next 06 weeks

---------Requirements---------
*FFFFFFFFFFFFFFFFFFFFFFFFFFFFFFFF*MMMMMMMMMMMMMMMMM

Item #	Descr.	Cap. u/m		Current + Past due	Week 2/8	Week 2/15	Week 2/22	Week 3/01	Week 3/08	Next 04 wks.	Next 12 wks.
13579	Plate	2.5	Qty.:		100				100	100	300
			P.O.#:		B1146						
			Cap.:		250				250	250	750
24680	Panel	10.0	Qty.:	20	20	20	20	20	20	80	340
			P.O.#:	B1122	B1146	B1180	B1203				
			Cap.:	200	200	200	200	200	200	800	3400
42457	Tube	1.0	Qty.:	300			200			1100	3500
			P.O.#:	B1122			B1203				
			Cap.:	300			200			1100	3500
77543	Frame	3.0	Qty.:			40		40			
			P.O.#:			B1180					
			Cap.:			120		120			
Total capacity requirements:				500	450	320	400	320	450	2150	7650
Weekly average:									536	538	638

Performance summary–prior wks.	Last wk	2 wks ago	3 wks ago	4 wks ago	4-wk tot.	*Ytd. Volume	%
Capacity units required:	580	495	520	565	2160	22427	
Received:	582	580	406	573	2141	22298	
Cumulative deviation:	2	87	-27	-19	-19	-129	-1.0
Deliveries missed:	0	0	1	0	1		10.0

Figure 4.8 Supplier Schedule with Supplier Performance Summary.

4. Since the schedules are valid, the plants operate on the principle of "Silence is approval." This means that, as long as they will hit the schedule, nothing needs to be said. When something goes wrong to cause a missed schedule, then suppliers' plants need to give feedback.

In companies doing supplier scheduling well, routine follow-ups of suppliers have become a thing of the past. Suppliers know that the due dates are valid. They know the company needs the items at those times. When suppliers have a problem and can't ship on time, they know it's necessary to notify the company at once. Otherwise, they say nothing and ship on time. Silence is approval.

ELECTRONIC DATA INTERCHANGE (EDI) AND THE INTERNET

There are several hot issues in purchasing today. They include JIT, which allows the buyers to receive parts more frequently; Electronic Data Interchange (EDI), which allows companies to do electronic purchasing with the suppliers; the Internet, which is a new way to communicate with suppliers; and Purchasing Cards that simplify some buying activities. There are many forms of JIT scheduling (see Chapter 5) and electronic approaches (see Chapter 10) that can give companies and their suppliers instant access to purchasing and scheduling information through either Kanban signals or computer-to-computer linkages. The key operating words for both JIT and electronic systems are "well managed"; you can take the fanciest JIT and EDI system in the world and obtain terrible results if the schedules are invalid and people misuse the tools. As with anything else in business, the mere presence of the computer will not guarantee excellent results; computers in manufacturing are only as beneficial as the people who use them and the validity of the schedules they have to work with. If you are going to be successful, you need to recognize that fact and develop valid schedules first; then you can approach JIT and EDI in a sensible and realistic manner.

SUMMARY

- Supplier scheduling allows buyers the time to do what they do best—save the company money.

- Paperwork is significantly reduced when supplier scheduling is used, because the need for most hard copy is eliminated.

- Lower inventories, constant pricing, and shorter lead times are other benefits of supplier scheduling.

- Supplier scheduling, done properly, results in a reduced firm future commitment.

- Suppliers' one-time delivery improves significantly.

- While JIT encourages single-sourcing, the reality of the manufacturing world dictates that some multiple-sourcing must still be done. Multiple-sourcing is possible with supplier scheduling.

- Communication between the buyer's company and the supplier's company improves.

- If anyone asks, "Why help the supplier?" just remind the questioner that "the supplier's problems are your problems, too."

- Supplier schedules can be enhanced by showing capacity and input/output data.

- Electronic Data Interchange (EDI), which involves computer-computer linkups for electronic purchasing, is a useful means—but it is not an end in itself.

Chapter Five

Raising the High Bar

Chapter 4 described supplier scheduling. Companies that implement supplier scheduling achieve dramatic results, including improved credibility with the plant and suppliers, significant reductions in purchased part inventories, a reduction to 1 or 2 percent of orders past due, the elimination of expediting and hot lists, the communication of planning data to the suppliers, a reduction in supplier lead times, and improved service to the plant. In addition, companies that use supplier scheduling find that their buyers, instead of spending time expediting orders, can focus on carrying out value analysis, negotiations, and problem resolution with suppliers. Finally, supplier scheduling can lead to a highly motivated and professional Purchasing Department that has the time and information needed to do the best possible job.

While all these benefits are certainly desirable, they're not the end of the line; purchasing professionals should continuously challenge their level of performance today and strive for improvements tomorrow. That means asking: Is there something else we can do to further reduce lead times, inventory levels, and lot sizes, while providing better service to the shop? Is there anything else we can do to eliminate more waste— things that add cost but not value to the product?

A number of areas offer excellent potential for achieving such improved performance in purchasing: Kanban, supplier setup reductions, design for manufacturability, transportation issues, supplier assurance of quality, and Electronic Data Interchange. These areas will be discussed in this and in the following chapters. First, though, the Just-in-Time/Total Quality Control (JIT/TQC) process will be covered, in order to provide a basis for understanding how JIT/TQC drives continuous improvement.

THE JIT/TQC PROCESS

The philosophy behind JIT/TQC is the elimination of waste, waste being defined as anything that does not add value to the product. In purchasing, there are many kinds of waste that are encountered every day. We receive requisitions from Planning, we issue purchase orders and distribute the copies to several departments and the supplier, we write up receiving reports and get invoices for payment. None of those pieces of paper add value to the product, only cost. Purchased material is received by the Receiving Department, where the paperwork is checked and the quantity of the items verified. Those parts are then moved to Quality Control, where the items are checked against the specification. The material is then moved to the warehouse, where it is put away and stored until needed. When needed, the material is then counted out by the warehouse and moved to the manufacturing floor. None of these activities add value to the purchased material, only cost. The ultimate goal of JIT/TQC is the total elimination of waste.

To meet the JIT/TQC goal of zero waste, we must learn how to economically manufacture "one less at a time." (See Figure 5.1.)

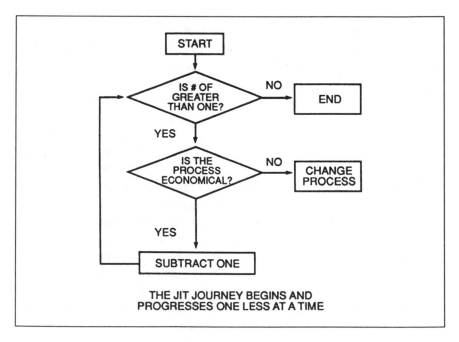

Figure 5.1   Just-in-Time.

Let's say you are manufacturing a product in lots of 500, and that is an economical run quantity for your company. The "one less at a time" flowchart states that if it is an economical lot size, subtract one. Could you manufacture in a lot size of 499? The answer is likely to be "yes"— it is such a small change. Could you manufacture in lots of 498, 497, 496, and so on? We continue the process down to 350. Is the process economical? It's not as economical at 350, and we are having trouble getting the work completed because of the increase in the number of set-ups. In other words, we have uncovered a constraint.

At this point, the flowchart states to change the process. Try to find out how to lower the setup time. When we get the setup time down, we then continue the process. Could we make 349, 348, 347, and so on? We get down to 250, and the material-handling process begins to become a constraint. We have increased the activity in the stockroom and the material handling on the plant floor. These costs are starting to go up, not down. The answer lies in changing the material-handling process. Maybe we can rearrange the equipment on the plant floor in a cellular flow, store the material at point-of-use on the plant floor, and greatly reduce the need for material handling.

When we reduce these costs, we again continue the process. Could we make 249, 248, 247, and so on? We get down to 125. Now we find out that we have four times the number of shop orders, purchase orders, and related transactions. The workload on Receiving, Quality Control, and the stockroom is now much greater. So the next step is to certify the supplier's quality, have the supplier deliver the material directly to point-of-use on the shop floor, have the personnel on the shop floor use a bar code reader to do the receipt, and eliminate the need for those departments. How about 124, 123, 122, and so on? The process continues until we eliminate all waste in the system.

Note that all these changes are small steps, and the process is under control the whole time. They are not radical changes. Companies that go from lot sizes of 500 to lot sizes of one overnight usually fail. Why? Because they do not have the time or experience to address the problems that come up along the way. They end up adding costs, not minimizing them, and eventually go back to the larger lot sizes. They say, "JIT does not work for us." JIT works; they just used the wrong process to implement it. And it is not just one less in the lot size. It is one less purchase order, one less piece of paper, one less in inventory, one less inspection in Quality Control, one less defective part, one less receipt in Receiving, one less supplier, one less move of material from Receiving to the warehouse, one less move of material from the warehouse to the plant floor, and so on. It is one less until all the waste (the non-value-adding activities) is eliminated.

MRP II AND JIT FUNCTIONS

How do MRP II and JIT function together? MRP II is the planning and control system that plans and controls the manufacturing and purchasing environment. MRP II gives us the valid schedules we use in purchasing. JIT, on the other hand, is the process used to change the manufacturing and purchasing environment, in order to execute those valid schedules quicker, faster, and better. Its goal is to eliminate any and all waste associated with executing these valid schedules.

KANBAN

One of the key techniques in the JIT process is Kanban. Kanban, or demand-pull as it is sometimes called, is a material movement and queue control technique that takes on the flavor of scheduling. The power of Kanban lies not in the use of the cards or signal but in the ability of the process to maintain a flow of work and defect-free products.

Figure 5.2 depicts a situation in which there are two operators. These operators could be in your own or your supplier's plant. Each is autho-

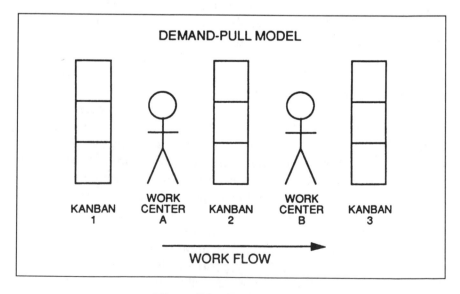

Figure 5.2   Kanban Setup.

rized to hold three jobs at his or her work center (represented by three squares to the right of the operator). If all the squares are filled with work, the operator is not authorized to manufacture any additional material. The Kanbans here are represented as squares, but they could also be cards or inventory locations on the manufacturing floor.

The rules of Kanban are fairly simple:

1. Don't start any work without an open Kanban.

2. Work to keep the Kanbans full.

3. Never pass on a known defect.

Figure 5.3 shows that each Kanban is filled with a job, so the operators are not authorized to do any work.

But at this point, along comes a customer who buys a product from the inventory on the right Kanban. (See Figure 5.4.)

The operator in Work Center B is now authorized to make another item, because there is an open Kanban square to the upper right. The operator pulls some material from the middle Kanban and starts to work on it. This causes the operator in Work Center A to be in demand mode, because there is an open square to the right of Work Center A and that operator begins to work on a purchase part from Kanban 1.

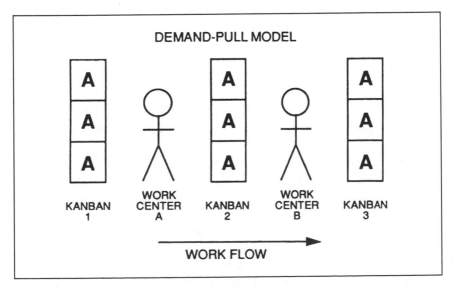

Figure 5.3 Generic Kanban, Filled (No-Demand Mode).

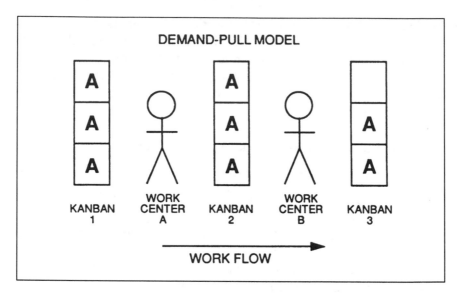

Figure 5.4   Generic Kanban (Demand Mode).

As both of the operators complete their jobs, both Kanban 2 and 3 are full, so the operators are not authorized to start on another job. There is an open square in Kanban 1, which authorizes the supplier to supply more material. This type of Kanban is referred to as "generic Kanban" because only one part was being produced in these work centers.

Where two or more products are built in the same line, a "brand-name Kanban" is used. Note in the example shown in Figure 5.5 that two products are being manufactured, A and B.

When all the Kanbans are full, the operators are in a no-demand mode. Now the customer buys Product B, which authorizes Work Centers A and B to produce another B. When they complete their respective jobs, more purchase parts would be required for B to fill the Kanban square. (See Figure 5.6.)

If the customer had purchased Product A, the open Kanban square would have authorized more purchase parts for A. This works if you have a limited number of part numbers that are used frequently. Where you have a large variety of parts, most companies use a final assembly schedule that gives the sequence of customer orders to be built. (See Figure 5.7.)

The final assembly schedule details the order in which the product is to be built. In this case, the order is A-A-F-E-A-B-D. The purchase parts would be pulled from A, then F, and so on. The open Kanban squares would authorize the supplier to replace the material in that sequence.

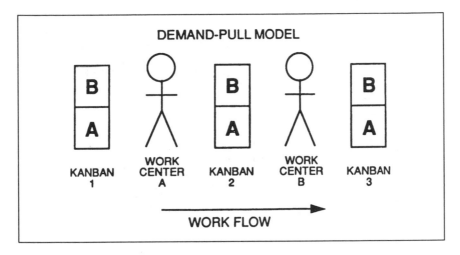

Figure 5.5   Brand-Name Kanban (No-Demand Mode).

Because the supplier is not next to the open Kanban, a card is used to indicate the open square and authorize the supplier to deliver more parts. The card would be similar to that shown in Figure 5.8. This Kanban card indicates which purchase parts to make next, the quantity of the parts to be made, and where to deliver the parts in the buyer's manufacturing facility.

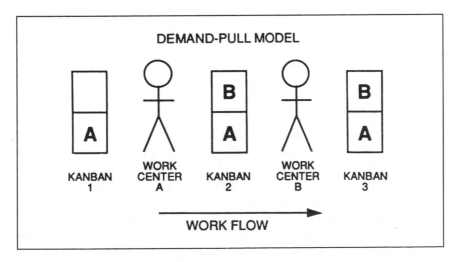

Figure 5.6   Brand-Name Kanban Authorizing More Purchase Parts for B.

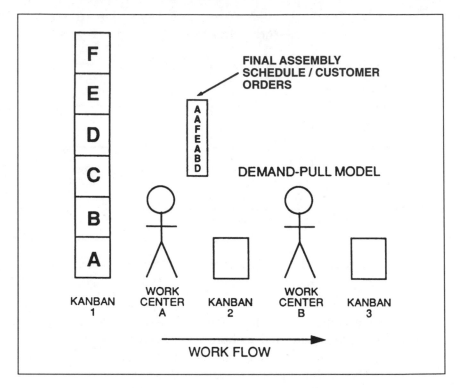

Figure 5.7   Final Assembly Schedule.

How Kanban Applies to Supplier Scheduling

To see how Kanban fits together with supplier scheduling, consider the following examples. The first is based on a company that makes casement windows for sale in the housing market. The windows are similar to those shown in Figure 5.9 and, for the purpose of this example, are available in 20 different sizes.

The company in this example produces 1,000 windows per week in its manufacturing facility and level loads the factory at 200 windows per day. From MRP, the supplier schedule would show 200 windows per day, and 1,000 windows per week in the future. This authorizes the supplier to purchase enough glass to deliver 400 pieces per day. (*Note:* The number is 400, not 200, because there are two pieces of glass per window. The supplier must therefore allocate enough capacity in the shop to cut 400 pieces each day from the master glass sheets.) While the supplier schedule tells the supplier how much product to deliver, the Kanban card

---

SUPPLIER KANBAN CARD

PART NUMBER _____ A 173

DESCRIPTION _____ LEG

SUPPLIER _____ 123

QUANTITY _____ 40

QTY / CONTAINER _____ 20

CONTAINERS _____ 2

NOTES:

Figure 5.8   Kanban Card.

specifies the sequence in which product should be made. The result is that purchased parts match the company's assembly operation.

The process works as follows. On Day 1, the manufacturer rough-cuts the wood pieces that will make the window frames from the long master pieces of wood. As the company rough-cuts the lumber, it establishes the sequence by which the windows are to be assembled. This assembly sequence in turn establishes the sequence by which the company needs to receive the glass. As the lumber is cut, a Kanban card is placed in a container to represent the two pieces of glass to be matched with the pieces of wood. At the end of the day, when the supplier's truck delivers glass for the next day's assembly schedule, the supplier picks up the Kanban cards from the container and returns them to the supplier's manufacturing facility.

On Day 2, the window manufacturer routes the desired contour on the window frames, drills all necessary holes for assembly, and cuts out

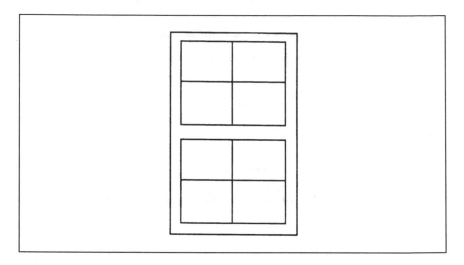

Figure 5.9   Casement Window.

the slot in which the glass will sit. Also on Day 2, the supplier cuts the glass in the same sequence as the Kanban cards and loads the glass into specifically designed carts, also in sequence specified by the cards. At the end of Day 2, the carts are delivered directly to the assembly line at the buyer's shop. On Day 3, the window frames and glass are assembled together in the order both were made, and at the end of the day, the empty carts are picked up by the supplier when delivering that day's shipment of glass. The carts are refilled in the following days.

Measurable Improvements

Now let's consider the difference between the old way this company purchased its glass and the new way based on Kanban. Before the company used Kanban cards and supplier schedules, it purchased glass in large lot sizes, had it delivered two or three weeks before it was needed in manufacturing, and averaged a month's worth of glass on hand in all 20 sizes. Despite the inventory, the company experienced occasional stock-outs on various sizes. The glass was delivered to Receiving in large heavy wood containers for protection. Receiving would open the containers, count the quantities, and write up a receiving report. The containers would then be carefully moved to Quality Control, where the size and specifications would be checked.

Next, the wood containers would be nailed closed again and moved to the warehouse and placed in special racks in order to minimize breakage during storage. These wooden containers consumed a lot of space in the warehouse, and despite the thickness of the wood, a fair amount of breakage still occurred.

A month later, as the glass was needed, it would be moved in the wood containers and a worker in the factory would stage the glass by size as required for the jobs. Broken pieces would be discarded but would not be charged back to the supplier, because there would be no way to establish who or what caused the breakage. Moreover, breakage was often not recorded correctly, so the inventory was usually incorrect, causing additional unexpected stock-outs.

Since the company implemented a combined approach using JIT and MRP II, in this case using Kanban cards and supplier schedules, it has experienced immediate positive results. Glass is brought in daily and delivered directly to the production line. Any breakage is noted and recorded before the supplier's truck leaves, and the stock is quickly replaced at no charge.

At the end of a day, if the manufacturing facility produces 200 windows and there is no glass left on the carts, the supplier has to have delivered 400 sheets that day, and is paid on the basis of the company's schedule completions in the shop. In other words, if the company produced 10 windows measuring 60 by 30 inches, the supplier must have supplied the company with 20 pieces of glass measuring 26 by 26 inches.

The benefits to the company, of course, include the elimination of Receiving inspection and Quality Control inspection, as well as the elimination of moves from the warehouse to the factory floor, with their attendant handling of the glass. The breakage in inventory due to poor handling has been dramatically reduced, which in turn has eliminated the need for a month's inventory on hand. And the reduced inventory need has reduced the need for all the warehouse space in which the glass was previously stored. Another benefit is that the buyer has negotiated a price over time for the various glass sizes based on the supplier scheduling requirements.

The supplier, too, has experienced significant benefits, including getting the information needed to plan the glass and cutting capacity well in advance of their needs. In addition, the supplier's paperwork is drastically reduced since there are no requisitions, no purchase orders, no receiving reports, and no invoices.

Just-in-Time is defined as the elimination of waste, waste being defined as anything not needed to add value to the product. In this example, the use of Kanban cards and supplier scheduling eliminated a good deal of waste.

FAXBAN

Where suppliers are more distant, the idea of sending the Kanban card to the supplier may not be practical and may take too long. In this case, buyers have started to fax a copy of the Kanban card to the suppliers. This is usually very easy to set up, and most suppliers already have fax machines.

Here is how it typically works. When an open Kanban occurs for a purchase part, the Kanban card that would authorize the supplier to make more material is sent to Purchasing. Purchasing faxes a copy of the Kanban card to the supplier and then sends the original Kanban card to Receiving. The supplier manufactures the material, attaches the copy of the Kanban card to the material, and ships the material to the buyer's company. Upon receipt of the material, Receiving replaces the copy of the Kanban card with the original and moves the material to the appropriate location on the manufacturing floor. If needed, the copy can be sent to Accounting to authorize payment or it can be discarded if the receipt is entered into the computer.

In some situations, because of the distance the supplier has to ship the material, weekly shipments might be preferable to daily or more frequent shipments. In these cases, the supplier accumulates a week's worth of faxes and then ships all the material at one time. When the entire shipment is received, the original Kanban cards are again attached to the individual lots of material and the material is moved to the appropriate location.

OTHER KANBAN TRIGGERS

In the above example, a card was used to trigger the production of more material, but other items can also serve that purpose. Companies have used golf balls, doughnuts, tubs, and other items instead of a card.

One manufacturer uses a warehouse tub to authorize more work. The tub is made of steel and measures 3 by 4 by 4 feet. The buyer sends 100 parts to the supplier per tub, the supplier paints the parts and puts them back into the tub, and the buyer's truck picks up the painted parts the next day. The tubs are color-coded. The supplier schedule indicates the daily quantity of parts the supplier will be required to paint, while the color-coded tubs indicate the color the parts are to be painted and how many of each color are to be produced.

A furniture manufacturer uses a variety of sizes of wood tops, depending on the size of the desks to be produced. The standard size is 30 by 60 inches, but tops come in sizes as small as 24 by 48 and as large as 36 by 76. The manufacturer makes up a final assembly schedule similar to the one shown earlier in Figure 5.7. Because of the weight of the wood core used in these tops and the large quantity used each day, the supplier has to make eight deliveries a day to satisfy the buyer's needs for wood core. In this case, the Kanban trigger or authorization for the supplier to produce more parts is a telephone call by the final assembly scheduler at the buyer's plant. Each hour the final assembly scheduler phones the supplier with the sizes and sequence of wood core to be delivered. The supplier then cuts the sizes from master sheets of wood core and sequences per the schedule. Two hours later the wood core is delivered directly to the top line by the supplier. The supplier schedule authorizes the supplier to purchase master 4 by 8, 5 by 10, and 6 by 12 sheets of wood core, and the telephone call (Kanban trigger) tells the supplier how to cut the individual pieces.

Here's another example. A manufacturer of office chairs sells a line of products that offers the customer the option of having the arms powder-coated in a choice of eight different colors. The manufacturer sets up eight separate racks in the chair assembly area, each one containing different color arms. The arms are put in the racks in pairs of left and right units.

At 7:00 A.M., the supplier goes to the chair assembly area, counts the number of openings in each of the eight racks (an opening represents a left- and right-hand arm pair that has been used and needs to be resupplied), and records the number of openings by color. The supplier then walks over to the weld department to a large rack that contains the arm weldments and removes the number of arm pairs needed to fill the powder-coated racks.

Next, the supplier takes the arm assemblies back to the shop and powder-coats the arms that same morning. After the supplier leaves, the weld department counts the number of holes in the arm weldment rack and replaces those with new weldments during the morning. At 1:00 P.M., the supplier delivers the powder-coated arms and puts them in the appropriate colored racks. The powder-coated arm racks are not full at this point because the chair assembly department has been pulling arms during the morning to make chairs.

At this point, the supplier counts the holes in the racks, goes to the arm weldment racks, and pulls arm weldments that are then powder-coated during the afternoon and delivered at 7:00 the next morning. The weld department replaces the arm weldments again in the afternoon to ensure that there will be sufficient arms for the supplier at 7:00 the next morning. In this case, the MRP supplier schedule tells the supplier how many arms will be needed daily and authorizes the purchase of the powder in the eight colors; the openings in the racks tell the supplier the actual sequence in which to powder-coat the arms.

A food manufacturer used two to three truckloads of sugar per day in the manufacture of its products. A study of its inventory revealed that at any one time there were seven to eight truckloads of sugar in inventory, or about three days' supply. The sugar supplier was one hour away, and also carried several truckloads of sugar in inventory at any one time. It could easily deliver a truckload of sugar within a few hours of an order from the food manufacturer. Using yellow paint, the food manufacturer painted two rectangles, each the size of a 42-foot semitrailer, on the receiving dock. The sugar supplier filled each rectangle (Kanban) with a truckload of sugar. As the food manufacturer needed sugar in manufacturing, it removed containers of sugar from the first Kanban, a palletful at a time. When the first rectangle of sugar was empty, the Receiving Department called the sugar supplier and requested another truckload of sugar, which usually was delivered in two hours. The truckload of sugar was stacked on the empty rectangle on the dock and the receipt was entered in the computer system. As the second Kanban rectangle was emptied, the supplier was notified and the process repeated. The food manufacturer reduced the sugar inventory by 75 percent, simplified its ordering and receiving process, eliminated the need to move the sugar inventory into the warehouse racking system, and never ran out of sugar—all because of the Kanban process.

Probably the most unique use of Kanban I have seen recently involved the railroad and the movement of material from a supplier in the Southeast to a manufacturer in the Northeast. The supplier and manufacturer both used the same railroad for car movement and switching. In this case, the railroad car itself was the Kanban. The manufacturer typically used one or two railcars of material per day. On rare occasions, three railcars of material were used. Five railcars of material were staged just inside the fence at the manufacturer's plant and five railcars of material were staged on the siding next to the supplier's plant. Around seven in the evening, the railroad would stop at the manufacturer's plant and remove the empty railcars from the siding next to the manufacturer's plant. If there were two empty cars, the railroad would telephone its Southeast office and authorize the shipment of two full cars on the evening train heading north. The railroad would pick up two full cars from the supplier's siding, drop two empty cars, hook the two cars of raw material on a train moving north that night, and have the cars in the Northeast late the next day. The supplier, having seen that morning that only three of the cars on the siding were full, would fill the two empty cars to complete the authorized Kanban at five cars. That night, the railroad would deliver the two full cars to the manufacturer, pull the empty cars, and repeat the process. Although the supplier was physically a long distance away, the manufacturer was able to get daily deliveries because of an excellent partnership with the railroad.

When combined with the supplier schedule, a Kanban system in Purchasing can be a powerful tool. Why not pick a supplier who gives you a variety of parts and see if you can develop a Kanban mechanism today? You won't regret it.

TOOLING CHANGEOVERS

One of the biggest obstacles in most companies to reducing order quantities and getting more frequent deliveries is the time it takes to set up the tooling or change over the equipment to run the items. If your supplier takes eight hours to set up the tooling or change over the equipment, the supplier won't get excited about producing and shipping very small shipments to you. Therefore, another area that the buyer will need to work on with the supplier is reducing changeover times.

Let's first discuss how the setup affects the purchase quantity you buy, and then talk about how to reduce setup costs. Most companies use a form of the economic order quantity (EOQ) to calculate the quantity they need to produce. Figure 5.10 graphically demonstrates how the EOQ calculation works.

Line A represents the fact that the total cost of the material increases incrementally as a larger lot size is produced. The parts cost $.10 each. If you produce one, the total material cost is $.10; if you produce 10, the total cost of the material is $1; if you produce 100, the total cost of the material is $10, and so on. Line B represents the cost of the setup allocated to each piece. If the setup costs $100 to complete and you produce 10 parts, the cost of the setup is $10 per piece. If you produce 1,000 parts, the cost of that same setup is $.10 per piece. If you produce a lot of 10 pieces, the material cost is $1 (10 pieces times $.10 each), and the setup cost is $10 per piece. The sum of A and B is $11. At a quantity of 30, that cost drops to $6.33, and by the time you get up to 50, the cost is back up to $7 each.

Therefore, the lowest cost to produce that part is with an EOQ of between 30 and 35 units. If you could lower the setup or changeover cost to $50, the EOQ would drop to between 20 and 25 units. The lower the

where A = cost per piece times the quantity
       B = setup cost divided by quantity
       C = sum of lines A and B for each quantity
       D = EOQ quantity or the lowest cost to produce the item

Figure 5.10   Ordering Costs.

setup cost, the lower the run quantity. Ideally, if you could lower the setup far enough, the run quantity would become one.

A major lift truck manufacturer in the United States had a series of 600-ton presses in the shop. The average setup time per tool was eight hours. The Japanese competition had the same 600-ton presses, but they had reduced the setup time to three minutes. The U.S. manufacturer had to produce a large quantity to justify the setup, while the Japanese company produced daily what was needed. The U.S. manufacturer was not able to get product out of the machine while the tool setup was in progress, while the Japanese company was able to produce parts all day long. Guess who had the competitive advantage in the marketplace? Purchasing has to work with its suppliers to reduce setup times so the buyer can purchase smaller, more frequent shipments at a lower cost. That means buyers need to understand the techniques to reduce changeover times.

One of the key techniques in setup reduction is to videotape the setup process and put the operators and setup people in a room to watch the video. Have them break the elements of time into types of activity, and then discuss which activities can be eliminated or reduced. One company did this and generated a rather entertaining video. People chuckled as they watched a lift truck remove the tool currently in the press, after which the lift truck operator drove to the tool room to exchange it for the next tool to be used. The next tool was not available (it was in Maintenance), so the lift truck operator drove all the way back to the machine to ask, "Which tool do you want as an alternative?" This took around half an hour. What were all the setup people and the operator doing during this time? Standing around waiting for the new tool.

The solution this company used was to put a two-way radio on the lift truck. Before leaving the press area, the lift truck operator called and verified that the tool was available. The tool was picked and staged while the lift truck operator drove to the toolroom, so there was no waiting time. The average setup was reduced by 20 minutes as a result.

The second technique is to separate those internal and external activities. An internal activity is one that requires you to lock out the power so you can't produce parts while the activity is occurring. An external activity is one that allows you to produce parts while it is occurring. In the preceding example, the lift truck operator could have gotten the new tool while the last production run was still going and brought it to the machine prior to starting the change. The object is to move as many activities to external status as possible.

One company purchased a few extra beds for the press they owned. This allowed them to completely set up the next tool outside the machine on one of the extra press beds, and then, by means of a series of roller tables, slide the new tool into the press and use a quick connect system for securing the tool. This cut the setup time from eight hours to 15 seconds! The company runs only the parts it needs each day now, not large lot sizes to justify the eight-hour setup.

Finally, let's take the example of changing the tire on your car to illustrate how you can improve the process. If you have a flat tire, you first need to open the trunk, get out the tire iron, jack, and spare tire and remove the hubcap. Second, you must put the jack under the car. You then loosen the five lug nuts, jack the car up the rest of the way, and remove the five lug nuts. Next, you take the new tire and reverse the process to put it on. Assuming you can find all the parts of the jack and that the spare tire has air in it, this process will take you around 15 minutes.

Now consider an Indianapolis 500 race car. Where is the jack? Built into the car. How many lug nuts? One, and it is mistake-proof so you can't put it on wrong or misaligned. Changeover time: 14 seconds. An Indianapolis 500 car going 200 miles an hour travels 105 yards in a second. If you delay your tire changeover four seconds, you are a quarter of a mile behind the competition. We need to challenge our suppliers (and teach them when necessary) to lower setup times. If they are successful, then we can get JIT deliveries weekly, daily, or hourly, depending on our needs.

DESIGN FOR QUALITY AND MANUFACTURABILITY

One of the key elements of JIT is in the initial design of a part. A company needs to make sure that the purchase part is designed so that the supplier can provide consistent-quality parts at the lowest possible cost. The simpler the design of the part and the fewer parts or processes needed, the better chance the supplier will have of making a quality part every time.

JIT philosophy says, "If you need a part, excel at producing it. Simplify the part and mistake-proof the process so you can't make it wrong." JIT philosophy also says, "If you don't need a part or a process step in making the part, eliminate it. It adds only cost, not value."

When we say mistake-proof (the term used for mistake-proofing is "poke-a-yoke"), think of a jigsaw puzzle; the parts can go together only one way. You can't put it together incorrectly. Figure 5.11 is an example of this.

Two parts need to be inserted into the plate. One is half round with a flat side. It can be inserted only one way, so that perfect alignment is guaranteed. The second part has a different configuration—rectangular—so it can't be inserted in the slot intended for the first part. With these simple design features, we have just accomplished two things. First, we have guaranteed the quality of the assembly because you can assemble the three parts only one way—the correct way. Second, you have minimized the operator training necessary, because the shape of the parts tells you how to assemble the product.

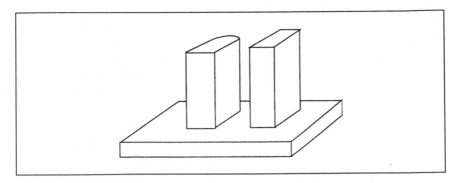

Figure 5.11   Mistake-Proof Three-Part Assembly.

Another example of mistake-proofing is the elimination of fasteners. Fasteners can be time-consuming to insert, can sometimes be difficult to align, and can back out if not tightened correctly. If the part can be designed to snap or slide together, the fasteners can be eliminated.

A manufacturer of copier machines made a major effort to eliminate the use of fasteners. It was able to reduce the number from 130 to 1, but couldn't seem to eliminate the last screw. The company offered a $5,000 reward to the first employee who could find a way to eliminate the last fastener. The fastener quickly disappeared from the design. All parts are now modular, and snap together with mistake-proof locking devices that can't come apart under normal usage and can only be put together in the correct sequence. As a result, the manufacturer has reduced the number and cost of the purchase parts, the assembly costs, and the indirect costs associated with ordering and inventorying all the fasteners, and at the same time they have significantly reduced the quality problems associated with incorrect assembly of the copier machines.

Many companies involve the supplier in the design of the parts. How often has a company designed a part only to find it nearly impossible to find a supplier who can manufacture the part to the specification? By involving the supplier in the process, you can assure yourself that the part can be manufactured to the specification. Also, because the supplier is typically an expert in producing that type of a part, it may be able to make suggestions on the design of the part to improve the quality and reduce the cost of your product.

In companies that are active in Supply Chain Management, the customer is also involved in the design process. There are many reasons for this; I will touch on four of them. First, Design for Manufacturability philosophy states that 80 percent of the cost of a product is determined in the first 15 percent of the design process. The initial assumptions used to design the product determine the majority of the cost of an item. We then spend the balance of the time trying to reduce the costs. By having the customer and suppliers in the room with your engineers, you can take advantage of the latest supplier technology and technical directions to design the product so that it not only functions well, but has the lowest cost initially possible. Second, by including the customer in the design process, you can assure yourself that the manufactured component, as well as the purchased component, will meet your customer's need. Third, the time to market is reduced because all of the design processes (customer to supplier) are taking place concurrently. Lastly, by working as a team and openly sharing information, you can build a strong foundation for supplier partnerships that truly become win-win relationships.

ONGOING IMPROVEMENT

As described earlier, JIT defines waste as anything that doesn't add value to the product. Paperwork, poorly designed parts, and setup times do not add value, only cost. Challenge these areas, lower or eliminate the costs associated with them, and you will enjoy solid benefits from putting JIT techniques to work in your company.

As we move to more frequent shipments—weekly, or possibly daily—two areas become critical. The first is transportation costs, which can escalate dramatically with smaller, more frequent shipment, if not managed correctly. The second is quality—essential in a JIT environment because there will be little or no inventory to serve as a hedge against rejections. Both issues will be covered in the next two chapters.

SUMMARY

- Purchasing professionals should continuously challenge their level of performance and strive for improvements.

- MRP II plans and controls the purchasing environment while JIT is the process to change that environment.

- The philosophy behind JIT/TQC is the elimination of waste.

- The "one less at a time" process is a key technique in the elimination of waste.

- Another key technique in the JIT process is Kanban, a material-movement and queue-control method.

- When companies have a combined approach using both supplier schedules and Kanban cards, they experience very positive results.

- One of the biggest obstacles to reducing order quantities and getting more frequent deliveries is the time it takes suppliers to set up their tooling and equipment.

- JIT companies involve their suppliers in the design of the items they buy in order to improve the quality and reduce the cost of their products.

Chapter Six

Organizing for Supplier Scheduling

The goal of supplier scheduling is to get the buyer out of the traditional mode of using paperwork and expediting into one in which he or she has the time to spend money well. The buyer's full-time job becomes one of value analysis, negotiations, supplier selection, alternate sourcing, quality negotiation, lead-time negotiation, integrating suppliers into the business, and developing long-term partnerships with the suppliers. In terms of the day-to-day buying, the buyer should be involved in the exceptions—those things that do not go according to plan. To do this, changes in the purchasing organization are necessary. Figure 6.1 shows the evolution that occurs in most companies as they evolve from a traditional organization of buying to an MRP II and then JIT organization.

THE TRADITIONAL METHOD REVISITED

As we saw earlier, most companies have a planner who determines the needs for purchased items. This person enters the quantity and due date on a requisition and forwards it to Purchasing. On receipt of the requisition, barring any difficulties, the buyer creates the purchase order.

Unfortunately, in many companies, regardless of size, the planner and buyer do not work in concert. The reason is simple: The planners are normally held accountable for the dollars in inventory. Therefore, they tend to requisition smaller quantities to keep the inventory low. In contrast, the buyers are accountable for price, so they tend to work at getting the largest quantity price break possible. If they're unable to get

Organization		
Traditional	Planner writes requisitions	Buyer places orders
Combined	Buyer/planner plans and also orders	
Supplier scheduler	Supplier scheduler plans and orders	Buyer negotiates contracts, solves major problems, etc.

Figure 6.1   Evolution to an MRP II and JIT Organization.

the maximum price break, they may go back to the planners and ask them to increase the order quantity. At this point, the company has unwittingly set conflicting goals for these people.

Another common problem with the traditional approach is the lack of a valid planning and scheduling system. Without valid schedules, the initial due dates on requisitions may be incorrect because they may not reflect when the material is *really* needed in the plant. Also, because of constantly changing priorities in the factory, it can be very difficult for the due dates to be kept valid during the life of an order.

In such an environment, the buyer doesn't really know when the orders are needed. And if the company runs out of a material before the next shipment from the supplier arrives, destructive finger-pointing begins. The planner blames the buyer for not respecting the dates on his or her requisitions, and the buyer fires off a return volley by accusing the planner of giving incorrect need dates.

Yet another problem with the traditional method is that, in most companies, planners are not allowed to talk to the suppliers. The reasons for such policies are threefold. First, purchasing people feel they don't get valid dates on the requisitions from the planners, so they don't want the planners passing the unrealistic dates on to the suppliers.

Many purchasing people also fear that planners may treat the suppliers unfairly, violating lead times or perhaps minimum order quantities. In other words, they're concerned that planners may break down the rapport the buyers have worked so hard to establish with their suppliers. Finally, since the planners in most companies are organized by product lines, not commodities, two or more planners could end up contacting a supplier at the same time and giving the supplier conflicting priorities.

The Combined Method (MRP)

As industry made the transition from manual to computerized inventory recordkeeping, a number of opportunities opened up for purchasing professionals. As the recordkeeping became less time-consuming, it became practical to allow one person, typically a buyer, to do both the buying and the planning. That person is often called a buyer/planner.

With this combined form of organization, buyer/planners receive computer-generated information on each of the purchased items. They review this output, reacting to the action messages on each item as needed. Once the planning is complete, they place the purchase orders with the supplier and perform all the normal purchasing functions.

This approach gives buyer/planners much better information than the traditional method. They can see the need dates on every item and can easily increase order quantities or combine items to get the desired price breaks. They're also freed from requisition paperwork, so their overall paperwork burden is reduced. Further, with an effective MRP II system in place, the dates can be kept valid, thereby sharply reducing the buyer's expediting workload.

Despite the benefits, though, the combined approach does pose some drawbacks. The buyers now have to do the planning in addition to their regular buying responsibilities. Some, possibly much, of the time gained by doing less paperwork and having better dates now must be devoted to the planning function. Once again, buyers may be confronted with the classic problem of having insufficient time to do the really important parts of their job: sourcing, negotiation, value analysis, and so forth.

The Supplier Scheduler Method (MRP II)

In today's manufacturing environment, supported by MRP II, there is a better purchasing approach. Since MRP II can generate and maintain valid need dates, much of the traditional conflict between the buyer and planner can be eliminated. Planners can be organized by commodity and can work directly with the supplier on details of the schedule. Often, they're given a new title: supplier scheduler. The buyer's job now changes to what it should have been all along: spending money well.

Note that it's not necessary to go through the combined method to get to supplier scheduling. A company should go right to supplier scheduling from whatever its current arrangement may be.

The Supplier Scheduler's Job

The supplier schedulers must carry out a number of important activities. First, they analyze the Material Requirements Planning reports and react to the messages out of the system. The types of messages they would review include:

- Release an order.

- Reschedule an order in.

- Reschedule an order out.

- Cancel an order.

- Resolve data problems.

Material Requirements Planning looks out into the future and calculates when the company will need to receive more material from its suppliers on each purchased item. It takes the date the company will need more material, backs up by the supplier's lead time, and then recommends when to place an order. This is called a "planned order" because it is only a recommendation from the system. For example, as time passes, a planned order release moves from Week 4 to Week 3, from Week 3 to Week 2, and from Week 2 to Week 1. When it gets into Week 1, the Material Requirements Planning system gives the supplier scheduler a message to firm up the order with the supplier. The supplier scheduler then converts that planned order to a "scheduled receipt," which authorizes the selected supplier to produce the item. If there is a problem from the supplier's viewpoint, the buyer may need to get involved and resolve the difficulty prior to the placement of the order.

Material Requirements Planning is also constantly reviewing the need date (when the first piece is needed) against the due date (when the supplier has been asked to deliver the item). If the need date changes, either in or out, the system gives the supplier scheduler a message to move the due date accordingly (reschedule in or reschedule out).

In either case, the supplier scheduler contacts the supplier and requests the change in due date. If the supplier agrees to the change, there's no problem. The scheduled receipt's due date on the computer is simply changed to reflect the new date. If the supplier cannot or will not change the date, the supplier scheduler may contact the buyer, who tries to resolve the differences.

On occasion, the system will also recommend canceling an order with a supplier. This can happen when a customer has canceled an order and the manufacturer no longer needs a scheduled purchased item. In such cases, the supplier scheduler contacts the supplier to try to stop the order. If there are problems, and perhaps cost implications, the buyer would need to get involved and negotiate the necessary settlement.

MRP II will also generate messages to indicate data problems. A good example of this would be the supplier's weekly capacity. Consider a supplier who works five days a week, eight hours a day, on one purchased item. In a typical week, the supplier produces 10,000 parts. This maximum of 10,000 parts would therefore be input into the system.

Now suppose business picks up and the manufacturer needs 11,000 of that item in a particular week. The system would give the planner a message that says, in effect, "This exceeds the supplier's stated capacity." The planner would contact the supplier and either get the supplier to produce the larger quantity or perhaps pull part of the 11,000 quantity into the previous week. If this is a problem for the supplier or a cost is involved, the supplier scheduler would once again involve the buyer to resolve the situation.

In short, the supplier scheduler does all the planning via MRP II, handling the 90 to 95 percent of the items that are routine. The few exceptions are handled by the buyer. Freed of all the traditional paperwork and routine replenishment planning, buyers now have the time and the opportunity to do their job of purchasing better.

The second area of responsibility of the supplier scheduler is to maintain the information in the system. If a price changes or the buyer negotiates a new lead time or selects a new supplier, the buyer passes the information on to the supplier scheduler, who inputs it into the system. After verifying that the master data are correct, the supplier scheduler lets the buyer know that the change has been completed. This allows buyers to exercise management control over the Material Requirements Planning system, but frees them of actually having to do the time-consuming transactions themselves.

The third area of responsibility of the supplier scheduler is to respond to changes to the schedule, to engineering changes, and to supplier delivery problems. "Can the supplier move the shipment of parts from Thursday to Monday?" "Can they give us the red ones before the blue ones?" "We just broke the tool. Tell the supplier we won't need the half-inch size until next week. What size can they move up sooner?" The supplier scheduler thus becomes the eyes and ears of both the supplier and the inside shop.

The last area of responsibility of the supplier scheduler concerns the actual generation of the supplier schedules. After all the necessary planned orders have been converted into scheduled receipts in the Material Requirements Planning system, all the reschedule messages completed, and all the changes updated, the system can then be authorized to generate the supplier schedule. The supplier scheduler is responsible for transmitting the weekly schedule to the supplier. Other responsibilities may include checking with the supplier to ensure receipt of the schedule and to verify that the schedule is practical and attainable.

THE BUYER'S JOB

The supplier scheduler has freed the buyer of the paperwork associated with requisitions and purchase orders and taken on the bulk of the day-to-day contact with the supplier. As a result, buyers can focus on spending money well, which is what they were hired to do in the first place. The buyer's full-time job becomes value analysis, negotiation, supplier selection, alternate-sourcing, quality negotiation, lead-time negotiation, and developing long-term supplier partnerships. Buyers now have time to sit down with members of the engineering team to understand the function of an item and its critical elements (tolerances, specifications, etc.). They also have new opportunities to work with suppliers to find ways to satisfy the function of the item at a lower cost. Finally, there's time to do effective negotiation on all the items, not just the high-ticket ones.

Appendix B details a survey of successful users of Manufacturing Resource Planning, focusing on their results in purchasing. In this survey, the companies using supplier schedulers reported an average 13 percent annual purchase cost reduction. Most likely, this is primarily because the buyers had the time to do their jobs (in addition, of course, to furnishing the suppliers with valid schedules generated by MRP). Those companies that have buyer/planners reported an average 7 percent annual cost reduction. Why the difference? Under the buyer/planner concept, the buyer has to spend time doing the planning and follow-up function. That takes time away from value analysis, negotiation, and so on. With supplier scheduling, the buyer's full-time job is getting the best return on the money available.

Buyers also have the time now for supplier selection. As will be discussed in Chapter 14, they can use supplier measurement reports to evaluate how well the supplier is performing. There's also time to search out alternative sources, either to assure supply or to replace a supplier who isn't performing up to expectations. In addition, buyers have the opportunity to negotiate quality and resolve differences between the supplier's specifications and their own. Quality measurement reports identify the parts below quality standards, and buyers have time to then work with the suppliers to install statistical process quality control. Finally, buyers have time to work with Engineering on tolerances, and to help Engineering with standardization programs so as to improve incoming quality.

When supplier scheduling is in place, buyers have the opportunity to negotiate lead times more easily. By visiting the supplier's plants, buyers can determine the real elements of lead times from the supplier's perspective. They can get answers to such questions as: When does the supplier need to order raw materials? When does the supplier set aside capacity to make the parts? How long does it actually take to produce the item? By using the supplier schedule to forecast raw material and capacity needs, the buyer can negotiate a shorter lead time based on the supplier's actual manufacturing time.

In short, buyers are given the time to do all the functions of their job well. Since they're now expert at buying, rather than at doing paperwork and carrying out expediting, they can become highly motivated professionals in the Purchasing Department.

A POTENTIAL DILEMMA

To whom should the supplier schedulers report? Purchasing managers may feel that the supplier schedulers should report to them, since they're in direct contact with the suppliers. Managers of production and inventory control might want the supplier schedulers reporting to them, since they're operating MRP. What's the solution to this potential dilemma?

The answer lies in the basic issue of accountability. The supplier scheduler should report to the manager who has accountability for the performance of the purchased material inventory. Inventory performance in this context has two aspects: service and turnover.

Service refers to manufacturing and the customers. This means keeping Manufacturing supplied with purchased items so it can operate efficiently and without interruption. It also means providing good customer service on purchased spares and finished goods. Turnover simply means keeping the inventory levels low.

The manager who can best be held accountable for purchased inventory performance is the logical choice to manage the supplier scheduling operation. In some companies, this might be the purchasing manager. In others, the production control manager or perhaps the materials manager might be the best choice.

All things being equal, it is important that the supplier scheduling group be a part of the Purchasing Department. In this arrangement, there's only one person to consult if there is a problem with a purchased item—the purchasing manager. It makes no difference if the item was ordered too late, if the supplier didn't ship on time, if the quantity is wrong, or if the inventory level is incorrect on a purchased item; the purchasing manager is ultimately responsible for all purchased item problems. If the supplier scheduler reports to Production and Inventory Control, there may be confusion on whom to call—the purchasing manager or the production and inventory control manager.

Also, if the supplier scheduler reports to Production and Inventory Control, there may remain some conflict between order quantity and price breaks. If the supplier scheduler reports to Purchasing, the purchasing manager is held accountable to manage pricing while staying below the total inventory dollar limit.

That's the theory. In actual practice, though, there are no absolutes regarding the issue of reporting. In the survey mentioned earlier (see Appendix B), about half of the companies had the supplier schedulers as part of the Purchasing Department, and roughly half had them in Production and Inventory Control.

In most companies, regardless of their reporting structure, the supplier schedulers sit in close proximity to the Purchasing Department. This makes it easy for supplier schedulers to update buyers on potential problems as they occur. In return, the buyers keep the supplier schedulers informed on key issues.

Quality problems can be handled jointly by the buyers and supplier schedulers. The supplier schedulers need to get a replacement shipment, while the buyers need to resolve the underlying reason for the quality problem. The buyers also need to keep the supplier schedulers up to date on pricing and lot size changes so they can input the data and replan as necessary. The supplier schedulers keep the buyers updated on engineering changes and new product timing so they can select suppliers and negotiate pricing prior to the effectivity date.

The buyers inform the supplier schedulers about pending changes in suppliers, new suppliers, and so on. This can enable supplier schedulers to help new suppliers with material and capacity planning information, and to begin building the core relationship.

In short, buyers and supplier schedulers work together to resolve problems and handle changes before they can cause a production short-age. When suppliers call to discuss quality or pricing, they contact the buyer. When they call to discuss delivery, they contact the supplier scheduler. But because buyers and supplier schedulers work as a team, often both deal with suppliers to be sure all bases are covered. Anything short of a team effort may cause a return to the old "your supplier, your schedule" finger-pointing routine, hot lists, and low performance.

How many supplier schedulers will a company need? Our survey showed an average of one supplier scheduler supporting two buyers. Since the buyers and supplier schedulers are set up on a commodity ba-sis, it is fairly easy to arrange the commodities so this 2:1 ratio can work smoothly.

A logical question at this point is, "Will we need to hire more people in order to staff the supplier scheduling function?" The answer is almost always "no." The supplier schedulers can often be drawn from the exist-ing planner group as a result of reassigning planning responsibilities from a product orientation to a commodity orientation on the purchased items.

MATERIALS MANAGEMENT

In many companies today, Purchasing, Production, Inventory Control, and other departments report to a person called the materials manager. This person's job is to coordinate and resolve the problems that can oc-cur between the various materials departments. Purchasing wants larger lot sizes. Production and Inventory Control want smaller lot sizes. Traf-fic wants truckload shipments. The warehouse wants even flow of mate-rial.

With MRP II, the company now has valid priorities, and many of the problems encountered with the informal system vanish. Hot lists disap-pear, expediting is dramatically reduced, inventory is lowered, weekly or smaller shipments of purchased items even the flow of material. Traf-fic is provided with advanced schedules of inbound freight with which to negotiate freight rates.

Consequently, much of the need for a referee is removed. The sup-plier schedulers are given the responsibility of scheduling purchased items and staying within their inventory target, and the production schedulers are given the responsibility of scheduling work-in-process and staying within their inventory target. Therefore, in many MRP II companies, the need for the materials management form of organization is lessened.

MULTIPLANT OPERATIONS

Many companies today have multiple-plant operations. They often have a Central Purchasing Department, but their manufacturing operations are decentralized. Typically, each operation does its own production scheduling and generates its own material requirements, then forwards them to a central buying group to be purchased. Normally, they would come to Central Purchasing on a requisition of some type, rather than as a Material Requirements Planning output, which makes it impossible for Central Purchasing to do supplier scheduling.

There are two approaches to this problem. If each plant has its own computer and its own MRP II software, the supplier scheduling function can be located at the plant site. Central Purchasing can be supplied with the annual quantities of all the parts used at all the facilities and would do annual contracting, based on the total combined requirements for each item.

Once the supplier is selected, and the terms or conditions negotiated, the supplier scheduling function at the plant site would do all of the supplier scheduling. Though they would be part of the plant staff, they might have a "dotted-line" responsibility to Central Purchasing in regard to supplier selection, order quantities, lead times, and so forth.

In cases where the company has a central computer and only one MRP II software package, and the central data processing group does all the Material Requirements Planning processing, Purchasing would have the option to do supplier scheduling at the central location or the plant site. Since all plant requirements are run on the same software, it would be very easy to get the combined requirements for every item for every location on one Material Requirements Planning report.

This would let buyers give each supplier a supplier schedule that showed the total requirements for each item, just as if there were only a single location. This would also be far simpler for the supplier than receiving five different plans from five different plants. At the same time, the supplier schedule would break down the total weekly quantity by plant location and tell the supplier how much to ship to each plant on a weekly basis.

Regardless of which approach is employed, it may be advantageous to generate one corporate supplier schedule in situations where there are common items used by several plants. This schedule would display the total requirements for that item, along with shipping and delivery information.

Some companies use a combination of approaches. Large-volume multiple-plant items are handled by a central scheduling group. A plant scheduling group handles items that are unique to a plant and purchased at a nearby supplier. In cases where some items are purchased overseas by someone located in an overseas buying office, those items can be scheduled from that location. MRP II can provide a great deal of flexibility in establishing "who does what and where." Chapter 13, which covers special situations, presents more examples of organizational flexibility.

SAMPLE JOB DESCRIPTIONS

Below you will find sample job descriptions for a supplier scheduler and a supervisor of supplier scheduling. Obviously, the descriptions would have to be tailored to meet the requirements of each company, but they do give an overview of the general functions related to each job.

JOB DESCRIPTION
JOB TITLE: SUPPLIER SCHEDULER

Job Function

Responsible for the planning and maintenance of the Material Requirements Planning system as it affects purchase parts. Monitors changes in the Material Requirements Planning system and notifies buyers of changed requirements. Works with suppliers on irregular orders to check on the status of current or future shipments of purchase parts as required.

Summary of Duties and Responsibilities

1. Records additions, deletions, and changes to the item master file and the material requirements file for purchase items.

2. Analyzes the Material Requirements Planning system and advises both the buyer and the supplier of irregularities or unusual demand.

3. Releases new orders to suppliers confirming delivery dates on the supplier schedule. This is accomplished by converting planned orders to scheduled receipts (or firm planned orders if quantities or dates are modified) in the Material Requirements Planning system.

4. Reschedules delivery dates as required by the Material Requirements Planning system and, if the change is inside the supplier's lead time, contacts the supplier before making the change to assure it is practical and possible.

5. Contacts suppliers on matters of current and past due shipments. Works closely with suppliers and production schedulers to assure that the master schedule is workable and valid.

6. Responds to routine questions from suppliers and inside employees via telephone.

7. Other duties as required by supervisor.

JOB DESCRIPTION
JOB TITLE: SUPERVISOR, SUPPLIER SCHEDULING

Job Function

To supervise the supplier scheduling function.

Summary of Duties and Responsibilities

1. Responsible for the purchase part inventory level.

2. Responsible for working with data processing to ensure the Purchasing Department of timely delivery of necessary computer runs, and for requesting and securing all "on request" management information reports, such as commodity buying reports, dollars purchased by supplier report, and so forth.

3. Responsible for ensuring that supplier schedules are provided to the suppliers on a timely basis (via mail, electronic data interchange, fax, etc.).

4. Supports the supplier schedulers in their contacts with suppliers on matters of current and past due shipments. Contacts with suppliers require tact and discretion, as the company image is at stake.

5. Responsible for providing long-range planning reports to suppliers to do capacity and raw material planning and to buyers to do negotiating and contracting.

6. Monitors flow of work through contacts with other departments, engineering change notices, and so on.

7. Coordinates new product effort, as that affects new purchase parts entering system.

8. Works on special projects as directed by purchasing manager.

One caution in regard to supplier schedulers should be kept in mind: The job is critical in terms of giving the suppliers a valid schedule. If the job is not done properly, the buyer will be forced to do a lot of expediting and get involved in problems that will pull him or her away from the primary task of spending the company's money well. Therefore, it takes a skilled individual to do the job correctly. If the job is rated as a clerical job and treated as such, the results will probably not be satisfactory. Supplier scheduling is a very important job and must be treated as such.

THE JIT METHOD

In Chapter 5, the Kanban method of scheduling suppliers was covered. To recap, the supplier schedule authorizes the purchase of raw materials and gives the supplier the overall rate at which the items are needed and the allocation of capacity at the supplier's facility. The Kanban mechanism, be it a card, a container, or a telephone call, tells the supplier the actual sequence in which to run the items. In companies with a level, steady, and consistent daily production rate, the supplier schedule is generated infrequently and is used for future capacity planning only. In those cases, the Kanban mechanism is the only trigger to authorize production at the supplier's facility.

Typically in companies using JIT extensively in manufacturing, both the generation of the Kanban card and the sequence in which items will be made are determined by Manufacturing. In such companies it is possible to have the production planner, final assembly scheduler, production supervisor, or the direct laborer schedule the supplier.

In some JIT companies that flow the product in a cellular manufacturing environment, the direct laborers in that cell have been given the responsibility to establish the daily manufacturing schedules. The direct laborers would look at the master schedule to determine what has to be produced, they would then determine the best sequence in which to produce it, and they would also be accountable for requisitioning the material from the warehouse as needed. They would also be responsible for scheduling the supplier, via the Kanban mechanism, for the material needed to complete that daily schedule. In the Kanban examples given in Chapter 5, the direct laborer on the saw at the window company schedules the supplier; in the company that uses color-coded tubs to determine the paint color, the direct-labor operator sends the empty tubs to the supplier; and at the chair manufacturer the direct laborer, by pulling the powder-coated arm out of the rack, in effect schedules the supplier.

The idea of having Manufacturing, and in many companies the direct laborer, schedule the supplier via a Kanban mechanism is a relatively new concept. But it is likely to be the norm for JIT companies in the future.

PURCHASING STRATEGY

There are two separate organization changes occurring today in many companies that directly affect purchasing strategy. The first is the move to put more areas of responsibility under the umbrella of the Purchasing Department. The second is a major move to outsourcing in Supply Chain Management organizations.

Traditionally, most Purchasing Departments have been responsible for buying only. Activities such as planning, inventory control, and receiving have reported to other departments in the company. As stated earlier in this chapter, with the move to supplier scheduling, the areas of planning and inventory control for purchased components and raw materials are now starting to fall under the Purchasing Department. Because of the need for timelines of receiving and accurate receipt information, some companies have also started to have the Receiving Department report to Purchasing.

Some companies have moved far beyond having just materials management functions report to Purchasing. A large Midwestern company, an excellent user of MRP II and supplier scheduling, did a study of its product costs. This very efficient manufacturer had engineered out all the labor content it could over the previous few years. The study showed that 80 percent of the cost of its products was purchased components and only 20 percent was labor. Consequently, the real opportunity for product cost reduction in the future would come primarily from the area of Purchasing. As a result of this study, the company realized that Product Engineering was not always concentrating its efforts to minimize purchase costs and that Purchasing did not have good costing information to make good decisions on make or buy initiatives. As a result, the company was reorganized to put the Product Engineering and

Cost Accounting departments under Purchasing. With the new organizational alignment, the company has been able to concentrate on purchase cost reductions. The result: purchase costs reduced by 40 percent over a three-year period.

The second major move is to outsourcing in Supply Chain Management organizations. As mentioned in Chapter 1, manufacturers are now specializing their operations to gain a competitive advantage. They are maximizing their core competencies to become very efficient and outsourcing high-level and intermediate assemblies, as well as the basic components. There is a move away from vertically integrated operations, where you build as much of the product in-house as possible, to doing only the final assembly. This is true in the electronics industry and the chemical industry, as well as in many assembled products companies. A large locomotive manufacturer used to buy the components for the wheel assemblies (wheels, axles, springs, paint, etc.) from several companies and assemble them in-house. The manufacturer now buys the complete wheel assemblies and has them delivered directly to the locomotive assembly line. To free up capacity to make finished product, a large chemical company is buying intermediates it used to make from a chemical specialty manufacturer that can produce smaller batches more efficiently. An electronics manufacturer is buying stuffed boards instead of inserting all the components on the board in-house, because the supplier specializes in this area and can perform the operations more efficiently. This allows the final product manufacturer to concentrate on its core competencies and outsource to take advantage of suppliers' core competencies. This movement to outsourcing will affect Purchasing and increase the demands on Purchasing. It will require Purchasing to be more involved in the entire manufacturing process, not just the components. Purchasing will need to form closer partnerships with suppliers, and evaluate suppliers to be sure they can perform in a JIT environment. As a result, Purchasing departments have started to add industrial engineers, Supplier Quality Assurance personnel, tooling engineers, and JIT experts to their departments to better support their supplier partnerships.

Review your company's Vision and Mission Statements, along with its core competencies. Review Purchasing's role as it relates to the Vision and Mission Statements, especially if your company is looking at Supply Chain Management, and develop a Vision and Mission Statement for Purchasing. Develop the purchasing strategies necessary to execute that role and then consider how you might creatively staff your Purchasing Department to accomplish that role.

SUMMARY

- The main problem of the traditional approach to purchasing is that it does not take into account the time when materials are actually needed.

- The combined approach puts buying and planning together, which solves the timing problem. But the new planning burden on buyers often prevents them from doing their jobs as effectively as possible.

- With supplier scheduling in place, the planner works directly with suppliers on details of the delivery date. As a result, buyers can focus on what really saves the company money: sourcing, negotiation, value analysis, and related actions.

- With MRP II in place, 90 to 95 percent of the items handled by the supplier scheduler are routine. The buyer handles the rest.

- In addition to generating the actual schedules, the supplier scheduler is responsible for maintaining information in the system, as well as responding to supplier delivery problems, engineering changes, and other situations that might alter schedule dates.

- The person to whom supplier schedulers report will vary by company. The only hard-and-fast rule is that supplier schedulers should not be placed in the position where they are given conflicting directives.

- In JIT companies, the trend today is to let someone in Manufacturing, the production planner, the final assembly scheduler, the production supervisor, or the direct laborer schedule the supplier via a Kanban mechanism.

- In an effort to improve Purchasing performance, companies are putting nontraditional departments, such as Product Engineering, under Purchasing.

- In Supply Chain Management companies, there is a major move to outsourcing of components and assemblies to take advantage of suppliers' core competencies.

Chapter Seven

Supplier Quality Assurance

SUPPLIER CERTIFICATION

In a typical company today, purchase orders are placed with suppliers for a certain amount of purchase material. The supplier ships the material to the buyer's company, where it is received at the Receiving Department. Receiving verifies the quantity and item number and writes up a receiving report, which is sent to several different departments. The material is then moved to the Inspection Department, where it is checked against the specifications and is either accepted or rejected. If accepted, it is then moved to the warehouse, stored, and at a later date moved to the Production Department.

If the material is rejected, it is moved to a hold rack in Receiving until the disposition of the material is determined. Each week, a Material Review Board meets to determine what to do with the rejected material. If it is desperately needed in Production and the bad material can be sorted out or reworked, the rejection is waived and the indirect operation of sorting or reworking is completed. The material is then moved to the warehouse and issued to Production as needed. If the rejected material is determined to be unusable, it is returned to the supplier and Purchasing then has to expedite in a replacement shipment of the material. What did all of these indirect activities add to the value of your product? Nothing—only cost!

In the case where the specifications on the shipment were waived and the rejected material was used, a dangerous message was telegraphed to the suppliers: It will be okay to ship defective material in the future also.

Let's say the specifications are stated as a range: We want a material that is .55 inches thick, but we can accept and use anything that falls between .50 and .60. The material that was waived is .70. We have therefore told the supplier that the true range we are willing to accept is now .50 to .70. The next time the supplier makes a batch at .70, guess what will happen? The supplier will ship it to the company knowing it is out of specification—but also knowing that if the company waived the specifications last time, it will probably waive them again.

To try and prevent this from happening again, the company sorts out the bad material from the shipment and deducts 15 percent of the invoice total for sorting. Many people assume that this sorting charge will deter the supplier in the future. In fact, all this does is tell the supplier that the company will be glad to pay 85 percent of the value for bad material. Now, let's say that the supplier has two buyers for a certain item. Buyer A will always return the items if they are bad, and Buyer B will sort the bad items and give the supplier 85 percent of the value for the items. What is the supplier's disincentive not to ship the bad items to Buyer B? There isn't any.

What is needed is a move toward certification of both the supplier and the material. If that can be achieved, it is possible to expect defect-free quality, frequent and synchronized deliveries to the point-of-use, and the elimination of waste in the Inspection and Receiving departments.

Supplier certification entails three steps. First, suppliers must be qualified. Second, suppliers must be educated in MRP II and JIT/TQC so they understand your expectations and how they can be successful. And third, suppliers must go through the certification process. Let's take a closer look at each step. (Education will be dealt with in depth in Chapter 15.)

QUALIFYING SOURCES

The recent trend is toward fewer suppliers and single-sourcing of components. This, in turn, makes it even more important to qualify sources. The following seven-step program can help you do that in an organized and professional manner.

1. Get management support.

2. Decide which suppliers to qualify first.

3. Assemble a cross-functional qualification team.

4. Agree on criteria for evaluating suppliers.

5. Gather and analyze your data.

6. Make an initial qualification.

7. Make the final qualification.

Get Management Support

Without management support, no qualification program will be successful. To gain that support, we recommend the following strategy. First, state the program's goals and timetables. The key objective is to find and develop single sources of supply capable of delivering defect-free product, on time, to the point-of-use, in frequent shipments, and cost-effectively.

Next, estimate the total cost of poor performance in terms of delivery, quality, and so on, and show the effect on the bottom line in black and white. What is the true cost of a line shutdown caused by a material shortage? What is the cost of inspecting, testing, and rejecting poor-quality material? Develop a solid cost/benefit number. Then excite management about the prospect of becoming partners with your suppliers. Provide case studies that demonstrate the results other companies have achieved through similar programs and share those with management. Finally, become a project champion—get the whole company behind the plan by showing them the benefits. Be prepared to sell the concept and to do it enthusiastically.

Decide Which Suppliers to Qualify First

If you try to qualify all your suppliers at once, the program will probably fail. A safer approach is to pick the items provided by the worst suppliers—those suppliers who seem least able to hit the specifications—because you'll be able to realize your greatest payback and savings. By either improving the performance of the worst suppliers or replacing them with excellent suppliers, you will quickly validate the program, achieve some quick financial paybacks, and reinforce your efforts throughout the company.

Assemble a Cross-Functional Qualification Team

To be effective, qualification must draw on a number of areas of knowledge. No one person can possibly be an expert in all of the categories that will be used to evaluate the suppliers, so your team should be multi-disciplinary and include key players from Purchasing, Quality Control, Receiving, Engineering, Finance, Manufacturing, Sales, and Marketing. The purchasing manager should head up the team to give it direction and ensure that the objectives are on target.

Agree on Criteria for Evaluating Suppliers

Chapter 3 described 10 criteria for a good supplier. Your qualification team can use them as a starting point, then add your own to tailor the list to your unique situation. For example, you might need FDA approval or have to meet minority hiring requirements.

Next, the team must decide what performance scores your company needs from its suppliers in order to not only stay competitive, but be the leader in your industry. This is a better approach than determining desired performance with respect to how the suppliers are performing today. In other words, determine the absolute performance that suppliers must demonstrate in order to participate in a partnership relationship. This step is sometimes called benchmarking.

Suppose one of your suppliers is performing at only 70 percent on-time. Don't approach the situation by saying, "We would like to see 85 percent by next June." Rather, start with your needs: "We want 99 percent on-time delivery." Period. Otherwise, you will wind up settling for something less than what you need to achieve your position in the marketplace.

The process of benchmarking entails five phases that most companies use to determine the absolute performance levels required.

1. *Planning Phase*. The team decides which items will be benchmarked and who is the industry leader in respect to those items.

2. *Analysis Phase*. The team studies competitors' strengths and weaknesses with regards to the items to be benchmarked.

3. *Integration Phase*. The team develops and communicates a strategic plan to capitalize on the company's strengths and minimize the weaknesses.

4. *Action Phase*. The team works with suppliers to implement the strategic plan.

5. *Maturity Phase*. Competitive benchmarking becomes a way of life and the company is able to maintain leadership in its industry.

Gather and Analyze Your Data

Qualifying suppliers is not just a subjective process—it's very much based on hard numbers. To obtain the necessary numbers, develop a checklist that enables you to compile standardized information about each supplier. Of course, in some cases you might have to ask some special questions of a particular supplier. Even so, the bulk of the data should be as consistent as possible. Use the list of questions in Appendix A.

Make an Initial Qualification

Once you run your existing suppliers through your qualification criteria, some will not be interested in being evaluated so rigorously. Some will say they don't want to share or give up anything, that they are the industry leaders (or believe they are). And some will just be beyond education or hope. The few good remaining suppliers will pass the muster in terms of (1) service, delivery, and quality; (2) financial stability; and (3) technical capabilities.

Make the Final Qualification

As in most things in life, common sense prevails in the area of qualification. If the best supplier is based in Europe and you are located in Florida, that supplier might not be ideal for frequent deliveries. If your company rates ethics as very important but your supplier has had some ethical problems in the past, you have a bad fit. If two of the suppliers you evaluated for a particular part both rate the same, you may choose to take both of them into the certification phase to determine which performs better.

Once you make your final cuts, you should give feedback to the winners and losers. You will do the losers a great service if you explain why they were not chosen. With this sort of information, they may come around and become the best suppliers during another round of qualifications. The same applies if you have to pull the business from a supplier that initially met your qualification criteria but later could not keep up with your standards. Say why you found the supplier to be deficient—that may help the supplier to tighten its operation and reach the top tier in the future.

SUPPLIER QUALITY EDUCATION

Once the qualification phase is complete, it is necessary to educate the chosen suppliers and provide a vision of what business will be like in an

MRP II and JIT/TQC environment. In these sessions, the company should lay out its new expectations for the future regarding quality, delivery, costs, certification, price reductions, teamwork, and so forth. (See Chapter 15 for a more detailed explanation of the education process.)

CERTIFICATION PROCESS

After the suppliers have been through the education program, certification can begin. To be able to deliver defect-free quality parts, suppliers will have to begin using quality techniques like statistical process control (SPC). Excellent TQC companies train their suppliers in SPC through in-house demonstrations. It is much more effective to show them how SPC works than to tell them about it. Moreover, the supplier realizes how serious you are about TQC because you are practicing it yourself.

First, visit the supplier and verify that its manufacturing processes and tooling can make a quality item to your specifications. Your quality and engineering people should accompany you and assist you in evaluating the supplier's capabilities. If you determine that the supplier's process is not capable of producing a quality item to your specifications, work with the supplier to change the process, the tooling, or, potentially, your specifications. If you don't visit the supplier's plant, the first time you will find out you have a quality problem is when you reject a shipment.

Next, your company and the supplier need to inspect the items for defects. The goal is to eventually eliminate the need for inspection, but practically speaking, that won't happen for a period of time. In the meantime, both parties need to identify and eliminate the cause of any defects.

The buyer's company should develop an inspection measurement system that identifies defects. Such a measurement system is described in Chapter 14. Likewise, the supplier should set up an inspection process during production. If the supplier runs a lot of 1,000 pieces and then inspects them, potentially all 1,000 could be defective. But if you insist that the supplier inspects the first, 25th, and 50th piece, and so on, and that the machine is shut off if a poor-quality item is produced, you greatly minimize the chances that you will get a defective item. There is no greater waste than taking good material and good labor and producing poor-quality material.

The effectiveness of such in-process inspection is illustrated by a manufacturer of aluminum die-cast parts, which occasionally produced a few bad castings. In some cases the castings were dimensionally incorrect because of warping. In others, the castings had porous areas or were not completely filled in, leading to surface problems. Prior to SPC, the operator of the machine would take each casting as it came out of the machine, remove excess metal, and toss it into a metal tub where it was later inspected by quality-control people. When SPC was put in place, the operator was given a check fixture that identifies dimensional problems. The operator now removes excess metal from each part, inserts the part in the check fixture to be sure it is dimensionally correct, visually checks the surface for problems, and approves only the good parts. Rejects are immediately melted down so they won't be shipped to the buyer. This is the goal you are trying to achieve through SPC.

Finally, as introduced in Chapter 3, you will want the supplier to chart the quality results of each lot of material produced to be alerted to potential problems before the process gets out of control. Figure 7.1 demonstrates this technique.

The acceptable tolerance on a certain element of the specification is .88 to .92. As long as the supplier produces product within this range, it is acceptable. The Xs represent the results of each lot of material produced. Note that over the six lots produced to date, the trend is pointing out a potential problem. The process is going out of control. Perhaps the tool is not sharp enough; something is allowing the quality of the part to get near the outer range. By charting the process, the supplier should be able to see this trend and correct the process to get future lots back in the center of the range as in Figure 7.2. This will help assure you of quality parts lot-to-lot from the supplier.

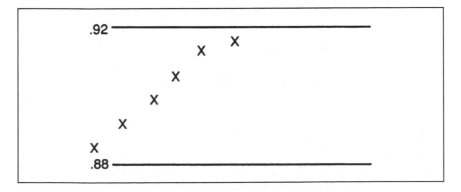

Figure 7.1   Control Chart—Trending Out of Range.

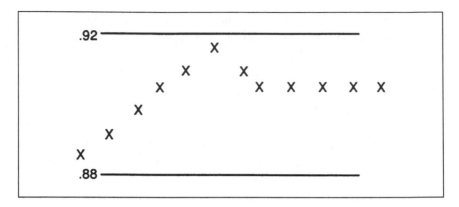

Figure 7.2   Control Chart—Trend Corrected.

Once the supplier is charting all the key elements of the specifications and has the process under control so it is producing only good material, the supplier should begin sending copies of the charts to your Quality Assurance (QA) Department. Your QA people should test those same elements and develop a confidence that the supplier has performed the tests correctly. After confidence in the supplier's charts has been developed, reduce incoming inspections and only randomly check the material for a given period of time. If no defects are found, certify the quality of that material for that supplier and eliminate incoming inspections (you will also eliminate the indirect costs that do not add value to the product).

Note that only the specific material is certified with the supplier. Don't assume just because the supplier can make one item with no defects that it can also make all other items defect-free.

In most JIT/TQC companies that accept control charts, periodic checks are done at the supplier's facility to verify that the quality-control tests are being run in an acceptable manner. It is a good idea to have your quality-assurance manager and your supplier's quality-assurance manager know each other personally. Then, if there are any questions on raw material, processes, testing, and so on, the two QA people can quickly discuss the problems before the supplier makes an unacceptable quality item.

Finally, if the supplier is going to put through an engineering change on your item, your QA people should check the change before it becomes effective. If that change causes you a problem in fit, function, or use, the supplier should not make the change. It is better that you know the effects ahead of time rather than when it is too late, when your product fails in the field because of the unknown change.

THE PROCESS WORKS

Tektronix had an ongoing series of quality problems with its suppliers. As a result, it employed 100 people in supplier quality control and acquired a good deal of very expensive test equipment to check incoming material. Although this company had 15 manufacturing plants, all purchase items were brought in through one central receiving/inspection area. After being checked for quality and quantity, the materials were stored at a central receiving area in a very large computerized warehouse and then shipped to the individual plants as required. Not only did this company have a very large Quality Control Department at the central location, but it needed more than 100 people in Receiving and Warehousing to move and store the items.

To improve the situation, the company formed a multidisciplinary team that included Quality Control, Receiving, Warehousing, Industrial and Product Engineering, Tooling Engineering, Finance, and Marketing. Purchasing chaired the team. The team's first step in addressing the quality problems was a series of "kickoff" education days for the suppliers' top management to explain the issues and the new Total Quality Control (TQC) approach to quality. The ultimate goal, they said, was defect-free product delivered frequently to point-of-use.

Once the suppliers' top management agreed to the program, a second series of kickoff meetings was held for the suppliers' operating managers. The team then started visiting each supplier to check the manufacturing processes and tooling and identify deficiencies that led to defects. As a defect was identified over the next several months, it was given to the supplier for cause identification and elimination. As the suppliers' quality levels improved, the expensive test equipment was transferred to the suppliers and the supplier was required to verify the quality and deliver only defect-free product. As the suppliers developed SPC and control charts, the company shifted to random inspections and, after a four-year process, certified the quality on the majority of their purchased items.

Today this company employs one incoming inspector at each of its 15 manufacturing plants and five source quality inspectors who visit supplier plants randomly. All certified items are delivered directly to point-of-use on the manufacturing floor as required, without going through Receiving or Inspection. The large central warehouse is currently for sale because the receiving, inspection, and warehousing functions are no longer needed on the majority of the items. The few items that aren't yet certified are delivered, as required, to the incoming inspectors at the plants. The goal is to eventually have 100 percent of the items certified.

As each supplier becomes certified for producing defect-free product, they are given a plaque to celebrate the occasion. This plaque is a symbol of an ongoing commitment by both companies to the highest levels of quality and performance.

SUMMARY

- In companies that consistently waive and use defective material, the suppliers are given the message that it is okay to ship defective material.

- Supplier certification entails a three-step process that consists of qualifying and educating suppliers prior to the certification step.

- Without management support, a supplier certification program will not be successful.

- To be effective, a cross-functional team should be used to qualify suppliers.

- To be able to deliver defect-free material, suppliers will have to begin using quality techniques like statistical process control (SPC).

- Control charts are a good way to visually alert suppliers to potential quality problems.

- Before making an engineering change on your item, your supplier should check with you first to verify that the change will not cause a problem in your product.

Chapter Eight

Supplier Base Reduction

Many companies today have a policy that states that Purchasing must have more than one supplier approved on each item purchased. The logic underlying this policy is simple enough. First, if you have more than one supplier, the price of the item can be regularly bid so that the company is assured that it is getting the lowest price for the item. Second, if the supplier has a production problem, the alternative supplier can step in and keep the company running.

In principle, that reasoning is sound. But it doesn't work in practice. The first reason mentioned for multiple suppliers is to get the lowest price. The idea of competition is good and we should always be looking for the "best" supplier. But that doesn't necessarily mean the supplier with the lowest price; you will never get to lowest cost by a quotation form. You get to lowest cost by working in a partnership with your suppliers to eliminate all waste and thereby develop the lowest cost *consistent with required delivery and quality requirements*.

Second, having multiple suppliers doesn't prevent stockouts. Regardless of how many suppliers they have per item, companies still have shortage lists and run out of purchase parts on a regular basis. Why? Because they don't have the best suppliers, they don't train those suppliers in what is expected as to performance, and they don't have valid schedules. It is difficult enough to find one good supplier that can consistently perform, let alone two or three suppliers. When purchasing people are forced by company policy to find multiple sources for all items, they usually have to dip into the pool of poor or marginal suppliers to make their quotas. This only guarantees that some of those suppliers will not perform up to expected levels. Also, it is impossible to adequately educate and train several hundred or several thousand suppliers. With a couple hundred suppliers, that becomes a more manageable task. One company's motto is "Make the suppliers so good they can't lose the business." Of course, that can't happen with a large supplier base.

How much can you reduce your supplier base? Consider Xerox, which cut back from 5,000 to 300 suppliers over a couple of years' time span. Then it invested heavily in training those 300 suppliers in MRP II and JIT/TQC. The results? Xerox cut its quality defect level from 10,000 (1 percent) to 122 (.01 percent) parts per million, cut its raw material inventory 75 percent, dramatically improved its on-time supplier performance, was able to link up with its key suppliers using EDI, and reduced the purchase content of a copy machine 48 percent. Not bad performance numbers! Tellabs, a manufacturer of high-speed telecommunications products based in Lisle, Illinois, cut its supplier base from 600 to 150 and reduced the number of trucking companies that carried the raw materials by half. With fewer suppliers to manage, the company can now give its MRP output directly to the suppliers and have them do the purchase material planning. The direct labor employees release purchase material as needed from those suppliers using Faxban. Purchasing now buys material by exception only, when there is a problem, and has time to work very closely with those suppliers on how to continuously eliminate waste and lower the total costs of acquisition.

Finally, Unisys, of New Jersey, cut its supplier base from 750 to 106 and reduced the number of trucking companies from 120 to 8. As a result, purchase costs dropped by 40 percent, freight costs were reduced from $.32 per pound to $.09 per pound, and transit times from the Far East were cut by two-thirds.*

If done correctly, reducing your supplier base can have dramatic results in purchasing. In Supply Chain Management companies, the direction is to form formal partnerships with single sources. In cases where the supplier cannot supply all the buyer needs because of capacity limitations, the partnership supplier is the major or dominant source of the material.

SINGLE-SOURCING VERSUS MULTIPLE-SOURCING

There are many excellent reasons why single-sourcing is more beneficial than multiple-sourcing. This section will cover only eight advan-

---

* *Purchasing Week*, July 16, 1987.

tages, but every company will be able to add some to the list due to its own particular circumstances and supplier base.

1. *Volume.* One of the primary advantages is consolidated volumes. If you split the business among three suppliers, the pricing typically will not be as good as buying the entire volume from one supplier. Whether you give each supplier 33 percent of the business or split the business 70 percent to Supplier 1, 20 percent to Supplier 2, and 10 percent to Supplier 3, the price will not be as good as if one supplier receives the entire volume. You also run the costs up by needing to negotiate more business agreements and have more receipts and quality inspections. You probably will have a higher freight rate because individual shipping quantities from Suppliers 2 and 3 are smaller, too. In addition, the costs of training and certifying multiple suppliers will be higher, and many JIT techniques such as point-of-delivery will be almost impossible to implement.

2. *Supplier performance.* It is often very difficult to find several good suppliers for an item. Many surveys have been published that show that the typical company experiences supplier performances that range from 70 to 85 percent on-time and 87 to 93 percent in terms of in-specification quality parts. A buyer in a supplier scheduling environment cannot tolerate that level of supplier performance, because the supplier schedule or Kanban mechanism is working to the need date of the item, not a replenishment date. Either the supplier hits the date with acceptable parts or the buyer has a potential stock-out situation. As the buyer is forced by company policy to buy from two or three suppliers, the chances for good supplier performance drops.

3. *Training load.* As mentioned before, buyers need to either train suppliers or ensure that they get training in MRP II and JIT/TQC. Many suppliers have little or no concept of how to produce defect-free items, make consistent on-time deliveries, or reduce lead times or lot sizes economically. Therefore, if the buyer wants better supplier performance, training must occur. (See Chapter 15.) If a company has 1,000 suppliers and educates 20 per day, that tallies up to 50 days, or 10 solid weeks' worth of training effort. If a company reduces the supplier base to 200, the training load drops to 10 days, or two weeks, a much more manageable workload.

4. *Synchronized schedules.* Chapters 5 and 9 cover the need to move toward more frequent shipments and the concept of synchronizing your

schedules with those of your suppliers. If you can get suppliers to set aside capacity to support your supplier schedules and then allow the buyer to select out of that capacity the material needed on a weekly or daily basis, then your company can become much more flexible at meeting its customer needs without carrying a lot of "just-in-case" inventory. The more suppliers a buyer has, the smaller the volume of parts per supplier, and the less sure the supplier can be about long-term guarantee of business. The latter means it will be more difficult to implement synchronized schedules.

5. *Communications.* Because there is only one supplier for an item, the communications between the buyer and the supplier are often much easier. Typically, with a large supplier base, the only person the buyer knows from the supplier is the salesperson. If a problem occurs, the buyer calls the salesperson to discuss the problem. The salesperson calls Customer Service, which calls Quality Assurance, which calls someone else. This is time-consuming and frustrating; it seems to take forever before an answer is provided. With only 150 suppliers, it may be possible to get to know the key people in Order Entry, Quality Assurance, and so on, at the supplier on a first-name basis. The problem can then be given directly to the correct person and resolved in a much more timely and efficient manner.

6. *Problem solving.* A smaller supplier base allows more of a joint approach to problem solving. The buyer and supplier are able to work more closely and, in effect, see themselves as a team fighting against the competition. The better the two perform together, the more business they are jointly able to generate. There is a joint commitment to get the order, to build a quality product on time that will get repeat orders, and to jointly make a profit off the order.

7. *Product development.* When there is a single source for an item, it is easier to get the suppliers involved earlier in the product-development process, which can result in significant improvements in quality, cost, and delivery. In addition, with fewer suppliers involved, it is easier to get your suppliers involved in problem-solving sessions. One Midwest company had the opportunity to bid on a onetime order for 125,000 units of a product it produced on a regular basis for other customers. The company normally made 500,000 of the units annually, so if it could get the order, there would be a 25 percent increase in volume for all the suppliers as well. The best price the company could come up

with and still make a small profit on the order was around $100 per unit, but at this price it probably would not get the order. To try to determine how to offer a more competitive price on this onetime order, the company held a meeting that was attended by all the key internal managers as well as all the key supplier personnel. They jointly discussed what could be done, on a onetime basis, to reduce the cost of the product both internally and externally. Approximately $20 in cost was identified and, in a team effort, removed from the product. The unit was bid at $90 each, the contract won, and everyone was able to share in added business and profit that would not have been realized otherwise.

8. *Buyer benefits.* Finally, the buyer is now able to purchase by exception only. With fewer suppliers, all working either to supplier schedules or Kanban, the buyer is removed from the daily routine of paperwork and expediting and only needs to get involved in the day-to-day routine when something goes wrong. The buyer now has time to spend developing and educating suppliers, negotiating long-term contracts, working with suppliers to simplify their products and processes, and integrating the suppliers into the business. If you can develop a partnership with a few good suppliers who deliver consistently on-time and in-specification with few problems, you finally can get the time to drain the swamp and uncover new opportunities to improve performance in the future.

SINGLE-SOURCING VERSUS SOLE-SOURCING

Sole-sourcing indicates that only one supplier is approved to produce a part. Single-sourcing indicates that more than one supplier may be approved to produce a part, but only one supplier is *used* to produce the part. It is not suggested in this discussion that you sole-source all your parts, but rather that you single-source.

Consider a multiple-source environment that involves nine suppliers. (See Figure 8.1.) In this example, you have three approved sources on each item, and purchase, where practical, product from each source during the year. Parts A, B, and C are all the same commodity, plastic injection-molded parts, but differ in either size, color, or type of plastic. Supplier 1 is your best supplier in terms of overall performance, followed fairly closely by Supplier 5, with the other suppliers significantly lower in performance. In a single-source environment, then, you would purchase all parts from Supplier 1. (See Figure 8.2.)

But note that you have a choice. You could consider Suppliers 2 through 9 as approved suppliers should a problem arise; or you could

Figure 8.1   Multiple-Sourcing.

Figure 8.2   Single-Sourcing.

approve Supplier 5, the second-best-performance supplier, on Parts A and C. That way you would not be sole-sourced, but you would be buying from a single supplier for all the reasons listed earlier in this chapter. The advantage for Supplier 5 in this situation is the potential for future business on other than Part B, and the opportunity for developing expertise using the training given by the buyer. In short, this becomes a win-win situation for all involved and eliminates a lot of time the buyer now spends trying to manage too large a supplier base.

OPERATING UNDER SINGLE-SOURCING

What is it like operating under MRP II and JIT/TQC with single-sourcing? One buyer indicated that she would never work for another company that didn't have it in place. When asked why, the answer was,"Quality of life." When you have valid schedules, a manageable supplier base, predictable performance, and time to do your job, work is certainly more enjoyable and rewarding.

One issue needs to be addressed at this point: pricing and profit protection for the supplier under a single-source arrangement. The concern is that the supplier, knowing it is the single source, will try to raise the price and make an excessive profit. On the other hand, the buyer, having been in the supplier's operation and knowing a lot about the supplier's costs, will try to drive the price down so the supplier makes an insufficient profit. The supplier deserves a reasonable profit and the buyer deserves a reasonable price.

With this in mind, there are three alternatives in pricing, which will be explored using the following supplier's cost breakdown:

Part A—Price $1 each
Cost Breakdown

Raw materials	$.40 each	(40 percent)
Direct labor and burden	$.40 each	(40 percent)
Supplier profit	$.20 each	(20 percent)

The first alternative says that the buyer demands a price reduction from the supplier and gives the need for this price reduction, but does nothing to help the supplier reduce the costs. To retain the business, the supplier reduces the price to $.90 each. Because the supplier has the same costs for raw materials and direct labor as before, the reduction must come out of the supplier's profit. The profit is cut in half, from $.20 each to $.10 each. The pricing would now be:

Part A—Price $.90 each
Cost Breakdown

Raw materials	$.40 each	
Direct labor and burden	$.40 each	
Supplier profit	$.10 each	(11 percent)

The supplier may try to cut corners to lower costs, but that may end up causing the buyer quality or delivery problems in the long run. Because the buyer's business has just become less attractive to the supplier, service, performance, and long-term relationships will suffer as a result.

The second alternative says the buyer works with the supplier to reduce costs on the item, but keeps the percentage of profit fixed on the part. Working as a team, the buyer and supplier are able to reduce both labor and raw materials by 25 percent. The pricing would now be:

Part A—Price $.75 each

Cost Breakdown

Raw materials	$.30 each
Direct labor and burden	$.30 each
Supplier profit (20 percent)	$.15 each

While the percent of profit remains the same, the actual dollars of profit are reduced for the supplier. While the supplier is still profitable and better off than in alternative one, the supplier will not be aggressive in reducing the costs because it reduces the total dollars of profit.

The third alternative says that the buyer and supplier work together as a team to reduce the cost of the item, but the amount of profit is fixed on the item. Like the second alternative, the cost of labor and raw materials is reduced 25 percent, but the supplier is guaranteed a $.20 each profit on the item. The pricing would now be:

Part A—Price $.80 each

Cost Breakdown

Raw materials	$.30 each	
Direct labor and burden	$.30 each	
Supplier profit (fixed)	$.20 each	(25 percent)

Note that although the buyer's price is slightly higher, the supplier's profit percentage is up and the total dollars of profit on the business is unchanged. The advantage to the supplier: guaranteed profit on the business and potentially more volume in business because the buyer's company can be more competitive in the marketplace. The advantage to the buyer: a 100 percent pass-through on all cost reductions to the buyer, a supplier who has no incentive to not reveal the cost breakdown on items, and a supplier who now has an incentive to work cooperatively with the buyer to reduce any and all costs that do not add value to the product. This is truly a win-win situation in which the buyer is able to secure lower costs with the supplier's complete support of the effort while the supplier is able to maintain a level of profit.

An East Coast buyer had a major problem with this concept. The item involved in that case was one in which, over four years, the raw materials and direct labor costs had been reduced by half. The buyer's objection was that the supplier was now making a 33 percent profit, and that was unacceptable to the buyer. The item quoted consisted of the following costs:

Part A—Price $.60 each

Cost Breakdown

Raw materials	$.20 each
Direct labor and burden	$.20 each
Supplier profit (fixed)	$.20 each (33 percent)

The buyer stated he would never allow a supplier to make that kind of profit on an item and felt the supplier's profit was the supplier's problem, not his as a buyer. He was proud of the fact that he often switched from supplier to supplier and had no need to develop partnership relationships. Upon further questioning, the buyer conceded that he had a fair number of past-due orders and quality problems, and had only generated about a 2 percent cost reduction for the year, which was less than the goal he'd set for himself. That is typical of an adversarial relationship with suppliers. The win-win partnership relationship yields nearly 100 percent on-time, in-specification parts, and a 13 percent annual cost reduction. The results speak for themselves.

Pick a group of like items, single-source those items, educate the supplier in what you are attempting to do, generate valid schedules for that supplier, use the win-win approach to pricing described here, and you will be amazed by the results.

SUMMARY

- You will never get the lowest cost by a quotation form.

- There are several reasons why single-sourcing is advantageous over multiple-sourcing.

- With fewer suppliers, it is easier to get your suppliers involved in education, synchronized schedules, problem solving, and product development.

- Single-sourcing is preferable over sole-sourcing.

- If a supplier partnership with single-sourcing is going to work, the supplier must receive a reasonable profit and the buyer a reasonable price.

Chapter Nine

Synchronized Deliveries

In earlier chapters, all the Kanban examples covered daily deliveries from suppliers. That is practical when the supplier is fairly close to the buyer's company and the travel time is short. When the supplier is further away, though, daily shipments may not be practical and cost-effective. Also, your company may not need daily shipments on all the items you buy. The objective is not to secure daily shipments, but frequent shipments that are synchronized to your production schedule in a cost-effective mode.

At some companies, for example, a box of a thousand screws might be a week's worth, so it would be overkill to have them delivered daily. On the other hand, consider a West Coast manufacturer of high-volume, expensive test equipment that consumes thousands of fasteners a day. This company has 30 different configurations of fasteners that are used at several locations on the shop floor. The cost of receiving, warehousing issuing, and keeping track of all these fasteners was very high. Therefore, the company sought to develop a daily delivery of all the fasteners, have the fasteners delivered to the point-of-use on the shop floor, and eliminate the need to receive and warehouse the fasteners.

The company now uses a technique called the "bread run." By analogy, consider how a bread truck arrives every morning at your local supermarket and replenishes the loaves on the shelf. The driver then reports to the manager how many loaves it took to restock the store. The West Coast manufacturer just referred to uses the same mechanism to ensure an adequate supply of fasteners, setting up Kanbans—small bins—at all the manufacturing floor locations where fasteners are used. It then developed a plant map to show which fasteners are used, and where they are used. Each day, the fastener supplier arrives, follows a predetermined path around the plant, fills up the bins at every location with the required fasteners, and then gives Receiving the counts the supplier delivered.

This process has eliminated receiving, warehousing, parts movements, and paperwork in favor of daily deliveries (which may or may not be appropriate for every item you use). The company then does a daily comparison in their MRP II system between what was used and what the supplier reported was delivered to each location. If the two numbers are within an acceptable tolerance, the Accounting Department pays for the delivery.

The same manufacturer buys one of its key components from Japan. Each part costs several hundred dollars, and the company uses about 200 of them per week. The company used to import the parts monthly through the West Coast but had many problems with customs clearance. The solution? A lot of inventory on the part, just in case additional shipments became snarled in red tape. After much time and effort, the company was able to locate and work with the customs officials at an East Coast port to smoothly and quickly move the parts through customs on a weekly basis. The customs officials have become used to seeing the parts arrive, and quickly release the shipments as soon as they hit the port. The parts are then moved from customs to the local East Coast sales office of the Japanese manufacturer.

Each Friday afternoon, the West Coast buyer for the parts faxes a release to the East Coast branch of the supplier, detailing how many of the parts are needed for the next week's production schedule. The West Coast buyer has established a contract with a trucking company to pick up the parts late Friday afternoon on the East Coast and deliver them to California Monday morning. The parts always arrive Mondays at 8:00 A.M., delivered to the point-of-use on the manufacturing floor, and the just-in-case inventory has been eliminated.

With this arrangement, the freight costs are actually lower than the total costs associated with the old method of shipping the parts from Japan to the West Coast plus the cost of the just-in-case inventory. Most important, the company now has a guaranteed weekly receipt quantity that is delivered directly to the point-of-use on the shop floor at 8:00 each Monday morning.

Shifting to daily deliveries in this case would not be necessary, nor would it be practical. But note that shipments are synchronized with the buyer's schedule (the amount needed for the week is delivered at the start of the week). As a result, they are more cost-effective (total cost now lower per delivery), and they are more frequent (weekly versus monthly).

Every company needs to decide on the frequency with which it wants—and needs—deliveries from suppliers. In general, though, most companies need to move toward more frequent shipments from their suppliers in order to reduce the costs ("waste" in JIT terminology) associated with the inventory investment it has tied up in purchase material.

FREIGHT CONSIDERATIONS

One of the major drawbacks to more frequent shipments can be the cost of transportation on the purchase material. If the transportation area is not managed correctly, freight costs can skyrocket and negate any benefits in purchase price reductions and inventory reductions obtained by adopting MRP II and JIT.

Let's look at a situation that illustrates this point. (See Figure 9.1.) A company based in Grand Rapids, Michigan, purchases forgings from a supplier in Detroit, a three-hour drive away. The forgings are purchased in a monthly lot quantity of 5,000. Each of these forgings weighs four pounds, so the monthly freight quantity, per shipment, is 20,000 pounds. The truckload rate for this shipment was $1.96 per hundredweight, or $392 for the total shipment.

Purchasing, in its initial JIT effort, cut the lot size to a weekly quantity, or 1,250 per week. It was able to negotiate the same price for the weekly shipment as for the monthly shipment, so the new approach seemed wise. But the weekly shipment weight dropped to 5,000 pounds, and the freight rate on that quantity increased to $4.43 per hundredweight, a 126 percent increase. In Purchasing's continued effort to reduce the lot size, it asked for and received daily shipments at the same price from the supplier. Again, everything appeared on target, except

Shipment Frequency	Weight per Shipment	Cost per Hundred weight	Monthly Cost
Monthly (1 per mo.)	20,000	1.96	392.00
Weekly (4 per mo.)	5,000	4.43	886.00
Daily (20 per mo.)	1,000	8.21	1642.00

Figure 9.1   Forgings Freight Costs.

that the daily shipment weight was 1,000 pounds. The freight rate on 1,000 pounds was $8.21 per hundredweight, a hefty 319 percent increase over the truckload rate. At the end of the month, the freight bill for the daily shipments totaled $1,642, which negated any inventory savings the company was able to obtain by going from monthly to daily shipments.

As you can see, the tradeoff can be problematic if transportation costs are not managed well. Most companies specify which common carrier they want to deliver the items and may negotiate the freight rate, but few go much further than that. Here are some JIT techniques being employed in the freight and packaging areas today.

Pooled freight rates is one technique that can be employed to lower freight costs. In this technique, all the shipments from a given area of the country are combined into one shipment at a consolidation point; then one freight rate is negotiated based on the total tonnage of that load. For instance, a Midwest-based company had several small suppliers in the Chicago area that had begun to ship to them weekly with less-than-truckload shipments. Each shipment ranged in weight from around 20 pounds to more than 4,000 pounds, depending on the supplier and part number involved. Because the company was getting weekly shipments rather than, say, monthly quantities, the average weight per shipment was less so that higher freight rates per hundredweight applied.

To remedy the problem, the buyer selected one common carrier based in the Chicago area that ran regular shipments into that part of the country. The buyer was then able to negotiate a pooled freight rate based on the total weight of the combined weekly shipments from the Chicago area to the buyer's location. All the suppliers were then instructed to arrange for that common carrier to pick up their shipments on Tuesday, and all of the small individual shipments were consolidated into one large shipment, which was delivered Wednesday morning to the buyer's plant. Because the total tonnage was now greater than the previous individual shipments, the buyer was able to get weekly shipments but pay less total freight costs.

Another variation on this technique is sometimes referred to as the "milk run." Instead of the consolidation occurring at the common carrier's location, the company hires the common carrier on a contract basis to carry out the consolidation. A Denver company, for example, has several suppliers located in small towns 200 or 300 miles from Denver. This company contracted with a freight company to stop at all those locations once a week and pick up the purchase parts. Monday morning the truck makes a pickup in Town A, Monday afternoon in Town B, and so on. The trucker stops at 10 companies during a three-day period and delivers the material back to the buyer's plant late Wednesday evening. The company pays the trucker a flat fee for the run, regardless of whether the truck comes back full. In effect, it rents the truck for the three days. The total freight costs to rent the truck for the three days are dramatically less than what they used to pay for the 10 individual shipments, and this allows the company to bring in what it needs to support the weekly production schedule without paying more in freight for the more frequent service.

Companies that own their own trucks would ideally like to transport purchase parts on the return trip so the trucks do not come back to the plant empty, but coordinating this backhaul scheduling is often difficult and not as productive as many companies would like. With Supplier Scheduling, though, the coordination is much easier. The supplier schedule is generated on a weekly basis for all their suppliers. The quantities due from the suppliers each week are multiplied by the piece weight of each part, and an inbound freight schedule is developed. This can be summarized by town code, county code, state code, and so on. Outbound trucks are then routed in a manner that achieves maximized backhaul potential. Those shipments that will not be picked up by your own truck are shipped by common carrier. In essence, the backhaul is free, so the freight costs are totally eliminated.

One Midwest company devised a very creative arrangement in this area. This firm had many small suppliers on the East Coast. It also had a large dealer for its product in the Boston area to which it delivered product on a weekly basis with its own truck. Purchasing rented 2,000 square feet of warehouse space from that dealer and instructed all its Northeast suppliers to ship to this dealer on a weekly basis. The parts had to arrive by each Wednesday, because on Thursday the company truck delivered product to the dealer and backhauled all the purchase parts. Consequently, the company was able to obtain weekly shipments from all its Northeast suppliers and yet reduce freight costs by more than 80 percent over the old, less-than-truckload way of doing business.

Another twist on the same theme occurred with a buyer in Minneapolis. His company had a supplier in central Wisconsin that shipped a truckload of purchased material each week. To reduce freight costs, the buyer attended several different purchasing association meetings in central Wisconsin to determine whether any companies had shipments coming out of the Minneapolis area. Fortunately, the buyer located a company that purchased a truckload of material a week from Minneapolis, and the two firms contracted with a trucking firm to do one round trip weekly, carrying the material each way for the two companies. Because the trucker was guaranteed a full backhaul for the trucks, they were able to negotiate a lower truckload freight rate. In the final analysis, both companies were able to lower their freight costs by 30 percent.

One other technique is being employed by JIT companies, whether common carriers or contract haulers are used. This is point-of-use delivery, rather than delivery to the dock. Most companies today have parts delivered to the dock, where they're counted, inspected, moved to the warehouse, and then later moved to the manufacturing floor. All of those operations add cost to the process, but no value. Ideally, in a JIT environment you can eliminate all non-value-adding processes. Where companies have certified the quality of their suppliers so no inspections are necessary, parts can be delivered directly to the point-of-use on the factory floor, thereby eliminating those non-value-adding operations. (See Figure 9.2.) In effect, all of their certified suppliers do a "bread run" type of delivery as discussed earlier in this chapter. Shipments to point-of-use on the manufacturing floor are typically smaller quantities than would be delivered to the dock, because the space on the manufacturing floor would be somewhat limited as compared to the dock. The material must be, therefore, available on relatively short notice and cannot be delayed by the need to inspect it for quality defects. Usually, Kanban is used in point-of-use delivery situations to signal the supplier to replenish the inventory.

A consumer goods manufacturer that packages all its product in plastic bags purchases large rolls of blown plastic film, preprinted in one of its eight patterns, each roll weighing several hundred pounds. The rolls of plastic film are mounted on a very large piece of equipment that both

Figure 9.2   Just-in-Time (JIT) Delivery.

produces the product and encloses that product in a plastic bag made from this film. There is very limited space in the area where the roll of plastic film is mounted, and because of its weight, a lift truck was used to load it onto the machine. Each roll of film lasts only around two hours and it was a hassle to move the film into the area and load the machine. The supplier of the film, located five miles away from the plant, designed a wheeled cart to solve the problem. The cart has a spindle that is five feet off the ground, the same height as the spindle on the machine that holds the roll of film. The film is mounted on the cart spindle, and there is a hydraulic cylinder mounted on the cart to push the roll of film off the cart onto the machine. Every two hours, the supplier delivers a roll of film on the cart, pushes the cart to the piece of equipment, and when the machine runs out of film assists the machine operator in loading the new roll of film on the machine spindle. The driver then checks with the machine operator as to which of the eight print patterns is needed next, takes the empty cart back to the plant, and refills it with the next roll of film. The supplier typically produces the rolls of preprinted film the day before shipment based on the supplier schedule, but delivers in the sequence the operator is running that day.

How can you get point-of-use delivery if you use a common carrier? Companies specify the driver they want, and then train that driver as to where the parts are to be delivered on the shop floor. To use this technique with a common carrier, negotiate a JIT contract stating that parts must be delivered to specific locations on the shop floor, and that John Doe is the only driver allowed under the terms of the contract. What happens if John Doe is sick or on vacation? Either train an alternate driver or specify that the parts must be delivered to the dock if John isn't available for that delivery.

Will more frequent shipments work if you import materials from overseas? Yes, but it will typically take a lot more time and effort to put the arrangements together. One East Coast manufacturer of computers purchases 85 percent of its components from Asian suppliers. The company selected a customs broker located in the Far East to coordinate the shipments. Here's how it works. Monday of each week, the buyer sends a Faxban to each of the Far East suppliers, detailing what is to be shipped that week. These suppliers then forward their components to the customs broker, who consolidates each of the individual shipments into a single container shipment. The shipment leaves the broker's location at the end of the week and arrives the next week at the buyer's plant. To do all this, the buyer has had to coordinate each shipment with the suppliers, customs broker, customs officials, the air freight forwarder, and the local trucking company. Is all the effort worth it? This company has been able to lower its incoming freight costs by over 40 percent!

The reverse situation also works. An Australian manufacturer of water heaters purchases virtually all of its components from suppliers in the United States. The company hired a firm in Los Angeles to consolidate the components from all of the suppliers into a single container and forward them to Australia each week.

Whatever your shipping needs, the basic message is be creative, challenge the way you're doing it today, and look for better ways to manage your freight costs.

PACKAGING AND LABELING

Very few companies take advantage of the benefits possible in this area by standardizing carton sizes and labeling requirements. They allow the supplier to package product in any size container and to vary quantities from container to container. The buying company asks the supplier to label the container with the part number and quantity, but it does not specify the location or type of label required. As a result, this company misses out on ways to reduce costs through packaging and labeling practices. This is illustrated by the following example.

A motorcycle manufacturer produces motorcycles in lots of 100. Every supplier ships in cartons that contain 100 parts. The company issues one container of each part to the assembly area, and at the end of the manufacturing run, no parts are left over. The stockroom doesn't have to count parts into or out of the stockroom; it issues and receives in cartons of 100, which makes its job a lot easier.

This system also makes receiving parts easier. Receiving counts the number of cartons and multiplies by 100 to ascertain the receipt quantity. How does it verify that the supplier counts are really 100 per carton? At the end of the manufacturing run, if there are none left on the manufacturing floor and 100 motorcycles were produced, there had to be 100 in each carton. Wherever possible, standardize carton sizes and carton quantities around your manufacturing lot sizes. This will eliminate a lot of wasted time and motion in receiving and counting the material.

As you move to JIT deliveries, the workload for Receiving will increase as you get more frequent shipments. You therefore need to develop JIT approaches that reduce workload, not increase it. To reduce the workload and make it easier for Receiving, companies have gone to bar coding. The buyer provides the supplier with bar-code labels that define the supplier number, item number, and quantity in each container. (See Figure 9.3.)

The supplier puts one bar-code label on each container. When the shipment arrives at Receiving, the Receiving person scans the bar code label on one container and records the number of containers. At this point, receipt is complete. This results in more frequent shipments but less total effort for Receiving. The bar-code label also facilitates point-of-use deliveries. The parts are delivered directly to the shop floor and the operator in that department can report the receipt directly to the computer using a bar-code reader. In deliveries made directly to the point-of-use, Receiving doesn't even need to be involved, so the cost of receiving is basically eliminated from the process.

The Advance Ship Notice (ASN) is another tool that is helping to improve the receiving process. The ASN indicates when the supplier will deliver product and what will be in the shipment. Usually the ASN details to the hour when the truck will appear at the dock and allows Receiving to preplan incoming shipments, schedule dock doors, and minimize carrier wait time. The ASN is usually sent at least 24 hours in advance via either Electronic Data Interchange (EDI) or the Internet. In many companies, Receiving is using the ASN to allow it to level load incoming receipts and set up appointments with suppliers on when their truck should be delivering. Because Receiving knows in advance exactly what is on the truck, often detailed down to the number of pallets and containers, it does not have to unload and count the shipment. Rather, it can have the material moved directly off the truck to either the warehouse or point-of-use location.

Again, the goal of JIT is the identification and elimination of waste in all functional areas of the company. That means constantly attacking

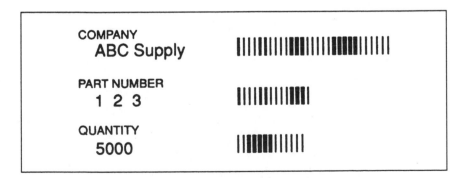

Figure 9.3   Bar-Code Label.

waste, making lots of little changes, and constantly improving procedures until there is no waste of any kind in the system. That also means looking for waste in the following areas: order quantity, safety stock, rejects, setup, receiving of parts, movement of parts to warehouse, issuing of parts to floor inventory, and, as we have seen in this chapter, transportation.

SUMMARY

- The objective is not necessarily to secure daily shipments from suppliers, but rather frequent shipments that are synchronized to your production schedule in a cost-effective mode.

- If not managed correctly, freight costs can skyrocket and negate any benefits in purchase price reductions and inventory reductions obtained by adopting MRP II and JIT.

- There are several techniques, such as bread runs, milk runs, and pooled freight rates, that allow the buyer to get more frequent shipments at a lower freight cost.

- Where companies have certified the quality of their suppliers so no inspections are needed, parts can be delivered to the point-of-use on the shop floor.

- By standardizing packaging and labeling, the costs of receiving can be reduced even though you are receiving more frequent shipments.

- The use of ASNs streamlines the receiving function and allows Receiving to schedule inbound shipments more efficiently.

Chapter Ten

The Customer/Supplier Relationship

Prior to developing partnership arrangements, buyers and suppliers often have adversarial relationships. One reason is that the buyer's schedules are not valid and as a result are constantly changing. The buyer knows that the dates on the purchase orders are replenishment dates, not need dates. The buyer therefore knows that even though an order might go one or two weeks past due, the company will not run out of material. The flip side of the coin is that the supplier knows the dates aren't valid. This is obvious to the supplier because no one is screaming for the past-due orders. Eventually, the buyer's company runs out of material, the item hits the shortage list, and the buyer aggressively expedites the past-due order. And who takes it on the chin for missing the invalid date? The supplier.

Another source of the adversarial relationship is that the buyer's quality specifications are not always representative of what is really needed. Let's say that a supplier shipment is initially rejected because it is outside certain tolerances, but since the parts are badly needed, the rejection is waived and the parts are used. At the time of the next production run, the supplier experiences the same quality problem. The supplier ships the parts to the buyer knowing they are out of specification, and they are again rejected. This time the buyer has a little time before the inventory of the part is depleted, so the buyer wants to return the parts to the supplier. The supplier then wants to know why the company could use the parts from the previous shipment, but not from this one. The relationship deteriorates a bit further.

At this point the buyer requests that the supplier consider lowering the price on the item purchased because of some vaguely defined competitive pressures. The supplier is not assured of any benefits by lowering the price and begins to question the soundness of a demand that only benefits the buyer. But the supplier also realizes that the buyer has several other sources for this item and could easily give some other firm the business. This transmits the message that the buyer has no real loyalty to the supplier, even if the supplier lowers the price. Both parties thus see each other as the aggressor, and the adversarial relationship becomes the standard way of doing customer/supplier business.

In a partnership relationship, there is a formal plan to which both parties have agreed. The dates on the supplier schedule are valid need dates. Moreover, the quality specifications define the minimum requirements and do not have unneeded or unrealistic tolerances. Common objectives form a win-win relationship. The supplier is assured of the business and a fair price for as long as the partnership lasts. The buyer is assured of on-time delivery of defect-free parts. A communication network ensures that information flows freely between the buyer and supplier.

Also, the supplier schedule is frequently communicated to the supplier and time fences are respected in a partnership arrangement. The supplier regularly communicates any problems or exceptions to the plan as they occur. Performance measurements that have been jointly agreed to are used to track how well both parties are doing. The measurements are not used for punishment or reward, but rather for planning performance improvements.

Partnership arrangements are characterized by a sense of teamwork, cooperation, and a shared goal of continuous improvement. This leads to more predictable performance, because all of the problems that have occurred in the past have been identified and eliminated. Finally, partnership arrangements improve the quality of life in the workplace by eliminating the adversarial basis of doing business.

GUIDELINES FOR EFFECTIVE PARTNERSHIPS

The following 12 guidelines should serve as the backdrop for all your supplier scheduling efforts. If you observe them in your supplier scheduling actions and plans, you will maximize your chances for a high return on your investment of time and energy.

1. *Trust and communication has to be open and honest.* This is by far the most important of all the rules. If the buying company or its suppliers have their own hidden agendas, you can be sure that the entire system will at some point fail.

2. *Suppliers are part of your organization—they just happen to be outside the gate.* The traditional organizational chart ensconces itself in a moat. For supplier scheduling to work, the moat must be bridged and suppliers brought back into the fortress. Only when suppliers are viewed as critical players can a scheduling system work.

3. *Shared risk means a fair price and a fair profit.* The traditional "zero-sum game" must stop. You can't always get the lowest prices and suppliers can't always seek the maximum margins. Everyone comes out a winner when they make concessions in favor of a long-term relationship. (See next point.)

4. *Long-term relationships are better than one-night stands.* When a company and its suppliers take their vows, they ensure themselves of sustainable profits and benefits—predictable quality, predictable cash flow, and predictable growth and development.

5. *Partnerships consist of a great deal more than signing papers or issuing some edicts.* A partnership between a company and a supplier is truly a culture change, a different way of running the business. But you can't just mandate a new culture and expect it to materialize. People must be educated about changes in the way they do their jobs. Systems must be in place. In short, management must regard itself as an agent of change, not just the authority that dictates change.

6. *You can't mass-produce partnerships.* Supplier scheduling won't work with all suppliers. You need to pick them one at a time and see which ones work and which don't. And don't start off with a written contract that may lock you into a relationship you may soon regret. Begin with a handshake and ease your way into a signature.

7. *Performance is the main criterion for picking a supplier.* Size is often irrelevant to whether a supplier can deliver the right goods to the right place at the right time. Look at performance first; everything else is a footnote.

8. *Internal accountability is a key factor.* When you develop a supplier scheduling system, it's critical to establish who's responsible for what. The system demands that everyone has an allotted role and knows what it is.

9. *Sell the concept to management and get the necessary leadership and support.* A supplier scheduling system will greatly reduce the number of suppliers your company deals with. This is a major change and requires top management support for it to be successful.

10. *Use an existing supplier to kick off the system.* Evaluate your current suppliers and pick the most likely candidate for a partnership arrangement. Sit down and negotiate the terms, conditions, and price (i.e., include everything you need to spell out in the partnership).

11. *Develop the working relationship.* All successful business relationships are based on ground rules. How do we communicate? How do we solve problems? These and other issues must be resolved on both sides of the partnership.

12. *Communicate constantly.* In anything involving human beings, on-going communication is crucial to success. Put every issue on the table and never make assumptions. That's a surefire formula for success.

The Chinese have a character in their written language that stands for the word *crisis*. There are two parts to this character. The first stands for the word *problem* and the second stands for the word *opportunity*. If the buyer does a good job of communicating needs to the supplier, and the supplier does a good job of communicating needs to the buyer, they can mutually work out all of the opportunities before they become problems. In doing so, they can look forward to a long, happy, and mutually beneficial partnership relationship.

ELECTRONIC PURCHASING

As mentioned earlier, electronic purchasing allows the buying company and the supplier to link up directly. In companies that are involved in Supply Chain Management, electronic communication is critical to quickly communicating the schedule to all levels in the supply pipeline. It is also critical for eliminating all the wasted time and costs associated with preparing purchase orders at each level in the pipeline. It makes good sense to use electronic purchasing to schedule all your suppliers. Three methods are commonly used to make the connection: electronic mail (e-mail), Electronic Data Interchange, and now the Internet.

Electronic mail is similar to sending a letter to someone. You can include as much information as you feel necessary to convey your message and the recipient can take as long as he or she likes to review the message. It is similar to voice mail, but much more powerful in that spreadsheets, graphics, and colored diagrams can be sent. Electronic Data Interchange refers to computer-to-computer exchanges of intercompany business documents and information. In contrast to electronic mail, this form of electronic purchasing is a two-way transmission of data, and is often based on reactive systems that "talk" to one another. The Internet is basically everyone's computer connected together in a large network. It is a good way to communicate with your suppliers as well as keep abreast of events that affect your key suppliers and the commodities you buy.

Electronic Mail

Electronic mail involves sending data or executable files from one computer to another via an information utility (such as MCI, the Source, and so on—more on these later). The data or files are actually sent to the recipient's "mailbox." When the recipient checks his or her mail, the person can retrieve the data or files and view them on-screen or print them out.

When used for supplier scheduling, electronic mail is a one-way transmission process in which you send an electronic message or file from one or more of your locations to the supplier's location(s). Either you can compose a message through the information utility and then send it to the supplier, or you can use the information utility to download a spreadsheet or word-processed document that you've created on your computer and transmit it to the supplier. The supplier can receive the message on a computer or a fax machine.

Transmitting to a fax machine does not require a system in which you type a purchase order and send a copy of it via electronic mail to your supplier's fax machine. That is the least desirable means of communicating information, because it still requires the preparation of a purchase order, which does little to reduce the paperwork. A more efficient way is to transmit the supplier schedule that appears on the personal computer (PC) screen directly to the supplier's computer or fax machine without the need to manually type a purchase order. Today, there are numerous fax "boards" that plug directly into a personal computer. These boards in effect allow you to use your supplier's fax as your printer.

Electronic mail offers three advantages over conventional correspondence: It costs less, it eliminates annoying and time-wasting "telephone tag," and it gives the buyer more time to buy. Let's consider each advantage individually.

1. *Reduced costs of purchasing materials.* The following cost comparison is based on 1997 average costs; costs will vary from company to company. Nevertheless, this comparison will give you a good idea of the potential cost savings involved.

	Average Cost Per
Purchase order	$40–$50
Business letter	$20
Long-distance call	$3
Electronic mail:	
Up to 1,000 characters	$0.50
Up to 3,000 characters (one-page document)	$0.95

A character is defined as a letter, number, symbol, punctuation mark, or space. For example, "400 EA. PART #125 *DELIVERY 10/15/91*" contains 35 characters. Remember, even though no characters are visible between the letters and numbers, the spaces count as characters and are factored into the character count.

As you can see, electronic mail is considerably less expensive than conventional means of communicating purchasing information.

2. *No more "telephone tag."* One of the great advantages of electronic mail is that the two parties don't have to be at their computers at the same time. You can send your message at 3:00 A.M. while suppliers are sound asleep, and they can pick it up first thing the next morning. The software needed to tap into an electronic mail service varies in price from $30 to $200, and the annual cost of a mailbox rental through an information utility is usually less than $50. These costs will be quickly paid back in terms of reduced long-distance calls and more effective communication with the supplier.

3. *More time to buy.* Ordering materials is much faster through electronic mail. When sending a purchase order to your suppliers through regular mail, you typically have to allow three or four days (or more

during holidays) for the paper to reach domestic destinations, and up to two weeks to reach international locations.

In contrast, electronic mail plunks the purchase order in the supplier's electronic "in basket" in three minutes. This, of course, reduces total lead time for purchasing items and should allow the buying company to reduce its inventory by at least the amount of time it usually takes for the supplier to receive your purchase order through conventional means.

Finally, if set up properly, electronic mail not only eliminates the need for the piece of paper the supplier schedule is printed on, but it obviates the need for receiving reports and invoices. This in turn frees up some of the buyer's time presently spent doing paperwork, and allows the buyer to do what he or she is paid to do: spend money well. An example of electronic purchasing in action will be presented shortly.

Electronic Mail Services

There are numerous suppliers of electronic mail services, some of the more familiar ones being MCI, Western Union, AT&T, Dialcom, CompuServe, and Digital Equipment. You simply call them and they will sell you the software you need and assist you in setting up the electronic mailbox network. This will require you to do all the work in terms of installing the software and making the arrangements to get your suppliers hooked up to the network; however, there are companies called third-party suppliers that can do this work for you. These companies have the necessary communications software on their computers and are already hooked up to an electronic mail service such as Dialcom. For a fee, they will set up all the standard inexpensive RS232 (ANSI 12) computer-to-computer interfaces for you and bill you a per-use charge. While the cost of using third-party suppliers is obviously higher than if you did it yourself, it may be well worth the added expense for several reasons: These companies have the experience to do it right the first time; they eliminate your having to get involved in the software issues; and they can get you up and running much faster.

Example of the Benefits of Purchasing via Electronic Mail

The following actual example will further put the benefits of electronic purchasing in perspective, in terms of inventory investment and cost reduction. A medium-sized Midwest company was purchasing $8 million in steel annually direct from mills, and had $2 million in inventory on hand (four inventory turns). This company averaged 140 hours per week of downtime, because it never had the correct steel items on hand. The company recognized that it had two problems: too much inventory and too many purchase parts shortages. The company went to a local steel service center and negotiated daily deliveries of all the steel part numbers through an electronic purchasing supplier schedule that was based on its MRP system. (See Figure 10.1.)

Note that the first five columns of requirements are displayed in daily increments across the total schedule horizon of seven weeks. Every day, the schedule would be updated so it would show the next five days' requirements. Thus, the first schedule would show Monday through Friday of Week 1. The schedule generated the next day would show Tuesday of Week 1 through Monday of Week 2. The following day's schedule would show Wednesday of Week 1 through Tuesday of Week 2.

Each day, the supplier was shown the next five days' actual requirements plus planning data for the next seven weeks. These supplier schedules were sent electronically to eliminate any delays that could be caused by the regular postal service. The company was able to reduce its steel inventory to less than two days on hand, from $2 million to $50,000—a reduction of 97.5 percent. And because the company brought in steel daily to meet its needs, it was able to drop the downtime for lack of parts to 15 hours a week—nearly a 90 percent reduction.

As a result, the company was able to improve service to the shop floor, reduce floor-space needs for warehousing the extra steel, free up $1,950,000 in cash from the inventory, which could be invested in the business, and save $390,000 annually in the cost of carrying the inventory (based on carrying costs of 20 percent).

Electronic Data Interchange (EDI)

In contrast to electronic mail, the EDI form of electronic purchasing is a two-way transmission of data, involving computer-to-computer exchanges of intercompany business documents and information. Three versions of EDI are in use today: One uses the supplier's computer, the second uses the buying company's computer, and the third uses both computers.

Supplier's Computer Provides the Information
This EDI technique involves using online, real-time systems for remote order entry and inventory status reporting. Typically, the supplier pro-

All tagged orders (*) are firm
Other orders are expected dates and quantities

Part Number	Description ECN No.	ECN Date	Buyer	Rec'd Last Week	Past Due	10/21	10/22	10/23	10/24	10/25	Week of 11/01	Week of 11/08	Next 4 Weeks
									Requirements				
167458345	Plate Steel 1337A	1X4X3/4 03/14/81	030	6245		1250*	1250*	1250*	1250*	1250*	6300	6400	25600
167458407	Plate Steel 1337A	1X5X3/4 03/14/81	030	2091	34*	425*	425*	425*	425*	425*	2125	2075	8200
167458456	Plate Steel 1337A	1X8X3/4 03/14/81	030	880		440*	440*	440*	440*	440*	800	1320	4400
167458554	Plate Steel 1548B	2X4X1/2 06/23/84	030	3488	122*		1805*		1805*		3610	3600	14400
168122764	Plate Steel 1232A	2 ft Dia. 11/21/80	030	84						84*	85	85	360

Figure 10.1 Electronic Purchasing Supplier Schedule.

vides the buyer with a terminal or software specifically written for the interface, which the buyer can use with a personal computer.

With this arrangement, the buyer can view the supplier's inventory system and, if the parts are available, simply place an order for the parts online. The supplier will then ship the parts immediately from inventory. Some of these systems allow the buyer to actually view the supplier's future production schedules and allocate production not yet sold to match the buyer's requirements. The order is confirmed online and displayed on the screen. If desired, a printer at the buyer's site will then produce a confirming acknowledgment in duplicate, simultaneously printing the same order at the supplier's location.

The disadvantage of this type of a system is that if enough suppliers choose to have this kind of direct linkage, the buyer could end up needing an entire room filled with terminals in order to handle all the items from all the suppliers.

Buyer's Computer Provides the Information

This arrangement is the reverse of the preceding one; the buyer provides the supplier with a terminal, so the supplier can look into the buyer's scheduling system on a daily or weekly basis. In some cases, the supplier actually does the purchase-part planning for the buyer and is required to advise the buyer in advance if it cannot meet the buyer's required delivery dates. Here's how it works. The supplier looks at the individual MRP planning reports for each part number it supplies. The supplier converts planned orders to scheduled receipts on the MRP planning report, which is a confirmation of the supplier's intention to deliver the parts on that day. If the date for the delivery is sooner or later than the need date in the MRP system, the MRP system alerts the buyer of the situation. The buyer then calls the supplier to determine why the delivery date is off.

When the supplier ships the parts, the supplier enters the shipping information, along with the quantity and part numbers, into the computer terminal. This shipping information establishes an inbound schedule for the buyer's receiving dock. When the shipment arrives at the dock, Receiving enters the receipt on the system and the computer compares the receipt information with what the supplier said was shipped. The negotiated purchase prices are already in the database, and if the receipt matches the shipment information, the buyer's company pays for the parts upon receipt without the need for an invoice. This eliminates the need for a requisition, purchase order, receiving report, or invoice. As a result, the buyer has more time to buy and the company has eliminated a mountain of paperwork that adds no value to its product.

Buyer's Computer and Supplier's Computer Interact

The third version of EDI currently in use, and one that represents excellent opportunities for further development in purchasing, entails an interaction between the buyer's computer and the supplier's computer. Nissan's automobile plant is a classic example of this type of scheduling arrangement. The automaker and 10 percent of its suppliers have MRP systems, which are all hardwired together.

When an automobile body enters the paint booth at the manufacturer's facility, MRP identifies the customer, the options, the color, and so on, and then schedules all downstream operations to assemble the proper options for that customer. At the same time, it downloads the schedule into the suppliers' computers that are hardwired into the system. Thus, the automobile maker not only schedules its own manufacturing operations, but, in effect, schedules its suppliers' operations as well.

The suppliers manufacture their respective purchase parts and deliver them directly to the assembly line at the automobile plant. The parts are installed in the automobile three hours after they were scheduled in the supplier's computer by the buyer's computer.

Each of the suppliers hardwired into the system delivers multiple shipments of purchase parts per day. As a result, this plant averages less than one day of on-hand purchase parts.

Figure 10.2 demonstrates how this scheduling works. When the car enters the paint booth, its options are defined for all the suppliers. Let's take the seat supplier as an example. The seat supplier knows that it is dealing with a brown vinyl four-door car with a specific model number. It takes the supplier's computer 20 minutes to digest that information and another 20 minutes to actually break it down to online schedules on the manufacturing floor. It takes the seat manufacturer 40 minutes to make the piece parts for that particular seat and another 40 minutes to actually assemble the seat.

In two hours, the seats are fully assembled, ready to ship. The car manufacturer wants to unload the seats directly out of the truck into the car on the assembly line, so the seats have to be staged and loaded into the truck in reverse order. In doing so, the first seat off the truck goes into the first car coming off the line. It takes 20 minutes to stage and load the truck and another 20 minutes to transport the seats from the supplier's assembly plant to the car assembly line. In this case, the seats arrive at the line about 20 minutes before they are put into the car. No requisitions, no purchase orders, and no receiving reports are necessary. Also, because the car manufacturer scheduled the seats and knows how

Figure 10.2   Supplier Schedule.

many of each style it scheduled, no invoice is necessary either—it pays on receipt.

This kind of timing would be impossible without EDI and computer-to-computer communication. The software needed to support EDI is approximately $50 per site and there is an annual fee of around $150. The cost per character runs from $.0017 for a one-page document to $.0005 for a 10-page document. This is more expensive than electronic mail ($.0003 per character for a one-page document), but the two-way computer-to-computer communication makes it worth the added cost. Both electronic mail and EDI have much lower cost than typing a purchase order.

Internet

Almost everyone has heard of the Internet and the World Wide Web, but very few are using it to conduct business. Up to now, the Internet has been basically used for information. The Internet is an easy way to search for news on a variety of topics that affect the economy, your suppliers, and the commodities you purchase. Using keywords, you can search for news articles that contain your search word. As software applications are developed, the Internet should be a good platform from which to conduct business in the future. Two MRP II suppliers, SAP America and Oracle, offer Web modules. Several suppliers of middleware offer packages to connect MRP II systems to other customer and supplier computers regardless of what software they are using. This will allow buyers an inexpensive way to reach smaller suppliers who are not set up for EDI. In the next few years, buyers will be able to send fairly complex programs to their suppliers via the Web.

Today, buyers using standard Web browsers can search suppliers' catalogs for products and get price and delivery information instantly. The buyer can view technical specifications, check the suppliers' inventory for product availability, and order product online. Payment can be made online using electronic funds transfer (EFT) technology or Purchasing Cards. Buyers can also track shipments and receive delivery information from transportation companies via the Internet.

Purchasing Departments are also creating Web sites to display their purchasing policy and list what each buyer purchases. Some of the more extensive Web sites include a Purchasing Mission Statement, what is expected of a supplier, and how the purchasing system operates. Some even request quotations from suppliers on needed items and list surplus materials being offered for sale.

Purchasing Cards

Several credit card companies are offering Purchasing Cards, credit cards that can be used online. These cards are similar to standard credit cards, but are designed for business-to-business purchases. The Purchasing Card allows the cardholder to make authorized purchases and usually has a maximum dollar limit. It is intended to be used on small-dollar purchases, such as Maintenance, Repair, and Operating (MRO) items or office supplies, where the cost to generate a purchase order would exceed the value of the item. The cardholder purchases the item from the supplier. The purchase is authorized electronically, according to specific cardholder criteria, preapproved by the buyer's company. The supplier receives payment for the item within a few days. The cardholder receives a detailed statement of all card purchases and makes one consolidated payment for all charges once a month. The major advantages of using EDI and the Purchasing Card are the elimination of paperwork, the reduction of administrative costs in that only one invoice is received monthly, better payment terms, and quicker payment to the supplier.

Several companies are moving to Vendor Managed Inventory (VMI). EDI and the Internet are allowing companies to make that transition. The next chapter will cover this new technology and how companies are using it to improve performance.

SUMMARY

- Prior to developing partnership arrangements, buyers and suppliers often have adversarial relationships.

- Partnership arrangements are characterized by a sense of teamwork, cooperation, and a shared goal of continuous improvement.

- The guidelines for effective partnerships should serve as the backdrop for all of your supplier scheduling efforts.

- Electronic mail is a one-way transmission of data from your location to the supplier's location.

- Electronic Data Interchange is a two-way transmission of data and refers to computer-to-computer exchanges of intercompany business documents and information.

- The Internet is being used basically for information, but will be a good platform for conducting business in the future.

- Purchasing Cards are typically used on small-dollar purchases and can be used online.

Chapter Eleven

Vendor Managed Inventory

The concept of Vendor Managed Inventory (VMI) is not new. For many years, buyers have asked suppliers to put inventory in the buyer's plant on consignment. They would require the supplier to come in periodically and take an inventory of the consigned stock and replenish it as needed. Usually, a minimum/maximum inventory level was suggested, and as long as the supplier stayed within that range, the buyer was happy. Some buyers would keep track of the inventory for the supplier and telephone the supplier when the inventory needed to be replenished. The buyer would pay the supplier as the product was used. This is very similar to the bread company delivering to your local grocery store. The bread delivery person fills the bread aisle in the grocery store and leaves the bread on a consignment basis. Every day, he or she returns to the store and replenishes the bread that has been sold. The grocery store is charged for only what is sold.

So, what is different about Vendor Managed Inventory? There are two major areas of difference—its technology and the role the supplier plays in the process. Vendor Managed Inventory depends on EDI to provide online visibility of the buyer's inventory and forecast to the supplier, and provides a direct input to the supplier's planning system. The supplier's role changes in that the supplier takes over the entire responsibility for planning and replenishing the inventory at the buyer's facility. Given better planning data, the supplier is expected to respond with perfect order fulfillment.

Vendor Managed Inventory started in retail businesses (mass merchandisers, grocery chains, health and beauty aids, etc.), but has slowly spread to industrial companies. Mass merchandisers such as Wal-Mart and Kmart were early users of Vendor Managed Inventory. They gave the entire responsibility for planning and replenishing their warehouses to their suppliers. They shared their future business forecasts—including promotional and new product introduction data, their point-of-sale scan data on daily store sales, and their inventory levels—with their suppliers. Their suppliers used this data as an input to their planning systems. The suppliers would develop a production plan to support the forecast and any variances from forecast as recorded daily with the point-of-sale scan data.

The benefits are obvious. First, coordinated planning with the supplier should ensure that the buyer never misses a sale due to a stock-out. Second, inventory is reduced because there is accurate planning information—you do not need as much inventory in the supply pipeline if you can see what your customer is actually selling on a daily basis. Third, by eliminating purchase orders and simplifying the planning process, you should be able to reduce administrative costs. Lastly, the supplier should be able to lower manufacturing costs by level loading its facilities and providing better information to its own purchasing department.

Vendor Managed Inventory is similar to or considered a part of several other concepts: quick response (QR), efficient consumer response (ECR), Just-in-Time (JIT), and Supply Chain Management (SCM). All of these concepts aim to share information among the trading partners, eliminate waste and redundancy in the supply chain, reduce lead times to the customer, and develop strong partnerships between buyers and suppliers.

ANSI

The American National Standards Institute (ANSI) has developed a series of standards for communicating business processes electronically. These standards allow data to be transferred between various systems. The two main ANSI transaction sets used in Vendor Managed Inventory are the ANSI 852 report that lists product usage and adjustments and the ANSI 855 report that covers the suppliers' acknowledgment of the order. See the following page for the ANSI transaction standards that are involved in electronic purchasing and Vendor Managed Inventory. They are listed to help clarify the discussion of how Vendor Managed Inventory works.

ANSI Number	*Description*
810	Invoice
820	Payment Order/Remittance Advice
830	Planning Schedule with Release Capability
845	Price Authorization Acknowledgment
846	Inventory Inquiry/Advice
850	Purchase Order
852	Product Activity Data
855	Purchase Order Acknowledgment
856	Ship Notice/Manifest
860	Purchase Order Change
861	Receiving Advice
862	Shipping Schedule
865	Purchase Order Change Acknowledgment
869	Order Status Inquiry
870	Order Status Report

HOW VENDOR MANAGED INVENTORY WORKS

In VMI, the buyer and the supplier negotiate the terms and conditions of the contract and spell out that the supplier will be responsible for all planning and scheduling activities associated with the items to be purchased. The buyer develops either a sales forecast (if a retail business) or a production schedule (if a manufacturer). This sales forecast or production schedule should spell out what the buyer's company intends to sell or manufacture for several weeks into the future. The forecast is transmitted to the supplier via an ANSI 862 transaction to cover the scheduling of the finished item to be sold in a retail environment. The ANSI 830 transaction, the supplier schedule, is transmitted to the supplier for the purchase of the component the manufacturer is going to use. The supplier uses this information to put together its production plan. Planning parameters such as minimum/maximum inventory levels, lead times, safety stocks, and target inventory balances are defined in the contract between the buyer and the supplier. Changes to contract pricing are authorized and acknowledged using ANSI transactions 845 and 865.

The supplier then monitors the buyer's inventory levels and daily usage of the components and plans when a replenishment shipment is needed. In some cases where the inventory is set at a low level, such as two or three days' usage, the supplier delivers daily what the buyer sold or consumed the day before. Where inventories are set at a higher level (e.g., two weeks' usage), the supplier need only ship weekly. The daily usage is transmitted via an ANSI 852 transaction and the supplier can view the current inventory levels via ANSI 846 transactions. The supplier reviews the usage and inventory level data and plans a replenishment order.

The supplier will either ship out of inventory or manufacture the component and ship, depending on the lead times negotiated in the contract. The supplier will notify the buyer of the replenishment order via an ANSI 855 transaction. This transaction spells out the product to be shipped, the quantity, and the estimated ship date. The buyer can use this transaction to do some transportation and receiving planning if needed. When the components are ready to ship, the supplier notifies the buyer of the shipment via an Advance Ship Notice, ANSI 856. This ship notice defines the carrier, the trailer number, and product being shipped. It includes a manifest detailing the number of containers and what is in each container to simplify the receiving process.

The buyer receives the shipment via an ANSI 861 transaction, the Receiving Advice. Where the supplier owns the inventory until it is used, the buyer pays for the material based on the ANSI 852 daily usage report plus any inventory adjustments made at the buyer's plant. Where the buyer owns the inventory when received, the supplier generates an invoice, if required by the buyer's company, via an ANSI 810 transaction. Because the buyer can compare the Advance Ship Notice with what is received, an invoice is not required in most cases. The payment is then made using an ANSI 820 transaction.

Several companies have started to develop their own Vendor Managed Inventory systems using various types of groupware. Shell Chemical has recently developed its own system, called SIMON, which stands for Supplier Inventory Managed Order Network. The company is offering it to its customers and providing both the technical services and training to assist them in its use. Shell Chemical's system uses Lotus Notes running on a Windows PC that simplifies the transactions and makes the system easier to use than standard EDI systems.

OBSTACLES

While there are many benefits to Vendor Managed Inventory, there are also some obstacles that need to be addressed if the concept is to work. Some of these were covered in Chapter 2 but bear repeating here.

First is the need to share information openly. To enter into a Vendor Managed Inventory arrangement, the buyer's company must be willing to share sales forecasts, production plans, promotional plans, sales plans, inventory plans, new product plans—almost their entire set of business plans for the items—with the supplier. Not all top management personnel are willing to share that data outside their corporation. Vendor Managed Inventory will not work without the sharing with suppliers of what was considered in the past to be company-confidential information.

Second is the cultural adjustment needed in the buying organization. Prior to Vendor Managed Inventory, buyers were heavily involved in the day-to-day buying and scheduling activities. They knew how much was being ordered from each supplier and were up-to-date on changes in the business. With Vendor Managed Inventory, the supplier has taken over much of the planning and scheduling responsibilities and the buyer is removed from the day-to-day involvement. Likewise, the supplier's salesperson no longer needs to call on the buyer, because the business is firm for the life of the contract. This change in the role of the buyer vis-à-vis the salesperson may be a threat if the buyer sees the role as placing orders and expediting product only.

Third, the supplier's administrative costs will increase, because the supplier has taken over from the buyer the responsibility of planning and replenishing the inventory. Assume you buy 50 different parts from the supplier. The supplier will get 50 forecasts, 50 supplier releases, 50 daily usage reports, and so on. If the supplier has automated the processing of this data so it enters the supplier's system without having to reenter the data each time, it will not be a problem. But if the supplier has to manually enter that data daily, it will add to its order entry and production planning costs. The supplier must see this as a value-added process—that the data will improve its operations—or the supplier will complain about the additional workload.

The last potential obstacle relates to the fact that the buyer's organization must have confidence in the supplier's ability to perform. If the supplier has had periods in the past where the performance was deemed unacceptable, the buyer may feel the need to get too involved in the process and the essential trust may be broken. The buyer should use only those suppliers that have proven their ability to perform and are quality-certified if Vendor Managed Inventory is to be successful.

PARTNERS' RESPONSIBILITIES

The buyer's role is to provide the daily usage information to the supplier and ensure the inventory records are accurate and available. The buyer needs to provide accurate forecasts that go at least four or five months into the future and must try to minimize changes inside the 30-day window. The buyer should communicate all promotion and new product plans well in advance to give the supplier time to plan for them. The buyer should maintain valid delivery schedules to enable the supplier to schedule deliveries efficiently. The buyer should use all available technology including EDI, point-of-sale scan data where appropriate, bar coding, and so forth. The buyer should measure and give feedback on performance to the supplier.

The supplier should deliver 100 percent on-time to the buyer's schedule. The supplier should use the usage data or point-of-sale scan data to manage orders and provide Advance Ship Notices on all shipments. The supplier should involve the buyer in product development and provide total team support to the buyer. The supplier should expedite the processing on all claims or returns. The supplier should maintain efficient and effective communications and notify the buyer of all potential problems as they arise. The supplier should use all available technology needed to support the buyer. The supplier should measure and give feedback on performance to the buyer.

SUMMARY

- The concept of Vendor Managed Inventory is not new.

- In Vendor Managed Inventory, the supplier takes over the entire responsibility for planning and replenishing the inventory.

- The American National Standards Institute has developed standards for communicating business processes electronically.

- A cultural change is needed in most organizations if Vendor Managed Inventory is to work.

Chapter Twelve

Profile of a Good Buyer

A company's effort to develop excellent suppliers to support an MRP II and JIT/TQC process requires more than a Supplier Education Day, special memos that direct suppliers to participate in new product design, or instructing them to deliver future shipments in small lots to the assembly line just when needed. Unfortunately, that is all that happens in many companies. Today, there is very little incentive for suppliers to change their relationships with customers. As buyers come up with new programs, the suppliers see it as a one-way relationship that amounts to "I have to change, but the buyer does not" and "I have to give up something, but I get nothing in return." And if the supplier does not go along with the new program, there is a veiled threat of potential loss of business. The relationship becomes adversarial, and the supplier becomes the villain for not supporting the program. The search then begins for a new supplier that will give the buying company what it wants.

To succeed in developing excellent suppliers, buyer and supplier must engage in a win-win relationship. That means the buyer's company must change the way it views its suppliers, must make changes in the way it schedules its suppliers, and then must show and train its suppliers in MRP II and JIT/TQC. When companies work to combine the strengths of their suppliers with their own internal strengths, a mutually beneficial and long-term partnership emerges. Chapter 3 described the attributes of a good supplier; the present chapter covers the buyer's responsibility in creating a win-win arrangement.

QUALITY AND RELIABILITY

There are four quality and reliability requirements on the buyer's side. The first is a well-defined specification. This specification should define the minimum requirement of the item as simply as possible. If you do not need a tolerance or a certain requirement, it should not be on the specification. This only adds to the cost of the item you are buying and makes it more difficult for the supplier to conform to your spec. The specification should also take into account the discipline of Design for Manufacturability. (See Chapter 5.) In other words, the part should be designed in such a way as to eliminate areas of potential quality and reliability failures.

The second requirement is having a measurement system in place that identifies the defects in the incoming material. Ideally, you want to eliminate all incoming defects and certify the quality of all your suppliers, but achieving this level of quality requires a lot of work. When material is received, Quality Control should pull and inspect a sample of the shipment. All defects and the reasons for defects should be noted. This report then serves as the basis for determining the cause of the defect. Was it the supplier's process, equipment, employees, or suppliers that caused the defect to occur? What needs to be done to eliminate the cause so the problem does not occur again? The buyer must have a measurement system in place to identify defects if they are to be eliminated at the supplier's. A detailed discussion of quality measurement can be found in Chapter 14.

Third, with a well-defined specification and defect-measurement system in place, the buyer must be willing to become part of a joint approach to defect elimination. That means a willingness to send whatever resources are available to assist the supplier in the identification and elimination of the causes of the defects. If the defects stem from a tooling problem, can your tooling engineers assist the supplier's engineers in correcting the situation? If it is a problem of identifying how to eliminate the defect, maybe your quality-control people can assist. If there is a financial implication in solving the problem, maybe you can jointly share the cost. A good buyer will be agreeable to participating in the solution and not lay all the burden on the supplier.

Fourth, the buyer should be willing to train the supplier, if necessary, in various quality approaches. Today, the reality is that most suppliers do not have a meaningful Total Quality Control program in place and don't know how to go about setting one up. If the buyer's company has that expertise, it should be willing to share it with suppliers. If you do not have Design for Manufacturability, Statistical Process Control, or Total Quality Control in place, it is unreasonable to expect your suppliers to be using them either.

Finally, the good buyer will respect the supplier's expertise. Many of your suppliers are leaders in their industries, and the sooner you can tap that expertise, the better off the buyer will be. A good buyer will allow the supplier to participate in the original design of the part, which results in better-quality designs in a shorter time frame. Suppliers can anticipate tooling and equipment requirements, allowing them to get an early start on the long-lead-time items. They can anticipate quality and yield problems before the design is finalized. They can also make recommendations and participate in the identification of alternatives and trade-off analysis. This joint approach to defect elimination and supplier participation in the design process can provide excellent opportunities for building sound partnership relations with suppliers.

DELIVERY

A good buyer will give suppliers valid (i.e., correct and attainable) schedules. In the traditional method of buying, the supplier is given a purchase order with a replenishment date. Both the supplier and the buyer know the date is earlier than when the first piece of the shipment is actually needed. Therefore, everyone knows the supplier can be late and the buyer will not run out of the material for a period of a few weeks. A good buyer will not only give the supplier valid need dates, but will continuously update the schedules as they change, via a supplier schedule, so the dates remain valid. The schedule must also be attainable in respect to the supplier's capacity. The buyer should not ask the supplier for a quantity of material in excess of the supplier's capability.

Beyond the short-term needs, a good buyer provides long-term visibility of needs to the supplier. If the supplier's quoted lead time is four weeks, the buyer should be willing to give the supplier visibility of needs for at least three months in the future. This would allow the supplier to plan raw materials, capacity, and equipment as productively as possible over time. The better the supplier is able to plan, the better chance the buyer's requirements will be met. (See Chapter 4 for a discussion of supplier scheduling and how need dates and future visibility can be given to the supplier.)

Time Fences

In addition, a good buyer has respect for the time fences established with the supplier. (See Figure 12.1.)

The typical supplier has three time fences that a buyer needs to respect. These are the time fences at which raw material is purchased, capacity is allocated on the manufacturing equipment, and the actual manufacturing lead time. Consider the manufacture of fabric, which was mentioned earlier. Although the supplier quotes 10-week lead times, the 10 weeks is made up of 4 weeks to purchase the yarn, 4 weeks to weave the fabric, and 2 weeks to dye the fabric. The critical time fences are 10 weeks and 2 weeks. If the buyer wishes to increase the rate of fabric deliveries on a weekly basis, it will take 10 weeks for that to occur. If the buyer wishes to change the color mix of the fabric on order, the colors can be switched at the two-week window.

A good buyer understands the supplier's time fences, schedules around those time fences, and does not expect the supplier to do something that is impossible. The good buyer would not ask for a color change one week out, because he or she knows that the dyeing process takes two weeks. A good buyer would not expect a rate increase in three weeks, because it takes the supplier six weeks to allocate capacity and weave and dye the fabric. Again, a good buyer respects the supplier's time fences and does not ask the supplier to do something that is impossible.

Delivery Specifications

A good buyer has well-defined packaging specifications that the suppliers have participated in developing and have agreed to meet. The buyer also negotiates all the terms and conditions in respect to the traffic issues so that pickup and deliveries are convenient and economical for both parties.

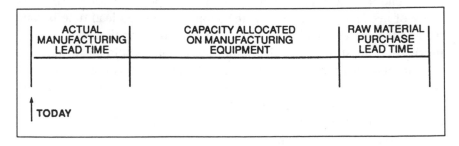

Figure 12.1 Time Fences.

Finally, a good buyer must be flexible. There are going to be problems in any relationship—things are not going to happen according to plan. The supplier's tool could break, it could have a quality problem, and so forth. The buyer needs to be flexible in either altering the schedule to work around the problem or assisting the supplier in any way possible to get the problem resolved. In the old Greek wars, when the battle was lost, a messenger was sent back with the bad news. What happened to the messenger when the bad news was delivered? They killed the messenger. The buyer needs to avoid searching for the guilty party to blame when something goes wrong and look with the supplier for a joint solution. In a partnership arrangement, the supplier will notify the buying company as soon as possible if a problem is encountered, and the buying company will quickly move to help develop a solution.

PRICE

A good buyer enters into a partnership arrangement knowing that the buyer's company must share any risks jointly with the supplier should problems occur. If the buyer asks the supplier to build up inventory prior to a new-product introduction and the sales do not develop as forecast, the buyer may need to share in the cost of the buildup until it is worked off.

On the other hand, if a joint value analysis project reduces the item's cost dramatically, both sides should benefit. If the current cost of the item is $1 and the supplier makes a 10 percent profit, the buyer would pay a price of $1.10. Jointly, through a value analysis project, the cost of the material content of the item is reduced 20 cents. The current cost is now $.80 plus the 10 percent supplier's profit, putting the price at $.88 each. The buyer has netted a $.22 savings and the supplier has watched its profit drop from 10 to 8 cents each. How excited will the supplier get about the next value analysis project? Not very. If the relationship is to be a win-win situation, then the buyer must be willing to share in the risks and the savings with the supplier.

In addition, a good buyer will allow for fair pricing that lets the supplier make a profit. Many buyers look at only the lowest price and constantly push to lower the price even more. If the supplier accepts the lower price in order to stay competitive, but is unable to lower the costs, it may be forced to cut corners to keep the ship afloat. This could cause delivery or quality problems in the future and would probably reduce the supplier's ability to be full-service, as described in Chapter 3. If you want a good supplier, you have to allow fair pricing.

Lastly, a good buyer will promptly pay the supplier for all shipments. Too often companies push their suppliers for quicker deliveries, better quality, and lower prices, and then pay them in 45 to 60 days as a "reward." If you expect good service, if you want a win-win relationship, then prompt payment is mandatory.

RESPONSIVENESS

Just as the buyer wants the supplier to be very responsive to questions asked and to quickly follow through on problems and complaints, suppliers expect the same in return. The buyer should provide a list of the various personnel in the company (i.e., quality control manager, technical services manager, tooling manager, supplier scheduling manager) along with telephone numbers where these people can be reached in the event of a problem. If the buyer is out of the office and the supplier does not know whom to call, the supplier may make a decision that is the opposite of what your quality control manager might make. The supplier needs to be able to talk to someone who will understand the problem and provide a good answer.

In short, when the supplier calls, he or she should not get the runaround. This is part of working as a team dedicated to the quick resolution of problems.

LOCATION

The buyer that has multiple manufacturing locations should be honest about their capabilities and shortcomings. This will assist the supplier in understanding the various requirements at each plant and how to deal with the various messages received from each location. If one plant is significantly advanced in terms of SPC, JIT, and scheduling, it will be wanting more frequent shipments in smaller lot sizes, and will be interested in discussing the possibility of working toward certified quality. Another plant may be looking for truckload pricing only and may not be interested in a closer relationship with suppliers. The good buyer will be candid and open in communicating these differences and will work to assist the suppliers in developing the correct working relationship with each location.

TECHNICAL CAPABILITIES

Often, the buying company will have developed certain technologies that have allowed it to become a leader in its field. It may have developed certain tests that are used to measure quality and performance of its products that no one else has developed. The buyer's company should be willing to transfer certain of these technologies to suppliers to allow them to produce better products and to better understand the requirements of the items. One producer of high-quality, cutting-edge electronic devices, Tektronix, had developed several pieces of very specialized test equipment for monitoring its products. These pieces of equipment were developed and manufactured in-house and were not commercially available. Their suppliers did not have the same level of sophisticated test equipment, so they were not able to detect many of the defects that the buyer's company claimed existed. Realizing the situation, the buyer duplicated its test equipment and provided it free of charge to suppliers. As a result, the suppliers were able to track down the causes of defects. Today, 95 percent of the suppliers are certified and deliver direct to the production lines.

Research and Development

Many companies spend a significant amount of money on research and development of new products. Six months to a year after the development process starts, specifications for the purchase items are finally developed and sent to the suppliers for quotation. If the supplier is unable to produce the item as designed or has some suggestions for improving the item, Engineering then has to decide whether to delay the introduction or go with a less than desirable item.

The good buyer will get the supplier involved very early in the design process. Experience has proved that early involvement of suppliers who are experts in their commodity lines will result in better-quality designs in a shorter time frame. Suppliers can anticipate tooling and equipment requirements, allowing them to get an early start on long-lead-time items. They can also anticipate quality and yield problems before the design is finalized, and as team members they make recommendations and participate in the identification of alternatives and trade-off analysis. A good buyer not only asks the supplier to participate in the early phases of concept/design of the new product, but also provides that supplier with pertinent information such as pricing targets and benchmark information on quality reliability. This early supplier involvement provides excellent opportunities to cement sound partnership relationships with suppliers.

TWO-WAY STREET

As we said at the beginning of Chapter 3, a partnership is a two-way street. The relationship must be open and honest in terms of information. It must be based on a commitment to available resources, and it must share the risks as well as the rewards. Therefore, the buyer and the supplier must change the way they do business today if the relationship is to be win-win and long-term.

SUMMARY

- Developing excellent suppliers means more than scheduling a Supplier Education Day and mailing out special memos.

- To develop excellent suppliers, the buyer's company must change the way it views its suppliers and how it schedules its suppliers, and then show and train the suppliers in MRP II and JIT/TQC.

- A good buyer will be agreeable to participating in the solution and not lay the burden on the supplier.

- A good buyer will give suppliers valid schedules, not ask the supplier to do something that is impossible, and respect the supplier's expertise.

- A good buyer is flexible and realizes that problems are going to occur.

- A good buyer realizes that a partnership is a two-way street and is willing to share the risks as well as the rewards.

Chapter Thirteen

Supplier Scheduling in Special Situations

Up to now, the book has discussed supplier scheduling only as it applies to somewhat routine production items. This chapter will cover special applications of this technique, first addressing the topic of buying scarce commodities (such as integrated circuits) and then covering some of the issues involved in small companies and in "process" and repetitive manufacturers. This chapter will also discuss using supplier scheduling in a distribution company as opposed to a manufacturing firm. It will conclude with an overview of planning and scheduling Maintenance, Repair, and Operating (MRO) supplies.

BUYING SCARCE COMMODITIES

Depending on business conditions, all commodities can become difficult to acquire from time to time. Lead times for integrated circuits, for example, can vary dramatically over a year's time, creating special problems. As the demand for the commodity increases, its lead time may lengthen dramatically. Individual items within the commodity, as well as the commodity as a whole, may go on allocation.

The supplier has a certain capacity, which can be represented by the bottom of a funnel. (See Figure 13.1.) The maximum rate at which the supplier can produce is the amount of work that can flow out through the bottom. Obviously, if orders come in at a rate greater than the supplier's capacity, the level of orders in the backlog will increase and the supplier's lead time gets longer. At a certain level, represented by the top of

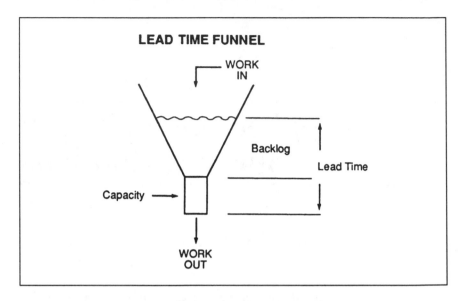

Figure 13.1   Maximum Production.

the funnel, it becomes nearly impossible for the supplier to add more orders to the backlog. At that point, the supplier will probably put all customers on allocation. Everyone is forced to take a percentage of what they might otherwise need. The funnel is now as shown in Figure 13.2.

The allocation can be very serious for a company if it is less than its real needs. An excellent way to attempt to avoid this situation is to work out an agreement with the supplier to set aside a certain percentage of its capacity before the allocation situation occurs. Let's suppose that a buyer requires four hours a week of the capacity of a particular piece of equipment. If the supplier runs it for 24 hours a day, 7 days a week, the total output from that piece of equipment is 168 hours. Using the capacity planning information, the buyer needs to contract for 2.4 percent of that capacity each week. That is represented by the thick line at the bottom of the funnel in Figure 13.3.

Now it makes no difference if the supplier's quoted lead time goes from 6 weeks to 60. The buyer is still able to schedule 2.4 percent of the supplier's capacity on a weekly basis. Even if the supplier goes on allocation, the company should get 2.4 percent of that equipment's capacity because of the contract the buyer has negotiated. That scarce commodity is now much easier to manage. Based on individual needs for the items the buyer has scheduled capacity for, the buyer always counts on getting the four hours of capacity each week from the supplier.

Figure 13.2   Allocation Situation.

Be aware, though, that this approach to scheduling capacity and se-lecting out of that capacity what is needed is not a panacea. It will take a lot of work, in some cases, to understand how the supplier schedules the item and how many work centers are involved at the supplier's facility. If multiple work centers are involved at the facility, this approach may be difficult to negotiate with the supplier. But if a capacity reservation can be negotiated, supplier scheduling will be much easier for those scarce commodities.

SMALL COMPANIES

It is often claimed that supplier scheduling is a good concept for large companies but not for small ones. Buyers for smaller businesses may believe they have no clout with their suppliers and that the system there-fore will not work the same way for them. This belief implies that clout is all it takes to get supplier performance—that unless someone buys in high volumes, the supplier really isn't interested in the business. This is simply not true in most cases. If it were, the large companies would never run out of any parts and would always get first call on supplier ca-pacity. Yet almost everyone has heard about large companies that have missed their monthly production goals for lack of purchase parts.

Figure 13.3   Capacity Percentage Contract.

It is not always clout that counts, it is the quality of the schedule that does. Small companies with good supplier schedules often get excellent supplier performance in all types of market conditions. In fact, the findings reported in Appendix B show that 80 percent of these companies surveyed purchased less than $30 million annually, with two companies spending only $4 million annually. These companies spent little with each individual supplier, but were able to get good service because they had valid schedules. When suppliers understand what the supplier schedule means and how they can use it to maximize their planning to meet customer needs, company size becomes far less important. Even small companies have found that supplier scheduling improves supplier delivery performance dramatically.

"PROCESS" COMPANIES

Companies in process industries, such as chemicals or paper, typically run on a continuous basis, and shutting down equipment—such as a glass furnace—is very expensive. All raw materials required must be continuously available. Since they are always running, such plants tend to use very large quantities of basic raw materials quickly. It is quite common to bring in tank cars or trucks of chemicals weekly or even more frequently. Often, the storage facilities for these basic chemicals cannot hold more than a few days' supply, so inventory turnover tends to be very high. Supplier scheduling fits well into this type of environment.

Most process plants have a daily production schedule, which becomes, in effect, the master production schedule in MRP II. They also have formulations or recipes (bills of material) for their products. Because of the need to maintain continuous production, process companies regularly verify the on-hand inventory of all raw materials. These elements, of course, are the key ingredients for Material Requirements Planning: a master schedule, bills of material, and the inventory status. By breaking the supplier schedule down into a daily schedule on purchased items, the Purchasing Department can schedule deliveries to arrive on the day needed. Here also, supplier scheduling handles the daily scheduling tasks and allows the buyer to spend time on negotiations, alternate sourcings, and so forth.

One potential variable in certain process companies is the yield of the end product. Process variables or process problems may cause the yield to differ from day to day. In other words, it may take more raw materials than expected to produce the total batch weight desired. This is somewhat analogous to the scrap some manufacturers in nonprocess industries experience on raw materials. If the company can forecast scrap or yield variances, they can be expressed in the bill of material. If they cannot be anticipated, the replanning feature of MRP will take these yield variables into consideration. If production takes more of a particular raw material than anticipated, the on-hand inventory will reflect this. MRP would then recalculate the need date based on the lower inventory and advise the supplier scheduler accordingly. Therefore, the supplier schedule can reflect the true need date on each item bought, taking into account all the variables of the process.

Replanning is one of the strong features of MRP II. It not only plans the first time, but replans based on the current situation. Reorder points and other ordering systems don't have this replanning capability. The MRP-generated supplier schedule in a process company can be a natural to support a continuous process.

REPETITIVE MANUFACTURERS

High-volume repetitive manufacturing is another natural for supplier scheduling. By definition, the same parts are being used over and over, day in, day out. High-volume repetitive situations lend themselves readily to Just-in-Time scheduling, as discussed in earlier chapters. In many repetitive environments, where the items required are fairly simple to manufacture, the supplier schedule can actually be used as the supplier's own production schedule.

As an example, suppose a company uses wood in its product and the only variable is the length of the piece. The buyer's company makes 1,000 end items per week and requires the wood pieces to be either 6 inches, $6^{1}/_{2}$ inches, or 7 inches in length, depending on which version of the end item is scheduled for production. The supplier would set aside the capacity required to make 1,000 cuts on a table saw. The supplier schedule would be given directly to the operator of the table saw, and it would tell the operator how many of each length to cut each day or each week. The other alternative, as mentioned earlier, is to use a Kanban card or similar mechanism to break down the schedule on a daily basis.

Since the purchase parts are repetitive, the supplier schedule tends to be much more stable in these cases. This makes the supplier's planning of capacity and raw materials much more efficient and should allow better pricing stability. If a company produces 20,000 chairs per week and each chair takes 1 yard of fabric, the supplier knows it needs the yarn and capacity equal to 20,000 yards every week. The supplier is able, therefore, to do a better job of planning internally and to secure stable pricing and supply with its suppliers. This further assures its customers of a constant product at a consistent price over time. Supplier scheduling is well suited to highly repetitive companies. Figure 13.4 is an example of a supplier schedule in a repetitive manufacturing company.

DISTRIBUTORS AND RESELLERS

Distributors and resellers are different from the companies discussed so far in this book. With few exceptions, they do not manufacture any of the items they sell. Typically, they purchase finished items from various manufacturers and resell them to retailers.

Distribution companies can develop supplier agreements for all the items they buy from a manufacturer, and then schedule in the items as they are needed. Sound familiar? That is what all buyers do, whether they are purchasing castings, fasteners, or finished items for resale, such as hammers or cosmetics or whatever.

Let us look at the sources of demand on a distribution company's buyer using Distribution Resource Planning, part of an MRP II system. In this example (see Figure 13.5), there are three regional distribution centers (DCs) and one central distribution center. The central DC re-

All tagged orders (*) are firm
Other orders are expected dates and quantities

Part Number	Description ECN No.	ECN Date	Buyer	Rec'd Last Week	Past Due	10/21	10/22	10/23	10/24	10/25	Week of 11/01	Week of 11/08	Next 4 Weeks
								Requirements					
167458345	Plate Steel 1337A	1X4X3/4 03/14/81	030	6245		1250*	1250*	1250*	1250*	1250*	6300	6400	25600
167458407	Plate Steel 1337A	1X5X3/4 03/14/81	030	2091	34*	425*	425*	425*	425*	425*	2125	2075	8200
167458456	Plate Steel 1337A	1X8X3/4 03/14/81	030	880		440*		440*		440*	800	1320	4400
167458554	Plate Steel 1548B	2X4X1/2 06/23/84	030	3488	122*		1805*		1805*		3610	3600	14400
168122764	Plate Steel 1232A	2 ft Dia. 11/21/80	030	84						84*	85	85	360

Figure 13.4   Supplier Schedule for Repetitive Manufacturer.

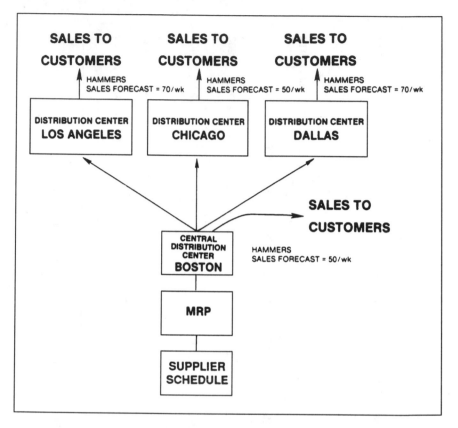

Figure 13.5   Central and Regional Distribution Centers.

plenishes the regionals, which ship to customers. In addition, the central DC services customers in its area. Each regional DC would have a sales forecast and an on-hand inventory for every item and would also know what is in-transit from the central DC.

Figure 13.6 shows that on the hammers it stocks, the Dallas DC has a forecast of 70 per week, 120 currently on hand in inventory, and 200 in transit from the distribution center due next week (Period 1). Distribution Resource Planning would calculate when Dallas will need more hammers (planned orders).

Dallas will need a shipment of 200 hammers in Week 4 and another shipment of 200 hammers in Week 7, to avoid going below the safety stock of 100. Given the two-week replenishment lead time, the central DC will need to ship to Dallas in Weeks 2 and 5; hence the planned order releases of 200 in each of these weeks. These Dallas planned orders

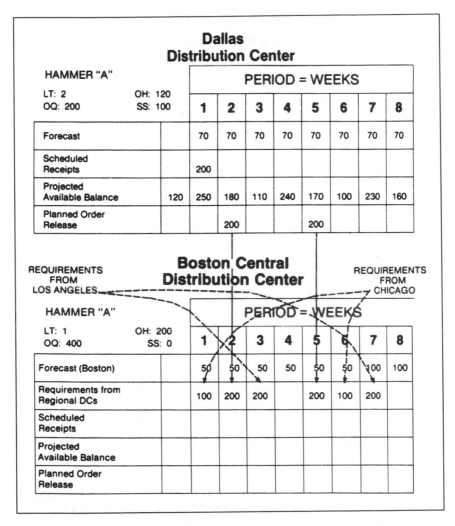

Figure 13.6   Distribution Resource Planning (DRP) Schedule.

are input to the central DC's Material Requirements Planning system for the hammer, along with the planned orders from the other two DCs and the regional distribution center.

Note that Los Angeles orders in quantities of 200 and Chicago in quantities of 100. DRP then calculates a schedule of the total requirements for hammers to be delivered from the manufacturer to the distribution center. (See Figure 13.7.)

The planned order information for Hammer A at the central distribution center is consolidated via MRP onto the supplier schedule along

**Boston Central
Distribution Center**

HAMMER "A" LT: 1 OH: 200 OQ: 400 SS: 0		PERIOD = WEEKS							
		1	2	3	4	5	6	7	8
Forecast (Boston)		50	50	50	50	50	50	100	100
Requirements from Regional DCs		100	200	200		200	100	200	
Scheduled Receipts									
Projected Available Balance	200	50	200	350	300	50	300	0	300
Planned Order Release			400	400			400		400

Figure 13.7   DRP Schedule (Totals).

with planned orders for all other items purchased from that supplier. The supplier scheduler at the central DC would review the schedule and forward it to the supplier.

If the hardware distributor in this example were purchasing hammers from more than one manufacturer—for example, both Stanley Tools and True Temper—then each of their respective supplier schedules would list their portion of the total hammer requirements. The buyer has negotiated master purchase agreements for hand tools, which includes the hammers just planned. The supplier schedule can be used to schedule the hammer and all the other hand tool deliveries to the distribution center.

MRO ITEMS

The typical Maintenance, Repair, and Operating (MRO) buyer is drowning in paperwork. Consider that the purchase of 20,000 items an average of three times a year creates 60,000 requisitions, 60,000 purchase orders, and 60,000 receiving reports. It is no wonder the MRO buyer has little time to do anything but shuffle paper. Because of this time constraint, the buyer typically finds it hard to do systems contracting or value analysis on the MRO items.

These items, however, can be handled and scheduled in much the same way as production items. To schedule any item on MRP, three things are needed: a master schedule on the end item, an inventory record on each item, and a bill of material that includes every item to be scheduled. Let us look at the bill of material.

First, every item must have an item number so the system can keep track of it. This may be a problem for some companies that do not currently have item numbers assigned to MRO items. Those companies would have to assign item numbers for all the MRO items that they want to schedule on MRP II.

The second requirement of the bill of material is the quantity of each item to be scheduled. For example, suppose that a piece of consumable tooling, such as a drill bit used in manufacturing an item, needs to be replaced. On average, the drill bit is replaced after producing 10 parts, so the quantity per for that drill bit would be one-tenth. For every 10 parts required, the MRP II system will require one drill bit.

The third requirement of the bill of material is a structure showing how the item is used. This structure is represented by Figure 13.8.

If the job demands a hundred of Part A, the system would plan a requirement for 10 drill bits and 100 undrilled parts (B), then schedule the drilling work center to complete the drilling operation. Likewise, if the drilling operation requires cooling oil, that could be scheduled by making it a component of Part A as well. See Figure 13.9.

By including the cost of the consumable tooling or the operating supplies in the product costs, a company can get a more accurate total cost of producing a product. On the other hand, some companies may not want these expense items in the product cost. By setting the costs of the drill bit and cooling oil at zero, they can be scheduled using MRP II and not affect the product cost.

Figure 13.8 Bill of Material Structure.

Figure 13.9   Bill of Material Structure.

An inventory record on the drill bit and cooling oil is required to determine the starting on-hand balance. If there are eight drill bits on hand and the MRP II system requires 10, it would indicate that at least two more must be acquired to meet the production schedule. The master schedule, the schedule of the end items to be built on a weekly or daily basis, would then drive the week-by-week drill bit requirements. These drill requirements would then be scheduled from the supplier on the supplier schedule. The buyer would negotiate a contract on drill bits, and the supplier scheduler would release the individual weekly quantities to the supplier. In this way, the operating supplies would be scheduled exactly the same as the production items.

Here is an interesting twist on organization. In one company, the supplier scheduler for consumable tooling—drill bits, saw blades, reamers, and so on—is a member of the Industrial Engineering Department. In another company, the supplier scheduler for packaging material is in Shipping. Good basic systems (knowing what is needed and when) and short, clear lines of communications (supplier scheduling) permit organizational flexibility, one aspect of which is being able to put functions "where the action is."

The maintenance items for the equipment in the factory can also be supplier scheduled. Many companies have a regular preventive maintenance schedule. This can be included in the master schedule. Each piece of equipment is given a number, such as Press 1 (P1), Press 2 (P2), and so on. When the maintenance staff plans the preventive maintenance on an individual piece of equipment, they intend to replace certain items. These items are then structured into the bill of material as shown in Figure 13.10.

If the lead time on each of these items to be used is one week, and the maintenance on Press 2 is scheduled for the week of July 15, MRP would schedule the items needed from the supplier releasing the orders in the week of July 8.

Figure 13.10   Bill of Material Structure.

This approach can also be adapted to work for items that aren't replaced consistently. Suppose that when the company does preventive maintenance on a piece of equipment, it's not always necessary to replace the V-belt. By checking the maintenance records, it is possible to see that it is necessary to replace it only 80 percent of the time. The company can put a .8 fractional quantity in the bill of material. MRP will then compensate for this and schedule in the correct quantity of the V-belts.

By inputting the annual preventive maintenance schedule for all the equipment in the factory into the master production schedule, preventive maintenance parts can be placed on a supplier schedule. Now that the buyer knows the annual requirements for oil, grease, V-belts, and so on, the buyer can negotiate annual contracts on these items with releases as required. Like the production item buyer, the MRO buyer is spending time contracting, not handling pieces of paper.

This technique can be extended to office supplies, hand tools, pipe fittings, ad infinitum. Here is an illustration: Most companies have a central stockroom that contains all the office supplies. Every item in the stockroom can be assigned an item number, which could, if desired, match the office supply supplier's catalog number for every item. An inventory record is created and a minimum inventory established for each item (such as one dozen ballpoint pens). When someone needs a pen, it is issued from stock. When the inventory drops below the minimum (in this case, to 11), the MRP system schedules a replacement shipment from the supplier in an appropriate lot size. If the company inputs a forecast on each item based on either expected future usage or historical usage, it is possible to get a time-phased requirements plan like that for all the other items being scheduled on MRP II.

This idea works equally well for in-plant construction. A simple example would be to build a wall to divide a conference room. A work order would be generated and assigned a number, such as W0137. The maintenance manager would develop a parts list of the materials needed to complete the wall. This parts list would be input to the computer in the form of a bill of material. The end item number would be the same as the work order number. See Figure 13.11.

Purchasing has negotiated a "list-less" contract with the local lumberyard covering all purchases for the year (that is, the published price on all the items, an across-the-board discount on all purchases). The Maintenance Department determines that it can do the job in six hours, and schedules the job for September 15. The lead time on the purchased items is two days. On September 13, the supplier schedule triggers the delivery of the various items required from the lumberyard. On September 15, the maintenance dispatch list would schedule the wall to be built. When the wall is completed, the work order is indicated as complete and the onetime bill of material is removed from the system. Again, the supplier schedule has been utilized to bring in the purchased parts on time.

Permanent tooling—both new tooling and preventive maintenance of existing tooling—can be scheduled in much the same way. By structuring a bill of activities (see Figure 13.12), it's possible to schedule all the activities necessary to have the new tool on the date required. When the tooling request is completed on June 1, the operation is reported as complete. The MRP system then schedules the Design Engineering Department to complete the design, a draftsman to complete the drawing specification, and lastly, the actual building of the tool.

MRP II is fundamentally a network scheduling system. Project activities of a onetime nature, such as designing and building a tool, typically scheduled by PERT (Project Evaluation and Review Technique), CPM (Critical Path Method), or other scheduling systems, can be scheduled

Figure 13.11   Bill of Material Structure.

Figure 13.12   Bill of Activities Structure.

via MRP II. A planning bill of material, or bill of activities as in Figure 13.12, is used instead of the PERT or CPM chart. Once established, this planning bill of material or bill of activities is entered into the computer just like a standard bill of material. Then, as each step is completed, the MRP system schedules the next operation in time to meet the completion date of the project. Companies have even erected buildings using MRP II scheduling techniques. MRP II has the capabilities to schedule all of the resources needed in a company and shouldn't be seen as just manufacturing resource planning.

MRP II and supplier scheduling works as well for the distributor and reseller as the manufacturer, in large companies and small, process, repetitive, or one-of-a-kind manufacturing companies. It represents a universal solution to a universal problem in purchasing: too little time to do a professional buying job. Supplier scheduling is limited only by the user's imagination and perception of what it can do.

SUMMARY

- An excellent way to manage scarce items is to work out an agreement with the supplier to set aside a certain percentage of its capacity.

- When it comes to excellent supplier performance, it is not always clout that counts, it is the quality of the schedule that counts.

- Supplier scheduling works well in a process type of environment.

- Replanning is one of the strong features of MRP II.

- High-volume repetitive situations lend themselves readily to Just-in-Time scheduling.

- Distributors and resellers can use supplier scheduling the same as manufacturers can.

- MRP II can free the typical MRO buyer from the massive paperwork normally associated with buying these items.

- Supplier scheduling is limited only by the user's imagination and perception of what it can do.

Chapter Fourteen

Performance Measurements

Many factors go into the successful use of MRP II and JIT/TQC. Two important ones are performance measurements and a commitment to continuous improvement. Performance measurements provide a window into areas that can be improved on in the future. In successful companies, continuous improvement becomes a way of life for employees, suppliers, and customers. It is also a key tool in maintaining a competitive advantage in today's manufacturing and purchasing environments.

PERSPECTIVE ON MEASUREMENTS

If MRP II is working correctly, need dates are being given to the supplier by either the supplier schedule or a Kanban card. If education has been done properly, users should start noticing a marked improvement in supplier performance. The only way to be absolutely certain of real progress, however, is to measure that performance.

Going by the Numbers

The first step is to establish objective measurements. The buyer should sit down with the supplier, set realistic goals, and develop a timetable for reaching them. These goals cannot be stated in subjective terms like "do better" or "work harder." This just leads to great philosophical discussions about what "do better" means and whether the supplier did in fact "do better." It leaves open to subjective opinion whether, in fact, the performance did improve. But if the goal is set in objective, numerical terms, the answer to the question "Did performance improve?" is obvious. If the goal was 95 percent and the supplier improved from 90 to 93 percent, the performance did improve but is still short of the goal. As the saying goes, "If you don't know where you are going, any road will get you there." The objective of performance measurements is to establish which road you want to take, where you currently are on the road, and where you ultimately want to end up.

Companies often need to make some basic changes in the way they reward performance. For example, if two buyers receive the same percentage pay raise at the end of the year, when one had suppliers who were 70 percent on-time and the other 98 percent on-time, the incentive to perform to the maximum level is diminished. Compensation systems, therefore, should reward people for good performance. The same principle is applicable to suppliers. If the 70 percent on-time supplier receives the same percentage of the business as the 98 percent on-time supplier, there is little motivation to work harder and improve performance. Both buyers and suppliers must realize that they are expected to meet certain standards of performance, and should be made aware of the unpleasant consequences of missing their targets.

Goals should also reflect current realities. If a company has just begun measurement reporting and finds that a particular supplier's on-time delivery performance is 70 percent, it is neither fair nor realistic to expect that supplier to achieve 95 percent by next month. Measurements are a starting point—they help people learn how to improve performance by pointing out where they are deficient and by establishing achievable timetables to reach desired levels.

Measurement reporting represents an opportunity to develop a better understanding between the supplier and the buyer of each other's needs. In this way they can be used as a basis for improved performance. If measurements are viewed simply as a punishment/reward tool in supplier relationships, the results may be just the opposite of those desired.

Small Steps versus Giant Leaps

Progress toward performance goals should be monitored. This is done with a process that entails setting up intermediate goals as yardsticks for improvement. Let us say Supplier A is currently 70 percent on-time, and you would like Supplier A to achieve 95 percent on-time performance six months from now. This supplier agrees that six months is a realistic time frame. Your intermediate goals are 80 percent in two months and 90 percent in four months. Supplier B, on the other hand, is 85 percent on-time. Since your goal is to have all suppliers at 95 percent on-time six months from now, and Supplier B also agrees that that length of time is realistic, Supplier B's benchmark would be 90 percent two months from now and 93 percent four months from now. This approach allows you to measure all of your suppliers' improvements in performance on a regular basis, taking into account where they are today, with confidence that they will improve steadily and hit your 95 percent on-time goal within six months.

One other perspective on measurements is needed before we look at how results are measured. We normally talk about goals in terms of 95 or 98 percent attainment; that is, quality is 98 percent (98 out of every 100 lots received are accepted, while only 2 are rejected). Based on most companies' current level of performance, those could be very challenging goals. A nationwide survey of purchasing personnel, reported in *Purchasing Magazine*, revealed an average on-time performance of 82 percent and in-specification of 92 percent. Therefore, 98 percent sounds very good to most people in purchasing today.

But consider the remaining 2 percent out of specification in the context of parts per million. A 2 percent defect level means you are getting 20,000 defects for every one million parts you receive. For certain, 20,000 defects is totally unacceptable on a continuing basis. This is why the continuous improvement process is so important. But to use it, you must first put a measurement system in place to determine where you are today. Next, you need to establish goals and programs to get the purchasing environment under control—95 to 98 percent in terms of performance attainment. Finally, you need to put into action a program to continuously improve your performance beyond those "acceptable" levels of performance.

If you are at 20,000 defects per million (2 percent), you could use a tool such as Pareto analysis to identify the reasons for the defects, solve the problem for some defects, and lower the total number to 19,000 defects per million. If you can get down to 19,000 defects, you can achieve 18,000, and so on. A leading manufacturer of copier machines was able to drop its level of incoming quality defects from 10,000 parts per million to 122 parts per million. Although this represents 99.9988 percent in-specification, the company still is not satisfied and vigorously pursues its continuous improvement program.

HOW RESULTS ARE MEASURED

To get control of your purchasing environment, you must first identify areas that need improvement. A good purchasing performance measurement system should cover eight different areas, including:

1. Delivery.

2. Quality.

3. Price.

4. Lead times.

5. Inventory investment.

6. Schedule completions in the plant.

7. Cost reduction/value analysis.

8. Inbound freight cost reduction.

If your company is already measuring other areas as well, combine them with the eight discussed here to provide an overall picture of supplier, buyer, and supplier scheduler performance.

Delivery

Because the company is displaying need dates rather than due dates on its schedules, the supplier must deliver on-time or a shortage will probably result. The supplier, the buyer, and the supplier scheduler must all realize that the dates on the supplier schedule are "drop dead" dates. Some companies tell their suppliers that a shipment will be considered on-time if it arrives anytime from seven days before the due date to seven days after it. That tells the supplier that the need dates are at least seven days later than the due dates. Performance cannot be measured honestly when an order shipped five days late is considered on-time. Initially in such a situation, it is preferable to allow suppliers to ship up to two weeks early. This still provides the same two-week delivery policy as the "seven days early to seven days late" policy but without violating the validity of the need date.

Once the need date is understood by suppliers, and suppliers demonstrate their ability to routinely deliver in that two-week window, the continuous improvement process can begin. The window is first moved from 14 days to 10 days. When the supplier is able to live with 10 days consistently, the window is narrowed to 7 days.

Leading MRP II/JIT companies today allow the supplier to ship up to two days early, no days late. And it is now becoming common practice in some industries to actually tell the supplier the *time of day* the shipment is wanted, not just the day it is wanted.

If the trucking time for shipping a product varies between 3 days and 10 days, Purchasing can initially instruct the supplier to ship it 10 days before the need date, so it will always arrive on-time (before the need date). Once this performance level has been accomplished, the trucking company can be included in the continuous improvement process. Ask questions such as "What can we do to cut down the variability in transit times?" and "Do we need to work with a specialty contract carrier to get the transit time to a consistent three days?"

The buyer should also define the past due cutoff date. If the order is due on Wednesday afternoon, the supplier must realize that a Thursday-morning delivery will be considered past due. If the order is for 5,000 and the supplier ships only 4,000, the remainder of the order is also considered past due on Thursday morning. Suppliers must realize that companies are serious when they say an order must be delivered on-time. Once the ground rules for on-time delivery have been established, performance can be measured more objectively.

It may also be necessary to change the way on-time performance is calculated. Typically, in companies without supplier scheduling, on-time performance is measured by adding up all past due purchase orders and dividing that number by the total number of open purchase orders.

Unfortunately, this measurement technique has some major flaws. It is too general and does not reflect how well a particular buyer or supplier did in a particular week or month. Consider the following example. You have 1,000 open orders in Purchasing with your suppliers and 100 of them are past due. The current performance level would be 90 percent (900 not yet past due divided by 1,000 open orders). If the supplier's lead times were to increase, the buyer would need to release more orders further in the future to cover the longer lead times. Using this example, there may now be 1,200 open orders. At the same time, the on-time measurement would increase to 92 percent (1,100 divided by 1,200). Is that because the supplier and the buyer are performing better? Of course not—it is purely a paper improvement. Obviously, this technique does not provide a true measure of performance.

Here is another example. A buyer has 5 open orders with a supplier, each for 20 pieces. (See Figure 14.1.) One of those orders is past due, so the supplier is 80 percent on-time (one order past due out of a total of five open orders).

Current Date 7/1					
Due Date	6/25	7/5	7/15	7/25	8/5
Quantity	20	20	20	20	20

Figure 14.1   Open Order Report.

On July 10, the supplier ships the 20 pieces due on June 25. (See Figure 14.2.) The July 5 shipment is now past due, however, and another order, due August 15, is added. The supplier is again 80 percent on-time, because one is late out of five that are due.

On July 20, the supplier ships the 20 pieces due on July 5. (See Figure 14.3.) The order due July 15 goes past due and another order due on August 25 is added. Look at the open order report of July 20—the supplier is once again 80 percent on-time.

The problem here is clear: The supplier has shipped every single order late and, in fact, is zero percent on-time in terms of delivery. A delivery performance system must measure true on-time performance. The system should track the receipt date against the due date on the supplier schedule and give the buyer and supplier an objective score on performance against the schedule for that week or month.

Figure 14.4 shows an example of a format for such a measurement report. The buyer and supplier would go over the report each month. Orders considered past due would be displayed below the totals column for the supplier's review. The principle of "Silence is approval" applies; unless the supplier disagrees with the monthly performance percentage, the supplier is held accountable for it.

At this point, the continuous improvement process can begin. Part number 147 was received seven days late. By working with the supplier, the cause of the late shipment can be resolved. Your thinking and ques-

Current Date 7/10					
Due Date	7/5	7/15	7/25	8/5	8/15
Quantity	20	20	20	20	20

Figure 14.2   Open Order Report.

Current Date 7/20					
Due Date	7/15	7/25	8/5	8/15	8/25
Quantity	20	20	20	20	20

Figure 14.3   Open Order Report.

tioning should go something like this: "Was it a quality problem, tooling problem, scheduling problem, or something else that caused the part to be late? What can *we* jointly do to eliminate this problem from occurring again? If *we* can jointly eliminate the cause of the late shipment so it does not occur again, we should expect performance to improve toward our goal of on-time shipments." It is important to remember that you may have caused the problem by a late schedule change or engineering change that the supplier did not have enough time to react to. The key to continuous improvement is to identify the cause and prevent problems from occurring in the future. Finally, since each item is tied to a buyer, a supplier scheduler, and one or more suppliers, a similar measurement report could be generated for each of these people.

You do not need sophisticated online systems to get on-time measurements; a microcomputer and spreadsheet package will suffice. For that matter, you can collect and track the measurement data manually. When the shipment arrives, the personnel at the receiving dock can fill out a simple one-part form such as the one shown in Figure 14.5. This information can then be either entered into the computer or manually checked against the open order file or scheduled receipts on the supplier

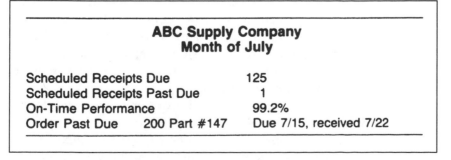

Figure 14.4   Performance Measurement Report.

DELIVERY

PART NUMBER _____

VENDOR NUMBER _____

DATE RECEIVED _____

LOCATION / DOOR _____

QUANTITY RECEIVED _____

UNIT OF MEASURE _____

Figure 14.5   Receiving Dock Form.

schedules to determine whether the supplier was on-time. The shipment was either complete and on-time or it was not—the measurement is as simple as that.

If you have only one receiving door, obviously you would not need such information. But for companies with many receiving docks, it is a way to see if the supplier delivered it to the particular door you requested (Door 7, Building 14), and if not, why not. In a continuous improvement effort where you are requesting the supplier to deliver product directly to the using department on the manufacturing floor, the measurement is a way of tracking its ability to do that. In that case, the department number would be input instead of the door number and the supervisor of the department would fill out the receiving form.

Reliable delivery is critical to MRP II. Since the supplier schedule is based on need dates, the goal should be a minimum 95 percent on-time. Now that suppliers are receiving the information they need to plan capacity and raw materials via the supplier schedule, they can reasonably be expected to meet the need dates. Those starting out at 70 percent on-time should be able to meet their immediate goals of 80 percent, then 90 percent, and then 95 percent. But don't stop there; 95 percent should be considered as the minimum acceptable level of performance. Why not 98 or 99 percent? Why not 100 percent?

The delivery measurement report will give Purchasing the information needed to identify the problem suppliers or items. When those problems are resolved, performance can be expected to improve. The challenge, then, is to make continuing improvement a way of life. The challenge is to get better and better. Some companies today are achieving nearly 100 percent delivery performance from their suppliers. They did not get there overnight; it has taken lots of hard work on the part of many people. But it is certainly worth it.

The survey in Appendix B indicates that Class A/B MRP II companies using supplier scheduling averaged 97 percent on-time supplier delivery performance. The average company took six months from the start of supplier scheduling to accomplish 97 percent on-time delivery performance. Those companies using a Kanban mechanism and receiving daily shipments from their suppliers averaged over 99 percent on-time delivery.

Quality

Out-of-specification material can represent just as many headaches as material that arrives late. Again, because supplier scheduling deals with need dates, the items must be of acceptable quality when they arrive at the receiving dock. It does not do a buyer any good to bring items in just in time if the quality is bad. It is equally disadvantageous to bring in good-quality material late; both the delivery date and quality level are critical to supplier scheduling. Companies need to work with their suppliers to assist them in developing a total quality approach that includes statistical process control and defect-prevention tools that will assure quality items every time. That means you will need to work with your suppliers to be sure they have the necessary tools, test equipment, and fixtures to make a quality item. Well-defined specifications on every item and a written agreement to those specifications from the supplier are critical. Even having done all that, though, the company will still need to be assured of the quality of incoming purchased material.

One way to gain this assurance is via source inspection; in other words, have all suppliers certified on quality and do a complete job of inspecting their output. Until a company has achieved this status with all of its suppliers, however, it will need formal and objective measurements of the quality level of purchased items coming in the door.

Traditionally, most companies measure quality based on lots accepted and lots rejected. The problem with this measurement is that it does not give the buyer the information needed to eliminate defects at the supplier's. With a lots accepted, lots rejected system, a sample of the supplier shipment is taken when it is received and measured against the specification. Tolerances are established on each measurement and a small amount of variant material is considered acceptable.

For example, if a particular test is measured to a 1.0 acceptable quality level (AQL), the shipment will be accepted if it has 5 or fewer defects in a sample of 125 parts, rejected if it has 6 or more defects. If it is measured against a 0.5 AQL, it will be accepted if it has 3 or fewer defects. In other words, the more critical the test, the fewer the defects allowed in the sample. A supplier shipment is received and contains only three defects in the sample, so it is accepted and recorded as a good lot. In a lots accepted, lots rejected measurement system, the buyer does not see the three defects, only the rating of accepted. Even though the shipment is acceptable, the buyer must see the defects so a program can be developed with the supplier to eliminate those defects in all future shipments. The goal is zero defects.

A good quality measurement system that records defects would work as follows. When a shipment is received, Quality Control would pull and inspect a sample of that shipment. Based on this inspection, a lot will be either accepted or rejected. The quality measurement would include a record of the number of defective parts in the sample taken and the type of defect, regardless of whether the shipment was rejected.

For example, suppose an inspector pulls 100 samples from an incoming shipment of 1,000 parts and 3 are found to be defective for various reasons. In this case, the shipment is 97 percent in-specification. Every shipment that arrives on the receiving dock would be inspected in this way. The results are recorded against the particular supplier who produced the shipment and summarized weekly or monthly. (See Figure 14.6.)

This report then becomes the basis for the continuous process-improvement effort in the quality area. The report has identified the reasons for defects (grease, rust, color, etc.). If, in working with your suppli-

ABC Company
Month of July

	Samples Pulled	Defective	%	Reason
Part #127	100	3	97	Grease
Part #213	150	3	98	Rust
Part #543	50	3	94	Color
Monthly Total	300	9	97%	

Figure 14.6   Inspection Report.

ers, you are able to determine the cause of the defect (machine setup, tool quality, operator training, etc.), in time you should be able to eliminate the cause of the defect. By eliminating the cause, you should expect overall performance to improve. In this way, companies can identify the parts and suppliers that are consistently a problem.

If the current supplier is unable to resolve the problem on its own, you have the option of either sending your quality and engineering people to the manufacturing facility to help resolve the problem, or finding alternative suppliers that can meet your quality objectives. The goal is to initially have a minimum of 98 percent of all items within specification to gain control over your purchasing environment. The ultimate goal is 100 percent.

Again, you do not need an online program to measure quality. As in the case of delivery, you can initially use a personal computer to gather the data. It would be difficult to manually measure quality because of the high level of detail numbers involved in the computations. A one-part form with the information shown in Figure 14.7 should be sufficient for collecting the appropriate data.

One last point needs to be made: Rejected shipments should not count as on-time shipments. A rejected lot means that the supplier receives a poor performance rating not only on quality but also on delivery. Only good parts are considered on-time.

QUALITY

DATA INSPECTED _____

INSPECTED BY _____

ECN NUMBER _____

QUANTITY INSPECTED _____

QUANTITY REJECTED _____

REJECT NUMBER _____

TOTAL QUANTITY DEFECTIVE _____

DEFECT CODE _____

DEFECT DESCRIPTION _____

Figure 14.7   Quality Record.

Price

Few companies measure price performance for each supplier and buyer to find out who is doing a good job of controlling costs and who is not. While many buyers can boast of their cost-reduction programs, few can talk about the total impact of all price increases and decreases on the bottom line of the profit and loss statement.

Is pricing, delivery, or quality a company's most important measurement of performance? For many companies, delivery and quality are probably more critical than price. It is far better to purchase in uneconomical quantities and keep the shop running than to get a "real buy" and shut the line down waiting for delivery. But price is still an important factor if a company is to remain competitive, so it is vital to measure performance in all three areas.

Many companies measure price against a standard cost. In these cases, the price measurement is actually more of a reflection of how well the standard was established than of how wisely the buyers are using the company's financial resources. Suppose that on January 1 a supplier's price is $1. Purchasing estimates an 8 percent inflation factor, so the estimated cost at the end of the year would be $1.08. If the standard cost was calculated as the average cost for the year, Purchasing would place the standard cost at $1.04. If, however, Purchasing guessed wrong and the inflation factor was really 10 percent, the buyer's price performance would likely show an unfavorable variance of 2 percent at the end of the year. The buyer has little or no control over this factor.

Companies should measure actual performance rather than measure against a standard cost; it's much fairer to the buyers to measure them in a way that takes into account all the price increases and decreases and gives a weighted price index of performance. That price index, calculated for each item, is shown in Figure 14.8.

Each item would be calculated the same way and the total would be summed by the buyer or the supplier. (See Figure 14.9.) Using this technique, Purchasing has an objective measure of price performance for each buyer and supplier. This makes it possible to determine that Supplier A (80 percent on-time, 80 percent within specification, and 112 percent on the price index) is not as good as Supplier B (who is 98 percent on-time, 97 percent within specification, and 103 percent on the price index). The same principle is equally applicable to buyers.

Lead Times

As discussed earlier, supplier scheduling allows companies to reduce their lead times significantly. Basically, supplier scheduling represents a

Price at end of year	$1.06
Price at start of year	1.00
Difference	.06
Annual Usage	10,000
Annual Price Impact	+$600.00

Figure 14.8 Calculation of Price Impact.

change from "paper" lead times to true manufacturing lead times. As the suppliers learn to use the information available to them in the supplier schedule to do a better job of planning raw materials and capacity, they will feel more comfortable working to manufacturing lead times. Purchasing should measure lead times regularly to see how well their suppliers understand the system. If the desired results aren't being achieved, more education may be necessary for the supplier or buyer involved.

Purchasing can measure two areas regarding lead times. First, of all the items purchased, how many have shorter lead times than before MRP II implementation? Once supplier scheduling is working, this answer should approach 100 percent. The second measurement would be the percentage of reduction in lead times. This would vary from company to company, depending on the commodities purchased, but the result should be fairly substantial in most companies. Companies that work with their suppliers in a continuous improvement program in which they (1) assist their suppliers in cutting lead times by showing them how to set up cellular manufacturing and (2) reduce tool setup times yield lead-time reductions of up to 90 percent.

Inventory Investment

Since Purchasing is able to bring in the items to true need dates, rather than invalid due dates, substantial inventory reductions are possible. The Class A/B users of MRP II surveyed reported they typically saw a 30 percent reduction in purchased material inventory levels—in the face of inflation and, in many of the companies, high growth. (See Appendix B.) Double-digit inventory turns (12 to 18) are very common in leading MRP II/JIT companies today.

Part #	Price EOY	Price SOY	Difference	Annual Quantity	Annual $	Price Impact
137	1.06	1.00	.06	10,000	$10,000	+ $600
243	.47	.45	.02	100,000	45,000	+ 2000
549	.03	.03	—	10,000	300	—
637	.63	.67	.04	6,000	4,020	− 240
					$59,320	+ $2360
					Price Index	104

Figure 14.9 Weighted Price Index.

Schedule Completions in the Plant

One key test of the success of any MRP II implementation is customer service—the number of orders being shipped complete and on time. That number should be measured weekly to ensure that all departments are executing the schedule correctly. The plant is a "customer" of Purchasing, so measuring Purchasing's performance amounts to measuring the "customer service" that Purchasing is providing to the plant. Similarly, the Sales Department is the "customer" of the plant, and the plant should be measured accordingly; its "customer service" measure is performance to the master production schedule.

Some of the best Class A MRP II companies publish weekly their schedule completions by product line. If a date is missed, it is recorded, as is the reason for the delay. This leads to identifying the root cause of the problem and solving it. Things that get measured get better. Do it right the first time.

Cost Reduction/Value Analysis

Purchasing should establish cost reduction/value analysis goals for each buyer and measure the buyer against those goals. MRP II helps the buyer in this area by identifying the items with the biggest annual savings potential. Purchasing can extract the annual usage of each item from the MRP II and determine its dollar value. Then, by printing the list of all the buyer's items in descending dollar sequence, the buyer can concentrate on those items with the greatest potential payback. Purchasing should measure the dollars saved against the goals set and routinely publish the results.

Inbound Freight Cost Reduction

In many companies today, inbound freight costs are a substantial part of the cost of materials. These costs can run up to 15 percent of the total dollars spent in Purchasing, although they are seldom broken out separately and typically are not visible to buyers. Because of the lack of visibility of these costs and the amount of money spent on inbound freight, there is a large potential for cost reduction in this area. You should see savings in this area when you implement an MRP II system for several reasons.

First, the buyers should have time to negotiate freight rates and study which mode of transportation is the most economical for a particular item. In the past this wasn't the case, and it was often left up to the supplier which carrier to choose.

Second, if a Traffic Department was assigned the task of specifying carriers or modes of transportation, or the buyer had time to do it, it was normally based on past experience. Traffic or the buyer would take bills of lading from previous shipments, and negotiated rates were based on what you did in the past. With supplier scheduling, you can give carriers future visibility of inbound freight by area and negotiate rates based on what is going to happen in the future. The way to do this is to convert scheduled receipts and planned orders into weight values by area. Figure 14.10 demonstrates how this works. A pooled freight rate based on a 15,800-pound shipment would be negotiated and all three suppliers would be instructed to arrange for pickup of their material on the same day of the week. The carrier would move all the material as if it were one shipment. As a result, your freight rate should be lower than it would be if these materials moved as five separate individual smaller shipments.

WESTERN MICHIGAN SUPPLIER GROUP

Supplier A Freight Plan in Pounds

	w/o July 15	w/o July 22	w/o July 29
Part 123	450	225	450
Part 456	730	0	730
	1180	225	1180

Supplier B Freight Plan in Pounds

Part 246	4500	7000	4500
Part 789	2000	2000	2000
	6500	9000	6500

Supplier C Freight Plan in Pounds

Part 137	7000	5000	7000
Part 973	1120	1150	1180
	8120	6150	8180

Summary—Total Freight Region

15,800	15,375	15,860

Figure 14.10   Pooled Freight.

The third reason for reduced freight is the reduced need for premium air shipments due to expediting shortages. With valid schedules, more time to plan, better on-time supplier performance and fewer quality rejections, the need for premium freight should be minimal. Documented savings of up to 40 percent of the total freight costs are not uncommon in good MRP II/JIT companies. (See Chapter 9 for a discussion on freight cost–reduction techniques.)

INTANGIBLE RESULTS

Purchasing can derive intangible benefits from MRP II. First, there is improved credibility. When the supplier scheduler tells the supplier that an item is needed on a certain date, the supplier believes it because he or she understands the MRP II system. When Purchasing tells the plant that an item will arrive at 8:00 A.M. on Wednesday, plant personnel believe it, and on Tuesday night they set up the equipment to run the part.

There is also a significant improvement in quality of life. Purchasing has valid data to work with and knows what is expected. Buyers have retired the old "fire truck" and are out in front, managing their commodities. If there is a problem, the suppliers are informing the company in advance so there is time to work out alternative solutions. Everyone is part of the same team and recognized for his or her contributions.

Finally, the Purchasing Department becomes more motivated and professional. With time to perform the really important parts of their jobs, buyers are more valuable to the company. They save the company money because they are negotiating contracts and tracking costs instead of putting out fires. Using the future visibility provided by MRP II, the buyer can make better decisions and take actions that will have very positive long-term effects.

SUPPLY CHAIN MEASUREMENTS

Supply chain performance measures are more difficult to determine because they involve the combined performance of several companies. While each company can report on its own on-time delivery performance, it is the on-time to the ultimate customer that really is important to the entire supply chain. While one company may be able to reduce inventory, if that reduction causes another partner to add inventory, the supply chain is not necessarily better off. The key measures in supply chains would be on-time to the ultimate customer, inventory and lead time reduction throughout the entire supply chain, the combined cost reduction of all the companies as a result of Supply Chain Management, and the reduction in time-to-market on new products.

CONTINUOUS IMPROVEMENT

The goal of any company should be to continuously improve their performance. No matter where they are today, they should seek to be better tomorrow. Purchasing should be a part of that drive to continuously improve. The problem is, many companies don't know where to start or what the ultimate goals should be. The Oliver Wight Companies have developed a series of questions, the ABCD Checklist, to guide a company toward excellence. Appendix C lists those questions to guide you in your quest toward excellence.

SUMMARY

- Performance measurements are the only way to gauge your and your supplier's effectiveness in today's purchasing environment.

- Performance measurements must be cast in terms of concrete, quantitative results and goals; subjective and generalized feedback cannot lead to improvement.

- Performance measurements are not designed to be used as a means of punishment or retribution; rather they provide feedback for buyers and suppliers to use to improve their performance.

- Measure performance in incremental steps against benchmarks, interim goals that will gradually move a supplier to the desired performance level at a realistic pace.

- A comprehensive performance-measurement system covers delivery, quality, price, lead times, inventory investment, schedule completions in the plant, cost reduction/value analysis, and inbound freight cost reduction.

- Supplier delivery performance must be gauged on need dates, not replenishment dates; otherwise, "on-time" becomes meaningless.

- A 2 percent defect rate may, on the surface, seem like good performance. But 2 percent means 20,000 defective parts out of every million, which is clearly unacceptable. Strive for 100 percent.

- Price should not be regarded as secondary to quality and delivery. An objective measure of price performance looks at *actual performance* rather than at performance against a standard cost.

- Lead-time reductions should be measured pre- and post-MRP II (all lead times should be shorter once supplier scheduling is in place). They should also be rated on an overall percentage basis.

- On-hand inventories of purchased parts should drop when items are delivered to true need dates.

- Scheduled completion dates are ultimately reflected in customer service, which should be assessed on a regular basis.

- Purchasing should develop a continuous improvement program and strive for purchasing excellence.

Chapter Fifteen

MRP II and JIT/TQC in Purchasing— Making It Work

Developing excellent suppliers to support MRP II and JIT/TQC means more than scheduling a one-time Supplier Education Day or mailing out instructions to the suppliers on their role in supporting your program. Rather, your efforts should be directed at assisting your suppliers in becoming excellent users of the same tools you rely on—MRP II and JIT/TQC—and to integrate their expertise with yours.

Unfortunately, when these tools first became available, many companies began to reduce purchase inventory, reduce purchase lot sizes, and increase frequency of supplier deliveries, while at the same time expecting their suppliers to ship defect-free product without first implementing the tools at their own facilities. These companies did not provide the suppliers with valid schedules, nor did they level production schedules, internally reduce lot sizes or lead times, stabilize product design, or implement a quality program. Not surprisingly, since the suppliers ended up carrying the inventory and all the extra costs, many of the early programs failed. And to add salt to the wounds, many of the suppliers involved became cynical about MRP II and JIT/TQC programs.

To avoid repeating such mistakes, companies must implement the programs internally first, find out how to correctly use MRP II and JIT/TQC, and then show their suppliers how to do it. This way, the suppliers will see the results at the buyer's company, understand that it is not just a program to push costs onto their ledgers, and be more willing to sign up to be involved. When the supplier sees how the buying company has developed valid schedules, improved internal quality, and reduced lead times and costs, the supplier will be more willing to support the program. Then it is time to start implementing supplier scheduling in purchasing.

A MAJOR CHALLENGE

When you implement supplier scheduling, whether you are going to use a supplier schedule or a Kanban mechanism and JIT/TQC philosophies, the effort must be integrated within your company's MRP II and JIT/TQC framework. As just explained, these items need to be in place so you can show your suppliers how they work. Implementing supplier scheduling is not something one takes lightly; it is a major undertaking that must be carefully planned and executed if it is to succeed.

Figure 15.1 presents a detailed implementation plan to help define the key tasks that need to be covered by the purchasing spinoff task force (the numbers on the right side represent first month, second month, etc.). Figure 15.2 provides a diagram and outline of the implementation plan. You will need to insert any additional steps that are needed at your company.

The purchasing manager must be a key part of the overall implementation effort. He or she must attend, as part of first-cut education, an in-depth class on MRP II and JIT/TQC. With this background, the purchasing manager can participate fully in the cost-justification process and should be able to make an informed commitment to the successful implementation of MRP II and JIT/TQC in purchasing.

In addition, the purchasing manager and perhaps other key people will require more specific education on how to design, implement, and operate an MRP system in purchasing. Also, the person selected to be the supervisor of the supplier scheduling group should attend both the MRP II and JIT/TQC class and the purchasing class.

The two educational experiences enable the attendees to develop a complete and valid implementation plan for MRP II and JIT/TQC in purchasing, and to assign responsibilities for the tasks in that plan. This gives them an opportunity to design the supplier schedule, the measurement reports, Kanban, and the other tools prior to beginning inside education for the rest of the department. With these in place in advance, the impact of the inside education process will be greatly strengthened.

TASK	MONTH
1. Outside Education	
A. Purchasing manager—MRP II and JIT/TQC class as a part of first-cut education	1
B. Other key purchasing people—MRP II and JIT/TQC class	3
C. Purchasing manager, other key people—class on MRP II in purchasing	3
D. Supervisor of supplier scheduling—MRP II class	4
E. Supervisor of supplier scheduling—MRP II in purchasing class	5
2. Inside Education	
A. Purchasing manager, along with all other department managers—a series of business meetings, over an eight-week period, based on an internal video-based education plan	3–4
B. All purchasing staff, buyers, and supplier scheduling supervisor—internal education, a series of business meetings, with purchasing manager as discussion leader	5–8
C. Supplier schedulers—internal education, a series of business meetings, with supplier scheduling supervisor as discussion leader	9–12
3. Specify the Tools	
A. 1. Design the supplier schedule	9
2. Supplier schedule due from systems group	10
B. 1. Design measurement reports—delivery, quality, price	9
2. Reports due from systems group	12
C. 1. Design management reports—negotiation report, purchase commitment report, other supporting reports	9
2. Reports due from systems group	14
D. Design Kanban mechanisms, JIT program	12
E. Design TQC program	12
4. Organization Defined	
A. Supervisor of supplier scheduling selected	4
B. Reporting structure defined—department to which supplier scheduling group reports established	5
C. Job descriptions developed for buyers and supplier schedulers	6
D. Supplier schedulers selected	8
5. Supplier Education	
A. Define if one session or three sessions (MRP II, JIT, and TQC)	9
B. Agenda for supplier education	10
1. Teaching materials selected	
2. Supplier education manual developed	
3. Supplier commitment and action plan developed	
C. Pilot supplier selected	10
D. Pilot supplier education with key supplier	11
E. Education of the 20 percent of the suppliers who represent 80 percent of the dollars	12
F. Education of the balance of production item suppliers	13–14
G. Education of the suppliers supplying MRO items (maintenance, repair, operating supplies)	20–23

(continued)

Figure 15.1   Purchasing Detailed Implementation Plan.

TASK	MONTH
6. Pilot and Cutover	
A. Pilot with key supplier and fine-tune the system	12
B. Cut over 20 percent of the suppliers who represent 80 percent of the volume (provided pilot is satisfactory)	13
C. Measure results	
1. Pilot measurement reports	12–13
2. Measure results—pilot and 20 percent of the suppliers	13–14
D. Cut over remaining suppliers—production items only	15–18
E. Measure results for all suppliers	16–18
1. Follow-up education—specific suppliers	18
2. Goals and action plans for all suppliers established and signed off by suppliers	18
7. MRO Items Added to MRP II	
A. Plan established	19
1. Operating supplies	
2. Preventive maintenance items	
3. Balance of the items	
B. Operating supplies added to bill of material	20
C. Supplier scheduling of operating supplies	21
D. Preventive maintenance bill of materials developed and master production schedule established	22
E. Supplier scheduling of preventive maintenance parts	23
F. Balance of items—office supplies, repair parts, etc.	23–24
1. Establish item numbers	23
2. Establish inventory location and on-hand balances	23
3. Establish desired on-hand inventory and forecasted usage for each item and load to MRP	23
4. Supplier schedule balance of items	24

Figure 15.1   (*Continued*)

Video-based education should begin in Month 3* and continue through Month 8. The purchasing manager, as a member of the project team, would take part in the "teacher's course" and then lead the education of the entire department. This would include all purchasing personnel, as well as the supervisor of the supplier scheduling group, and would follow an education plan tailored specifically for the Purchasing Department in that company. The purchasing manager, possibly assisted by the other key purchasing personnel who attended outside classes, would lead the discussions on how supplier scheduling will be done at this particular company.

---

*Throughout this chapter, there will be references to "Month 3," "Month 5," and so on. These are not intended to be hard-and-fast times, but rather to represent approximately when various activities should begin and end.

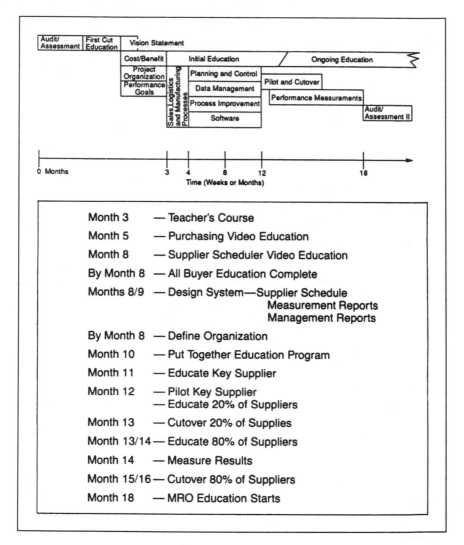

Figure 15.2   Implementation Plan.

Regardless of which department the supplier schedulers will report to (Purchasing or elsewhere), they will also require specific purchasing education. If these people were formerly planners in Production and Inventory Control, they probably would have already attended the internal education for Production and Inventory Control (P&IC). If they are new hires or have been transferred from an unrelated department, they should receive their P&IC education along with specific purchasing and supplier scheduling education. These sessions should be led by the supervisor of supplier scheduling.

Next, Purchasing has to specify the informational tools necessary to do the job. These include: the supplier schedule, the measurement reports, and the negotiation and management reports. These tools should be initially defined before and refined during the education process, and their design should be finalized by around Month 9.

Several MRP II software packages contain supplier scheduling capability. A company implementing supplier scheduling may have to design and program its supplier schedule and possibly create other reports depending on which software package it purchases.

On the positive side, though, many MRP II software packages do contain the ability to maintain purchasing and supplier-related data. The programming task, therefore, becomes primarily one of retrieval and display programming, which is typically less difficult than starting from scratch.

THE SUPPLIER SCHEDULE

The supplier schedule itself is the first tool that needs to be discussed. Purchasing will have to answer questions such as: What will the format look like? How many weeks are going to be displayed to the suppliers? Will capacity units of measure for suppliers be included? Will the report display the information horizontally (from the left side to the right side of the supplier schedule) or vertically (top to bottom)? Chapter 4 showed a horizontal format for a supplier schedule. Similar information, but in a vertical format, is shown in Figure 15.3.

The advantage of the vertical format is that it can display an unlimited number of weeks into the future, whereas a horizontal format is somewhat more limited in the number of weeks shown. A potential disadvantage of the vertical format is that it may reduce your ability to quickly see all the items due from a supplier in a given week. Purchasing must make these decisions early enough to allow the systems and data processing people time to program, test, and debug the supplier schedule.

SUPPLIER MEASUREMENT REPORTS

The second tool involves supplier measurement reports (discussed in detail in Chapter 14). Purchasing must answer questions such as: How is the company going to measure delivery, quality, and price? How often

JONES COMPANY SUPPLIER SCHEDULE FOR: SMITH, INC. WEEK OF 02/01			
Supplier Scheduler: AB Buyer: CD			
	Order Status	*Date Due*	*Quantity*
PART NUMBER 13579 PLATE	Scheduled	02/01	100
LEAD TIME 4 WEEKS	Scheduled	02/22	100
	Planned	03/08	100
	Planned	05/10	100
	Planned	07/12	100
PART NUMBER 24680 PANEL	Scheduled	03/01	50
LEAD TIME 6 WEEKS	Planned	04/19	50
	Planned	06/28	50

Figure 15.3   Supplier Schedule.

does Purchasing want the measurement reports and what should they look like? Are both suppliers and buyers going to be measured? How about the supplier schedulers? How long should data be kept? Which of this information should be accessible by computer terminal?

Finally, Purchasing needs management tools for use once MRP II and supplier scheduling are up and running. These can include negotiation reports, purchase commitment reports, and perhaps other supporting information to allow purchasing people to be effective negotiators and buyers.

On the sample negotiation report shown in Figure 15.4, all the items in the commodity group are displayed in a descending dollar sequence. The chart shows the annual usage of each in dollars, the average weekly usage, the safety stock and lot size information, the current on-hand inventory, and the unit cost, as well as the total dollars used annually in that commodity. This gives the buyer good information to allow negotiation of annual contracts and effective management of that commodity. This negotiation information could also be shown by supplier, plant, and so on.

Figure 15.5 shows a typical purchasing commitment report. This report takes the scheduled receipts (shown by *) and the planned orders (shown by P) and translates those orders into financial terms in the week they are due from the supplier. The right-hand column indicates to the

Negotiation report by commodity code
commodity code 01 and buyer code 80

Part	Description	Safety Stock Wks.	Qty.	Lot Size Wks.	Qty.	On-Hand Invent. Wks.	Amt.	Unit Cost	Annual Usage	Avg. Wkly. Usage
896890009	FIBERGLAS	1	75	1	75	1	$767	$ 7.67	$32,704	82
896890008	FIBERGLAS		5		15		$ 0	$13.50	$16,848	24
896890006	FIBERGLAS	5	25	5	25	7	$135	$ 3.87	$ 1,006	5
				TOTAL			$902		$50,558	

Figure 15.4 Negotiation Report.

PURCHASING COMMITMENT
BY SUPPLIER
FOR WEEK ENDING 01/21/XX

DATE 01/19/XX

(*) SCHEDULED RECEIPTS
(P) PLANNED ORDERS

SUPPLIER		CURRENT & PAST DUE	1/28	2/04	2/11	2/18	2/25	NEXT 4 WEEKS	FOLLOWING 4 WEEKS	SUPPLIER TOTAL
SMITH COIL EZ	*	2,975.50	743.00	100.50	1,772.50	525.00				6,116.50
	P						575.00	6,683.00	3,199.75	10,457.75
WILSON PLASTICS FA	*	388.36	1,431.10							1,819.46
	P			907.10	908.10	1,254.27	461.21	4,655.20	3,787.37	11,973.25
P B PECK FB	*	4,880.28	6,002.00	11,851.60	10,087.80	5,281.55				38,103.23
	P			1,467.30	1,164.68	1,849.74	8,052.28	44,064.24	40,538.33	97,136.57
HARTMAN FD	*	2,193.01								2,193.01
	P							1,737.60	1,685.60	3,423.20
TODSON FE	*	5,442.90	6,550.00	4,987.50	135.05	430.00				17,545.45
	P				5,435.95	4,988.35	5,675.40	29,272.01	36,917.51	82,289.22
JAMES FF	*	3,838.85	4,215.20	1,951.00	2,731.00	1,988.40				14,724.45
	P						925.00	5,687.00	8,172.74	14,784.74
TOTAL ALL SUPPLIERS		19,718.90	18,941.30	21,265.00	22,235.08	16,317.31	15,688.89	92,099.05	94,301.30	300,566.83

Figure 15.5 Purchasing Commitment Report.

buyer the total dollars committed to each supplier over the next 13 weeks. The bottom total indicates the total dollars committed to all suppliers in a given week. This aids the buyer in managing supplier commitments, future inventory dollars, and the company's weekly requirement for cash flow to support purchases.

Many other kinds of information are also available. The challenge, in terms of implementation, is to define specifically what's needed in reports, and with what frequency the information must be presented.

DEFINING THE ORGANIZATION

A clear definition of the supplier scheduling organization is also necessary for the implementation to succeed. Following the selection of the supplier scheduling supervisor, it is necessary to establish the reporting structure of the supplier scheduling group. As stated in Chapter 6, it is preferable to have this group report to Purchasing, all things being equal. But all things are not always equal; existing organizational structures, geography, the personalities and preferences of people, and other factors may play a part in this decision.

Following this decision, job descriptions for the buyers and supplier schedulers should be developed. The responsibilities of both the supplier scheduler and buyer, as discussed in several chapters, should be clearly defined in the individual job descriptions. Finally, the supplier schedulers should be selected by Month 8 so that their purchasing education and training can start the following month.

SUPPLIER EDUCATION

MRP II, JIT, and TQC education cannot be limited to only the people employed by the company. Suppliers are key to the success of each of these programs, and therefore they need to understand the disciplines involved in education and training.

The typical company would have three different education sessions for their suppliers. First, they would educate their suppliers on MRP II and work to get valid schedules and supplier performance to the schedules. Second, they would educate their suppliers on JIT, eliminating any waste in the supply pipeline. Lastly, they would do the TQC education on defect-free product delivered to the point-of-use in the shop.

You should consider bringing suppliers into the plant for a one-day supplier education program to kick off each of the programs whenever practical. In some cases, due perhaps to geography or other factors, it may be necessary to "take the show on the road"—that is, to conduct the education day at the supplier's plant. This approach can work well, although bringing the suppliers into one's plant and showing them how it works seems to have more overall impact and generate better results. It is important to have several people present from a given supplier at the training, and the mix of people in attendance would vary by topic.

For the MRP II education, supplier attendees should include their customer service/order entry manager, the manager of the scheduling group, and an executive who can commit to working from schedules rather than purchase orders, in addition to the local salesman.

For the JIT education, the group should include Engineering and Manufacturing, and the TQC education should include the quality group from the suppliers. Supplier education is a very time-consuming effort. If you have 400 suppliers and you educate 20 at a time, you will have at least 20 sessions on each topic. If you do one supplier at a time, you will never finish. The expectation and goal is that you will educate all suppliers on MRP II, JIT, and TQC.

The supplier education process should consist of basic education on each of these areas, plus more specific training on "how-to's" in each area. In MRP II, this would cover how the supplier scheduling process works, what is expected of a supplier under a supplier scheduling concept, and how the partnership arrangement will work. In JIT, this would cover how the Kanban concept works, how the supplier schedule and Kanban relate to each other, how waste can be eliminated in the system, and what is expected of a JIT supplier. In TQC, this would cover basic TQC principles, the concept of quality at the source, the ideal of defect-free product delivered right to the point-of-use, and what is expected of a TQC supplier. Each supplier education session would have a different purpose and a different agenda. It is hard to envision how a company could combine these topics and do justice to any one of the areas covered. The agendas for the Supplier Education Day on MRP II should be developed by around Month 10, as should outlines for what will be covered in the JIT and TQC Supplier Education Days.

It is also necessary to develop a supplier education manual for each of these topics. This is a document that the suppliers can take back to their companies for use in educating their own employees. It would cover the same topics as were covered during the Supplier Education

Day, although greater detail may be necessary to aid in educating people at the supplier's plant.

The following sample agenda for a Supplier Education Day is only a guide to demonstrate what some companies are doing today. Obviously, each company will vary somewhat from this agenda depending on the size of the company, the site of the education, the level of expertise in the company, and so forth.

Supplier Open House
Sample Agenda

8:00– 8:30	Registration
8:30– 8:45	Welcome
8:45– 9:45	Company vision
9:45–10:00	Break
10:00–12:00	MRP II or JIT or TQC education
12:00– 1:00	Lunch
1:00– 3:00	Factory tour
3:00– 3:15	Break
3:15– 4:15	Expectations and supplier schedules
4:15– 4:45	Panel question-and-answer period
4:45– 5:00	Commitment from suppliers and request for action plan from suppliers

An effective Supplier Education Day might be structured in the following way. (An MRP II example is used, but the same basic structure would apply if it were a JIT or TQC Education Day.) After the welcome of attendees, a top executive of the company would deliver a company vision presentation. This would outline the company orientation and its strategies, define why the MRP II program was started, what is taking place in the marketplace to cause the need for MRP II, what the competition is doing in this area, an overview of MRP II and what it will accomplish for the company, why the attendee has been asked to participate in the session, and how top management envisions the company's future relationship with suppliers.

After a short coffee break, the next two hours would be devoted to general MRP II education, based on some of the same material (videotape plus training aids) used to educate the buyers and supplier schedulers. This session should cover the following topics: fundamentals and applications of MRP II, the mechanics of executing the purchasing plan, and how to operate MRP II in purchasing.

After lunch, a factory tour would be a good idea. This would be the buyer's chance to show the suppliers that the company is serious about MRP II and is actually using it, not just talking about it. If done correctly, this will show the suppliers that they are not participating in just another program, but that MRP II is a way of life for your entire company. If this Education Day is not held at the factory, then a slide show of what you are actually doing, led by a supplier scheduler, master scheduler, and manufacturing supervisor, can often achieve good results.

Following the afternoon break, the emphasis would shift to the expectations for the future and the supplier schedule. The discussion should cover the format of the supplier schedule, what suppliers are authorized to produce (scheduled receipts), and how they can plan raw material and capacity, capacity units of measure, and other such areas. This would also be a good time to verify lead times, lot sizes, minimum order quantity, maximum weekly supplier capacities on each item number, supplier plans for vacation shutdowns, and so on. Time should be set aside to discuss the day of the week that the supplier schedule would be sent to the supplier, cutoff dates for the previous week's receipts, and the need for feedback on past-due orders.

The principle of "Silence is approval" should also be stressed during this time. Suppliers must understand that they will be held accountable for delivery on the dates shown on the supplier schedule, and it is imperative that they communicate in advance if they will miss a delivery date.

A quick review of the supplier manual should also be done during the after-break session. Since this is the document that suppliers will use to educate their people back home, they must have an overview of what is in it. The manual should cover MRP, how the supplier schedule works, and what is required of suppliers.

Some time should also be provided for questions from the suppliers. Questions are best addressed by a panel consisting of the day's presenters, as well as the top company executive who described the company vision.

The Supplier Education Day should be completed with a commitment from the supplier to work to the supplier schedule. After that commitment, the buyer and supplier need to work together to develop an action plan to bring performance on delivery and quality up to acceptable levels. Suppliers must realize that they will now be receiving valid need dates, and therefore that they must ship high-quality parts on time consistently. The action plan should spell out the supplier's current performance levels on delivery and quality. A timetable should be developed that shows when the supplier would be at acceptable levels of performance in the areas of delivery and quality to support the supplier scheduling program.

After designing the supplier education program, it is time to test it with a pilot exercise. This first trial run of supplier education should occur by Month 11. Month 12 would be spent educating the 20 percent of the suppliers who represent 80 percent of the dollars spent on purchased items.

PILOT AND CUTOVER

With the training complete, it is time to implement supplier scheduling, JIT, or TQC. It's usually best to start with a pilot exercise with a selected supplier to be sure the program is working correctly before cutting over a large number of suppliers.

The best choice for a pilot is a key supplier who is fairly close geographically, well organized, well run, and willing to work with you to develop and perfect your supplier education program for supplier scheduling, JIT, or TQC. This key supplier should be selected by Month 10 and, as said earlier, educated by around Month 11. This will give Purchasing a chance to get feedback on the first Supplier Education Day from the pilot supplier and make changes before educating other suppliers.

The actual pilot with the key supplier starts around Month 12 and normally lasts for three or four weeks (longer if the pilot is not working properly—in that case, stop and correct the problem before going any further). Based on the feedback from the pilot supplier, fine-tuning of the supplier scheduling system, the JIT Kanban pilot, or the TQC program occurs during the pilot period. The measurement reports should also be piloted with the key supplier at the same time.

Bear in mind that suppliers will not automatically become perfect the minute they start to receive their supplier schedules or Kanban mechanism. Initially, they will still have quality and delivery problems. The last thing a company needs when cutting over onto supplier scheduling or JIT is to have serious stock-outs on purchased items and to shut down production. Therefore, it is critical that Purchasing work closely with the suppliers during and after the pilot phase to quickly resolve any problems that do occur. In this way, the supplier scheduling concept has a good chance of succeeding.

It is often a good idea during pilot and cutover to make use of safety stock and/or safety time to protect against supplier problems. Then, as supplier performance improves, these cushions can be removed. Remember priority number one when implementing supplier scheduling: Run the business.

The 20 percent of the suppliers who represent 80 percent of the dollars spent on purchases should be cut over to supplier scheduling beginning around Month 13. During Months 13 and 14, you should be able to begin seeing the improved results of having the pilot supplier and the larger suppliers on the system. By this time, better on-time delivery, lower inventory, reduced lead times, and so on, should start to appear. If these results are not occurring, something is wrong, either with the supplier schedule itself or with the education program. Again, should this happen, go no further—fix what is wrong first.

When you begin to see some results, you can begin to cut over the 80 percent of the suppliers who represent the last 20 percent of the dollars spent on production items. This cutover would occur around Month 15, with all production items ideally on supplier scheduling by Month 18.

During Months 16 through 18, companies should be measuring results with all suppliers. They should determine which suppliers are not improving their performance on delivery and quality during the first three months, and provide these suppliers with follow-up education. Goals for all of the suppliers should be established on delivery and quality, and action plans should be established to get them up to acceptable levels of performance. The supplier should be in agreement with these goals and action plans and commit to them in writing.

MRO ITEMS

With all the production items on supplier scheduling by around Month 18, Maintenance, Repair, and Operating (MRO) items can be cut over during Months 19 through 24. (See Figure 15.6.)

The detailed plans to add MRO items to the supplier scheduling system should be established by Month 19. Operating supplies can be added to the bills of material by Month 20, with supplier scheduling of these supplies starting in Month 21. Bills of material for preventive maintenance items could be developed during Month 22, and the preventive maintenance schedule structured in such a way that it becomes, in effect, the master production schedule for maintenance. Supplier scheduling of preventive maintenance parts could then start in Month 23.

The balance of the items the company buys, such as office supplies and repair parts, could be added during Months 23 and 24. Part numbers would have to be established for all the remaining items, along with inventory locations. Inventory balances should be verified. Also during

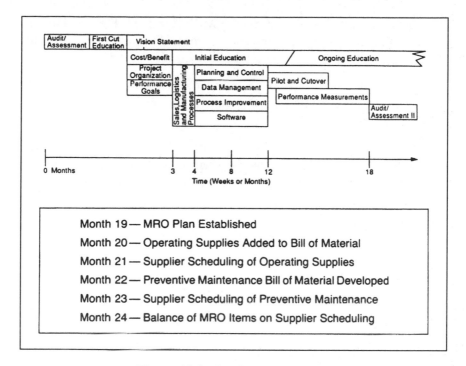

Figure 15.6   Implementation Plan.

this time, it is necessary to establish the desired minimum on-hand inventory and forecasted usage for each item and load them into the system. Supplier scheduling of those items could then begin.

Given this schedule, by the end of Month 24, all production and MRO items would be supplier scheduled with either a supplier schedule or a Kanban mechanism, or under a TQC program.

SUMMARY

- Without proper education, MRP II and JIT/TQC will not be as successful and will not generate their true benefits.

- Purchasing needs to define the formats of the supplier schedule, the measurement reports, and the management reports early enough to give systems time to program, test, and debug the programs.

- A clear definition of the supplier scheduling organization is necessary for the implementation to succeed.

- Suppliers are key to the success of MRP II and JIT/TQC, and therefore they need to understand each of these disciplines through education and training.

- It is advisable to develop a supplier education manual for each topic so the suppliers have a document to take back home and use to educate their own employees.

- It is recommended that a pilot exercise be conducted with a selected supplier to be sure the program is working correctly before cutting over a large number of suppliers.

Chapter Sixteen

Create a Spark, Ignite Change

As suggested at the end of Chapter 1, consider working on MRP II and JIT immediately. If your company is not currently operating under MRP II or employing JIT, spearhead an effort to get them under way. Perhaps consolidate your supplier base, spreading your volume over fewer suppliers. Then start more frequent deliveries, maybe shifting from once a month to once a week. Once you have gotten accustomed to this way of doing business, you can begin working with your best suppliers to improve quality, eventually eliminating inspection of incoming materials. Continue gradually until you accomplish your full range of goals and achieve excellence at your company.

Just-in-Time means one less at a time. . . .

One less supplier. Pick an item and try to go from using three suppliers to two. Once that is complete, go from two to one. Then pick like items and consolidate them under one supplier. Reduce the supplier base as much as possible.

One less hour in placing purchase orders. Pick a supplier and use a supplier schedule to eliminate the need for purchase orders. Then pick another and another until all suppliers are on schedules.

One less piece of paper. With all suppliers on schedules, look to EDI or a Kanban mechanism to eliminate the need for the printed schedule. Pick a supplier and try EDI or Kanban, then another and another until all pieces of paper are eliminated.

One less in the safety stock. Pick a part that has a good history of supplier delivery performance and reduce the inventory. Work with that supplier in a joint program to get more frequent shipments and eventually, if possible, eliminate the need for any inventory on the part.

One less day in supplier lead time. Work with the supplier to understand the elements of lead time that make up the total lead time on the part. Pick one of those elements and try to reduce it by one day, then another, until you get to the point of synchronized schedules.

One less supplier rejection. Pick an item that has a history of rejections and try to determine the underlying reasons. Eliminate one reason, then another, until there are no more rejections on that item. Then pick another item and another until all rejections are eliminated.

One less defect in quality. Once rejections have been eliminated, work to eliminate ALL defects. If you are at 1 percent defect level, 10,000 defects per million, try to lower that to 9,750, then to 9,500, and so on until all defects are eliminated and all suppliers and parts are certified for quality.

One less in the order quantity. Pick an item that has a fixed order quantity and ask why that quantity was selected. Challenge the reasons for the lot size (i.e., setup times, etc.) and reduce the order quantity as the reasons are resolved to match your internal lot sizes.

One less minute in setup at the supplier. Help your supplier understand the need for setup reductions. Then assist in taking a minute out of one setup, then another and another, until setup time is no longer an obstacle.

One less move on the shop floor. Pick an item, get the quality certified, then have the supplier deliver it to the point-of-use on the shop floor. Then do the same with another. The goal is to eliminate the need to move parts from Receiving to Quality Control to the warehouse and then to the shop floor.

Finally, one less at a time means seeking improvements over and over again in every area of purchasing and manufacturing, day after day, every day, until purchasing excellence is achieved.

Appendixes

Questions for a Good Supplier

DELIVERY

You should expect your suppliers to answer "yes" to the following questions:

1. Do you measure on-time delivery performance to your customers? What is that percentage?

2. As part of a formal program, do you document the reasons you deliver late and have action plans in place to prevent the underlying problems from recurring?

3. Are you willing to work in a JIT environment where you are responsible to plan to my supplier schedules and deliver within a window of, say, –0, +5 days of my need dates?

4. Do you have a documented policy/procedure that states that you are to notify customers in advance if their requested delivery dates will be missed?

5. Would you be willing to give me the names of two or three companies you currently service so I can verify your service levels?

Ask your suppliers the following questions to help determine whether they can meet your desired lead times.

1. Are you willing to deliver daily or weekly in small quantities as specified on the supplier schedule?

2. Are you willing to discuss the elements of lead time (raw material acquisition time, scheduling time, and actual production time) and establish stable lead times to your actual production time?

3. Are you willing to plan raw materials and capacity based on my supplier schedule?

4. What are your current lead times?

Questions for the suppliers relating to packaging and delivery include:

1. What is your standard container size per part number?

2. Would you be willing to modify package size or the number of items in my containers if required?

3. Do you deliver in your own truck or use a common carrier?

4. If you deliver in your own truck, are you willing to use the same driver every time you deliver to me and drop the material off at the point-of-use on my manufacturing floor?

5. If you use a common carrier, are you willing to specify that the carrier must use the same driver every time the items are delivered to my facility, and that the driver delivers the items directly to the point-of-use?

Questions to ask in the area of flexibility include:

1. Do you have any flexibility in your manufacturing processes or are they fixed once you start to manufacture the item?

2. At what points in the process is the flexibility built in and what are the limits of change you can handle?

3. Given that both of us will have changes in our schedules due to the demands of the marketplace, are you willing to handle last-minute changes routinely, and is there a written policy that defines how changes are handled?

PRICE

Ask your suppliers the following questions regarding pricing:

1. I'm looking for a long-term, win-win relationship; are you willing to reveal the cost elements of the materials that I buy?

2. In the same vein, are you willing to reveal your desired profit margin on the items I buy?

3. Are you willing to allow my engineering staff to assist you in reducing the cost elements of your raw materials and manufacturing process?

4. Do you currently have an established, documented value analysis/value engineering program in place, and, if so, what are the results of that program?

In terms of pricing for the long haul, ask the suppliers the following questions:

1. Are you willing to negotiate a price over time, say two years, based on my supplier schedule projections?

2. Are you willing to agree to a joint program to reduce the cost of the part over the life of the contract, with a lower price at the end of the contract period than at the beginning?

3. Are you willing to notify me in advance of all price increases, explaining what caused the increase, and work with me to either eliminate the need for the increase (i.e., alternative materials, etc.) or delay the increase?

QUALITY

Ask the following questions of suppliers to determine whether they are capable of giving you the quality and reliability you need:

1. Do you have a quality-assurance document guaranteeing me that material ready for packaging has passed final inspection and meets all of my requirements?

2. Do you have a quality-assurance document guaranteeing me that the material ready for packaging is the exact quantity I ordered?

3. Do you have a process for verifying that the shipping papers and the quantity to be shipped are the same?

4. Are special packaging and shipping requirements made available to and followed by the department personnel?

5. When a special marking, symbol, or bar-coded label is required, do you inspect it prior to packaging and shipping to ensure that it is correct?

6. Do your quality-assurance people periodically perform audits of the Packaging and Shipping Departments for conformance to approved procedures?

7. Will you guarantee that my material will not be damaged while in the packaging and shipping areas?

Typical questions to which suppliers should be able to say "yes" in the area of feedback include:

1. Do you conduct investigations to determine the cause of nonconforming materials?

2. Are corrective action plans initiated and the results of the corrective actions documented?

3. Do you routinely provide written feedback to your customers, documenting causes of problems, corrective actions, and the results of the quality-assurance program?

4. Is someone within your organization responsible for quality?

5. Do you document and file quality investigations in a manner that allows you to create a historical database for problem solving?

Some questions to ask suppliers to ensure that they are building quality into the product include:

1. Do you conduct quality audits of your sources of supply to assure you that *your* suppliers will produce only acceptable quality raw materials?

2. Do you verify that your incoming raw materials conform to the specifications?

3. Do you maintain performance history records on supplies and materials?

4. Do your in-process inspections and/or tests assure conformance to specified requirements?

5. Are your tests and/or inspections performed before and during process adjustments, machine setup, tool changes, and so on, to assure compliance to specifications?

6. Are there clearly written policies within your company stating that an operator is authorized to shut down the machine rather than make defective material?

7. Are control charts used to monitor your daily performance?

8. Do you initiate corrective action immediately when out-of-control or unstable processes are encountered?

Some questions to ask the suppliers regarding their process control are:

1. Do you perform process control planning on new products and on major changes to existing products?

2. Is quality planning a normal function of your quality management system for new products and for major changes in existing products?

3. Is the change control system governed by clearly written instructions and procedures?

4. Is it standard practice to notify all customers of changes to existing products in advance, allowing them time to evaluate the impact of the changes?

Here are some questions to ask suppliers regarding their attitude about the importance of quality:

1. Do you have an established quality organization?

2. Do you have clearly written directives that establish the responsibility, authority, and policy of your quality management system?

3. Have you established clearly defined quality goals and objectives?

4. Can you provide a case study that demonstrates your willingness to jointly resolve quality problems with your customers?

Questions you should ask suppliers regarding their full-service capabilities include:

1. Is quality planning a normal part of your quality management system for new products and for major changes in existing products?

2. Do you perform process control planning on new products and on major changes to existing products?

3. Is quality planning a normal function when you design or modify existing tooling, gauges, and equipment?

4. Can you provide a case study demonstrating your ability to take a concept, design and build tooling to actualize that concept, and then deliver quality items on time to the customer?

RESPONSIVENESS

Questions to ask your suppliers in this area of responsiveness are:

1. Who in Order Entry is assigned to my account? What is that person's telephone number?

2. Does that person understand how to read my supplier schedule and know what actions he or she is authorized to take based on the schedule?

3. Is there a customer service representative assigned to my account? What is that person's telephone number?

4. Is there a technical support person in my area assigned to my account? What is that person's telephone number?

5. Who is my quality contact if I have a problem, and what is that person's telephone number?

6. Can I have an organizational chart with telephone numbers of your company personnel?

LEAD TIME

In terms of lead times, you should be able to obtain the following information from your suppliers:

1. What are the elements of your lead time?

2. How do you schedule your suppliers and how much flexibility do they have in their lead times?

3. How long does it take to set up and actually run my items?

4. Are you willing to allow my engineers to assist you in reducing your internal setup and run times?

LOCATION

You should ask your suppliers the following questions regarding multiple locations:

1. Do you have more than one manufacturing location?

2. What is your capacity to make the items at each location?

3. Are all your plants equally automated?

4. Are any of the plants operating in a TQC/JIT mode today?

5. Do you have the ability to specify which location produces my material?

6. Who are your key subcontractors?

7. Do your subcontractors have TQC/JIT in place?

8. Can I talk to your subcontractors regarding quality, delivery, setup, and so forth?

9. How is capacity allocated by customer in your facility?

10. What other products do you produce, and would you be interested in additional business in other product lines if there is a fit between our two companies?

TECHNICAL CAPABILITIES

Questions about technical capabilities include:

1. Are you a leader in new technology, or do you wait until a new technology proves itself?

2. What is your track record for bringing on new products and product improvements on time? Give me an example.

3. What is your manufacturing strategy for the next two years in terms of new products?

4. Are you constantly looking for ways to improve the current products you manufacture? Give me an example.

5. Is Total Quality a standard operating principle of your Research and Development group?

6. Can you give me an example of where your R&D Department successfully developed a new product for a customer?

R&D

You will want to determine your suppliers' development commitment with questions such as:

1. What is your R&D budget as a percentage of your sales?

2. How many people have you assigned to R&D?

3. If necessary, are you willing to allocate development money to my account?

4. Are you willing to work on joint development projects with your customers? Give me an example.

FINANCIAL AND BUSINESS STABILITY

In terms of financial and business stability, you should ask your suppliers questions such as:

1. Can you supply me with copies of your annual reports for the last two or three years?

2. Can you give me an indication of your cash flow, receivables, and so on, to indicate your current financial stability?

3. Is there a high turnover in your management team or an expected change in ownership that could affect our long-term relationship?

SUPPLY CHAIN MANAGEMENT

You will want to determine your suppliers' willingness to participate in SCM by asking questions such as:

1. Are you willing to share information openly with all the members of the supply chain?

2. Are you willing to participate on cross-company teams to explore ways to add product and service combinations that add value to the end product?

3. Are you willing to share cost reductions with other members of the supply team?

4. Are you willing to integrate your supply and demand planning with the entire supply chain?

Purchasing Survey Results

BACKGROUND

A survey was taken of over 100 Class A and B users of MRP II (see Appendix C for a definition of Class A, B, C, and D), focusing on the results they had obtained in the area of purchasing. The respondents were primarily purchasing professionals, MRP II project leaders, and production and inventory control managers. This Appendix is a summary of the findings of that survey.

The businesses studied represent many different industries. The products they make include: floor sweepers, equipment for the telecommunications industry, cosmetics, pumps, diesel engines, hand tools, valves, forgings, pipe, wood kitchen cabinets, machine tools, instrumentation, trenchers, backhoes, power tools, office furniture, clothing, electronic instruments, cathode-ray tubes, autoclaves, chemical processing equipment, photocopiers, ball bearings, fabricated parts, process chemicals, and both high-volume and low-volume parts.

These companies also represent many different types of manufacturing, including make-to-order, make-to-stock, assemble-to-order, and design-to-order. Many of the companies surveyed are leaders in their respective industries; all are located in North America.

The sizes of the companies surveyed vary widely. Their annual volume of purchases ranges from a low of $4 million to over $1 billion. Eighty percent of them purchase less than $30 million worth of goods annually.

RESULTS

Organization

Fifty-five percent of the companies surveyed have one or more persons in the role of supplier scheduler—in other words, someone other than the buyer who schedules the suppliers. Thirty percent of the companies have buyer/planners—one person who does the MRP planning, the supplier scheduling, and the buying. Fifteen percent still cling to the traditional requisition method of scheduling, in which a material planner writes out a requisition based on the MRP output and the buyer converts it into a hard-copy purchase order.

Schedules

Of those respondents who do some form of supplier scheduling, 78 percent use a supplier schedule while 22 percent simply give their computer-generated MRP output sheets directly to the suppliers.

Interestingly, several companies reported some form of computer-to-computer linkage (Electronic Data Interchange) with their suppliers. One of those companies has placed CRTs in the offices of its key suppliers, allowing them to look directly into the company's MRP system at the requirements and orders.

Reporting Structure

The respondents were split neatly down the middle on the reporting structure of the supplier scheduling organization. In almost 50 percent of the companies, the supplier schedulers report to purchasing, and in the other nearly 50 percent, they report to production and inventory control. There was only one exception to the 50–50 split. In that company, the supplier scheduling group reports directly to the materials manager, who is on an equal level with the purchasing manager and production and inventory control manager.

Supplier Scheduler/Buyer Ratio

While the number of parts per buyer or per supplier scheduler varied widely from case to case, the average company surveyed reported one supplier scheduler as being able to support two buyers.

BENEFITS ACHIEVED

The benefits achieved in the Class A/B MRP II users' purchasing departments are impressive. The survey was designed to quantify benefits in four areas: on-time delivery, lead time reduction, inventory reduction, and purchase cost reduction. Respondents also commented on other areas of benefit, but these comments have not been quantified in any way.

On-Time Delivery

The keys to success in this area can be boiled down to a supplier schedule with valid need dates and intensive supplier education. On-time delivery was measured by comparing due dates with actual delivery dates. Companies using supplier schedules and supplier schedulers averaged an on-time supplier performance level of 97 percent. Those companies that used Kanban with supplier schedules averaged 99 percent on-time.

A few of the surveyed companies gave their MRP output directly to the suppliers. Those companies averaged 93 percent on-time service from their suppliers. One theory is that the 4 percent difference may be due to a small amount of misunderstanding by the suppliers' personnel on how to interpret the MRP reports.

Those companies that continue to use hard-copy purchase orders averaged on-time supplier delivery performance of only 76 percent. Apparently from the suppliers' viewpoint, where traditional purchase orders are used, there is not a great difference between their customers' old systems and MRP II. Therefore, supplier performance does not improve significantly until their customers change to supplier scheduling.

The typical respondent stated that 30 to 40 percent of the open purchase orders were past due prior to MRP II implementation. That figure was reduced to between 15 and 20 percent after one month of MRP II because purchasing "rescheduled-out" all the past due orders that weren't needed yet. Five months later, through a combination of supplier education and valid schedules, the level of past due orders was reduced to 3 percent.

Another way to look at supplier delivery performance is in terms of items short in any one week. Users typically cut purchased item shortages from 30 to 50 parts in a week to 4 or 5. As one buyer stated: "We cut the anticipated delay report from two pages to less than half a page, and we know about all those shortages in advance from our suppliers." Many companies also commented that particular commodities that had been troublesome before were no longer problems.

Lead Time Reduction

Most companies surveyed saw a dramatic decrease in lead times. Many stated they had no lead times greater than eight weeks. One design-to-order company that is buying capacity from its sand casting supplier has cut the lead time from 26 weeks to 8 weeks and eliminated shortages. They forecast capacity requirements to their suppliers at the eight-week window but show the actual configuration one week out, when the supplier is actually packing the sand in the mold box.

Inventory Reduction

The surveyed companies also reported significant inventory reductions made possible by MRP II. One company was able to cut its on-hand steel inventory from 13 weeks to 5 days, while simultaneously eliminating steel shortages. Another turned purchased item inventory 37 times a year, while a clothing manufacturer increased inventory turns on their purchased yarn from 50 to 125 turns. Responses of eight or more inventory turns per year on purchased items were very common. The average inventory reduction reported was 30 percent.

Purchase Cost Reduction

Companies with a supplier schedule and a supplier scheduler saw an average 13 percent annual reduction in the cost of purchased material. Those with a buyer/planner saw an average 7 percent annual cost reduction. One theory is that the difference in benefits is the result of the time the buyer/planner has to devote to material requirements planning and scheduling. Those companies still using hard-copy purchase orders saw a 2 percent annual cost reduction.

Comments

In general, the respondents were very positive about the use of MRP II in purchasing. Overwhelmingly, they reported they had better information and greater control over their departments than ever before. They knew exactly what was going to be built weekly on every product the company manufactured (through the master production schedule) and what the requirements were on every item they purchased (through MRP).

The only negative MRP II comments uncovered in the survey involved "nervousness" in the master production schedule. Several purchasing managers noted a stable master schedule is critical to purchasing and that their companies sometimes violated the established master schedule policies and time fences. However, all agreed that if the master schedule policies were followed, and all changes inside the firm time fences were reviewed with Purchasing first, this nervousness would be minimized.

One purchasing manager summed up the differences MRP II has made in his work life by saying: "If I know what I need to support manufacturing, I have a reasonable chance to get it. Before, I never knew, so we were always fire fighting. I would never work for another company that didn't have an MRP II system."

CONCLUSIONS

The results achieved in each of the four areas studied did not vary with the size or purchasing power of the company. Therefore, the effectiveness of supplier scheduling does not appear to be dependent on clout, but to be a function of the desire and the understanding of the people in the Purchasing Department.

One additional conclusion drawn from this study is that companies that stay with the traditional way of purchasing (hard-copy purchase orders) do not increase their on-time delivery performance dramatically and see little or no cost reduction.

Overall, the benefits of effective supplier scheduling include:

- Improved credibility with the plant and suppliers because everyone is working to the same set of numbers.
- Reduced inventory without reducing service to the plant. The right items can be brought in as needed.
- The ability to get planning data to the suppliers. The supplier schedule tells the supplier everything the customer knows about future requirements, both short-term and out beyond the supplier's quoted lead time.
- Ninety-five percent or better on-time supplier delivery performance.
- Buyers who can now spend time on value analysis, negotiation, and supplier problems, not expediting.
- Reduced floor expediting because manufacturing supervisors have the correct items when they need them.
- Reduced supplier lead times.
- A more motivated, professional Purchasing Department.

The ABCD Checklist

INTRODUCTION

PERSPECTIVE

Are we doing the right things? How well are we doing them? Are we on the right track to world-class performance? It's hard to imagine three more valuable questions for all managers to ask frequently. The answers reflect current levels of performance and reveal significant opportunities for improvement.

Finding the right answers, however, requires many more questions. This checklist raises those questions. As such, it's an important tool in appraising a company's effectiveness in utilizing the many technologies available to manufacturing companies today.

A good checklist does more than tell you where you are today—it helps managers focus on what's required to become more competitive and achieve world-class levels of performance. Periodic use of the checklist generates a consistent means of assessing progress. In addition, it identifies problems early, which allows the correction process to start immediately. Further, by comparing performance against established benchmarks, people are motivated to work in a more effective manner.

EVOLUTION

Ollie Wight created our first ABCD Checklist in 1977. It consisted of 20 items designed to evaluate a Manufacturing Resource Planning system, MRP II. The items were grouped into three categories: technical, to determine whether the design was proper; data accuracy, to determine how reliable the information was; and operational, to determine how well MRP II was understood and used within the company.

A few years later the original list was expanded to 25 items. This checklist is the accepted industry standard for measuring MRP II. By responding to these items, a person can objectively grade a company's use of MRP II into one of four categories: A, B, C, or D. These levels of potential have served as challenging goals, especially to reach the Class A level.

No Longer Just MRP II

During the 1980s, the third generation of the ABCD Checklist was created, which was broader in scope. It not only covered operational planning and control processes—MRP II and Distribution Resource Planning (DRP)—but also contained items in the important areas of strategic planning and Continuous Improvement. The third edition also contained entries for both the overview level, to facilitate review by the general manager and staff, and the detail level, to serve as a tool for operating personnel to diagnose and correct deficiencies.

The Fourth Edition of the ABCD Checklist

This new checklist is significantly more comprehensive than its predecessors. For this reason, we've organized the checklist into chapters based on basic business functions. These are:

- Strategic Planning Processes.

- People/Team Processes.

- Total Quality and Continuous Improvement Processes.

- New Product Development Processes.

- Planning and Control Processes.

It would be an overwhelming task for most companies to attack simultaneously all of these business processes and their underlying technologies. Implementing all of these major changes at the same time would call for too much work to be done by people who already have full-time jobs in running the business.

There are significant risks in trying to do too much at one time: Nothing gets done well, people burn out, and competitive advantage is lost.

The chapter organization of the new checklist allows a company to choose one or several of these basic business processes and concentrate its energies on that choice. An organization can choose to pursue as much, or as little, as it feels capable of pursuing.

Qualitative Characteristics and Overview Items

Each chapter begins with brief Qualitative Characteristics of the various levels of performance—Class A, B, C, and D—for the processes in question. Then listed are the Overview items, which provide an executive summary. They're designed to allow executives to evaluate whether necessary processes exist and, if so, how well they are being used.

Detail Items

Following this executive summary, the Detail Items are then spelled out, grouped under their respective Overview Items. These Detail Items provide additional information, guidance, and means for assessment, and make up the main body of the checklist. They're designed to provide operating managers with a tool for assessing the significant characteristics of each process, checking the vital how-to's of each process, and analyzing in greater detail how well the processes are being used. For most of the Overview Items, several Detail Items are listed that will help determine your position on the scale for each Overview Item. A few Overview Items, however, have no Detail Items, and these are noted in the text with an asterisk (*).

Duplication of Entries

This checklist covers multiple technologies, and there's sometimes overlap from one to another. For example, many of the Overview and Detail Items involved in effective People/Team Processes are necessary for Total Quality and Continuous Improvement Processes. Therefore, in some cases, it's been necessary to include the same items in more than one chapter. These have been noted in the text with a dagger (†).

Scoring of Responses

In prior editions of the checklist, responses were limited to "yes" or "no" (or, where appropriate, "not applicable").

The new checklist, however, enables responses to be made on a scale of 0 (Not Doing) to 4 (Excellent). This helps in identifying what's been done and what remains to be done, and can serve as an impetus for Continuous Improvement.

OBJECTIVE

Our objective in publishing the ABCD Checklist is to help companies become the best they can be. We hope you find this tool helps you to ask the right questions and determine the right answers to achieve absolute world-class performance, to become truly excellent in all operational aspects of the business. If so, then we have indeed produced a Class A product.

> Walter E. Goddard
> President
> The Oliver Wight Companies

HOW TO USE THE CHECKLIST

The best way to use the checklist is as a vision of what could exist in your company, and pursue it aggressively, systematically, and relentlessly. Companies using the checklist in this way are using it effectively, and are achieving the potential of their organization.

Not all companies use the ABCD Checklist this way. Some companies use the checklist merely as a results indicator in the later stages of an implementation program. While beneficial, this does little to ensure continuing improvement.

For this reason, we recommend the following steps to enable your company to use the checklist to achieve better results both in the short term and on a sustained basis in the future.

Performance Improvement Process

1. Assess current status.

2. Establish goals and objectives.

3. Tailor the checklist to your company's immediate needs.

4. Develop action plans.

5. Measure progress.

6. Conduct monthly management reviews.

With the ABCD Checklist, the performance improvement process begins with an assessment of the company's current strengths and weaknesses. Many companies start by answering the questions that pertain to their areas of focus. If planning and control systems are an issue for your company, then you might focus on only this chapter. It's not necessary to answer the items in all five chapters. On the other hand, you may choose to address all five chapters to get an overall assessment of the situation in your company. However you choose to use the checklist, remember to answer *all* the questions in each chapter that you select. The only exception to this is when the items are not applicable to your business.

Most companies meet in groups of 10 to 20 people to discuss the questions in the checklist. The groups allow for discussion and the comparing of differences. If one person feels the master production schedule is well managed but others can identify specific situations when poorly thought-out changes have been made, then a healthy discussion will take place. It's important to have several levels of management take part in these discussions, normally in several groups. It's typical for things to look better when viewed from the top of the organization.

There are a few prerequisites for these discussions to be useful. The first is that the participants must be knowledgeable. This means being familiar with the terms and techniques that are referenced and having an adequate understanding as to why the processes are important for the company to operate at a very high standard.

Second, it assumes that the answers will come from people of "good intentions." Knowledgeable people who are sincerely attempting to be objective can avoid seeing the world through rose-colored glasses or being overly critical to the extent that any minor imperfection leads to a negative response.

No matter how well phrased the items in this checklist may be, we recognize that degrees of interpretation are required to answer them. We also realize that a significant element of judgment is needed before answering many items. The combination of interpretation and judgment will, hopefully, lead to healthy internal discussion. The checklist will be productive if companies use it to review why these processes are important, what each process consists of, how the process can contribute to improvements, and how to accomplish these improvements.

SCORING THE RESULTS

The responses to both Overview and Detail Items are scored on a range from "Excellent" to "Not Doing," with three intermediate points. To determine where your performance falls on the range, use the following table as a guide.

Excellent
4 points

Highest expected level of results from performing this activity is achieved.

Very Good
3 points

Company is fully performing this activity and has achieved original goals associated with it.

Fair
2 points

Most of the processes and tools are in place, but company is not fully utilizing the processes and/or not getting the desired results.

Poor
1 point

People, processes, data, and/or systems are not at the minimum prescribed level, resulting in little, if any, benefit.

Not Doing
0 points

This activity is required but currently not being performed.

This method of scoring was chosen for the following reasons: It recognizes the work people have done, even though the company may not yet be at the "Excellent" level; it indicates where, and how much, additional work is required to achieve Class A results; it provides a means for Continuous Improvement—even at the Class A level, there is still room for improvement.

Most people answer the detail questions first, then use this information as a guide for answering the overview questions.

It's important to point out that the score for the overview questions is not an average of the scores for the detail questions. The detail questions are designed to help in determining the score for the overview question, but not all questions are of equal importance.

CALCULATING THE LETTER GRADE

Once the Overview Items have been answered, complete the process of determining the letter grade for the chapter by averaging the numerical scores for the Overview Items.

- Average greater than 3.5 means that you are at the Class A level for that set of business processes.

- Average between 2.5 and 3.49 qualifies for Class B level.

- Average between 1.5 and 2.49 means Class C.

- Average less than 1.5 indicates a Class D level.

Moreover, before any company can be rated with confidence, there should be *at least three months of sustained performance.* As we all know, there are periods when everything appears to be working well, but it does not necessarily mean that the company has implemented the right set of tools or has learned to manage effectively using them. A single point in time is not sufficient to arrive at a firm conclusion.

Even a Class A rating in a particular set of business processes, however, should not be interpreted as achieving full utilization of your potential. A company achieving a Class A level of performance can still get better.

For example, if the company has achieved a Class A level of excellence in New Product Development Processes, there are obviously other business functions in which Class A can be attained. In addition, achieving Class A in New Product Development Processes doesn't mean there is no room for improvement, even in that area.

Many companies take pride in attaining a Class A level and then use this accomplishment as inspiration for further improvements. In fact, all of the companies who have attained the Class A level of performance tend to be very self-critical. They continue to see what remains and what can be done, and are aggressively pushing forward.

"I know we can get a lot better and must."

"The competition is tough, but so are we."

"The emphasis in our business is to give the customer what it wants, when it wants it, with continually lower lead times and excellent quality."

These are quotes from companies that are remarkably good today, but will be even better tomorrow.

STEPS FOR OPERATIONAL EXCELLENCE

Establish Goals and Objectives

The next critically important step is to establish the goals and objectives based on the assessment. These goals lead to accountabilities for the areas that need improvement. Someone (or several people) would be assigned the accountability for meeting the goals and objectives in the planned time frame for each task in the action plan.

To prevent backsliding in areas where the assessment has shown good results, one person (or several people) would be assigned the accountability for maintaining the current level of performance on each of these items.

Tailor the Checklist to Your Company's Immediate Needs

Some companies tackle a number of areas for improvement simultaneously, while others go one step at a time. It used to be the norm that companies would start with one business function, for example, quality. Once they had made significant progress in that area, they would take on another initiative, perhaps Planning and Control Processes. Today the competitive pressures are such that many companies cannot afford to implement the new competitive tools one step at a time. Many companies are implementing several different business functions at once. For example, a number of companies have initiatives in progress on Planning and Control, Total Quality, and Continuous Improvement. Taking on this much work challenges a company's ability to manage change and puts significant strain on its resources. But the results are happening, and in less time than would be required if the different business functions were improved one at a time.

The new ABCD Checklist supports the implementation of one or many initiatives. You may choose to focus your implementation on one business function or several. When this implementation work is complete, one or more additional areas would be selected for implementation. By organizing the checklist into chapters, you can select one or several chapters to include in your current implementation plans.

In addition, we have created a database version of the checklist for personal computers. The database capabilities of this format allow a company to tailor the checklist to its implementation activities, creating a subset of the checklist containing the items being actively worked for improvement, and focusing attention on these items. In addition, the checklist software also includes a number of powerful tailoring and project management capabilities. These would be used to record the accountabilities, milestones, and target and actual performance levels for each item.

Develop Action Plans

With the goals established, the subset of activities defined, and the accountabilities in place, each person with specific accountabilities must now develop action plans for implementation. How are the goals to be achieved, what needs to be done to improve our ability to answer this question in the future, and what are the dates for completion and improvement? These are the questions that need to be answered in this phase of the improvement process.

Measure Progress

As progress is made, it should be recorded against the action plans created. Some questions can be measured quantitatively. For example, bill of material accuracy can be plotted, showing progress from the starting point to the agreed-upon goal. Other questions are more subjective, but still capable of measurement. An example would be surveying people's perceptions of top management's commitment to quality.

Conduct Monthly Management Reviews

Experience has shown it's important to conduct monthly reviews. The purpose is to monitor progress on currently active items and watch for slippage on established items. As with any implementation management review, the questions to ask are:

- Have the milestones been achieved?

- If not, what can be done to bring this aspect of the implementation back on schedule?

- What issues need to be resolved to continue our progress?

With these steps in mind as a method for improving the operational excellence of your organization, let's now look at the checklist.

SELECTED CHECKLIST QUESTIONS

We have only included the questions from the checklist that apply to Purchasing. The entire checklist is available from The Oliver Wight Companies at 1-800-258-3862.

Management regularly provides customer/supplier feedback and sets up opportunities for direct, face-to-face meetings between team members and customers/suppliers. These communication linkages are regularly used to identify process and product improvements.

Everyone in the organization can state who the key customers, key competitors, and key suppliers are, and can also describe what differentiates the product/service they build/support from others in the marketplace.

Top management is in routine contact with customers, suppliers, and employees.

The number of suppliers is being reduced, and single sourcing, where practical, is a stated company objective.

Just-in-Time/Total Quality Control are being encouraged throughout the supplier base.

Supplier selection is based more on the total cost of acquisition rather than on the lowest purchase price.

Long-term contracts (e.g., multiyear, life of product) are being established with the key suppliers who supply 80 percent of the purchased volume.

Purchasing by Kanban authorization, based on contractual agreement, is being aggressively pursued with an increasing number of suppliers. A significant percentage of the purchased volume is already under Kanban authorization.

Key suppliers participate in the development and design of new products.

Projections of future requirements for purchased items are shared with suppliers to ensure adequate capacity to support business requirements. These future projections extend out beyond the suppliers' quoted lead times.

Supplier are provided with output reports (e.g., supplier schedules) from the formal planning system.

Purchase order releases have been reduced or eliminated and replaced by Kanban signals for an increasing percentage of the purchased volume.

Suppliers are being certified to reduce/eliminate source inspection, receiving inspection, and count verification.

Delivery quantities are being economically reduced, resulting in more frequent deliveries of smaller quantities from suppliers.

Transportation costs from suppliers are being decreased even though delivery frequency is being increased.

Materials go directly from dock to point of use rather than from dock to stock. Central stockrooms are viewed primarily as overflow locations.

A supplier rating system has been developed and implemented, and is being used to trigger improvements in supplier performance.

Suppliers practice value analysis/value engineering techniques and make recommendations to improve quality, cost, and responsiveness for both current and new products.

Excellent / Very Good / Fair / Poor / Not Doing
4 3 2 1 0

Direct communications have been established to improve responsiveness between the company's operating departments and the suppliers' operating departments.

Valid, timely information is collected and analyzed on all products and services for external customers and significant and targeted internal customers and suppliers.

A data-and-information collection process exists, measuring all aspects of the organization's processes, customers, and suppliers. The data is focused and comprehensive. Any data and information collected has a specific purpose known by the data collectors and generators.

Objectives have been established for production and supplier defects. Performance is measured, and goals are being achieved.

Both intuition and quantitative information are used to identify areas of improvement. Benchmarking, customer requirements, process capability, and supplier requirements are regularly employed in this process.

Whenever possible, key suppliers are involved in the very early stages of new product development.

Specific programs exist to develop and maintain a list of preferred suppliers, and to specify these suppliers in the development process.

All financial systems (billing, accounts payable, cost accounting, purchasing, receiving, inventory, etc.) are fully integrated with all transaction systems.

Accounts payable, purchasing, and receiving tie to material receipt transactions.

At least 80 percent of the suppliers have been educated in MRP II and/or JIT and understand the supplier scheduling process.

Suppliers agree to plan raw material and capacity to meet the requirements displayed on the supplier schedule.

There is a clear policy statement of the respective responsibilities of the supplier scheduler and buyer, including at what point each becomes involved in problem resolution.

The supplier schedule displays planned orders and/or scheduled receipts over the planning horizon for all items provided by the supplier.

Commitment zones are established in the supplier schedule representing firm commitments, material commitments, and capacity planning commitments.

Time periods on the supplier schedule are weeks or smaller for at least the first four weeks displayed.

The supplier schedulers and/or buyers meet with production planners as frequently as required to maintain a valid schedule.

The suppliers understand the principle behind "silence is approval" and agree to notify the buyer in advance if a due date will be missed.

Supplier schedules are communicated to suppliers at least weekly.

For nonsupplier schedule items, 95 percent of purchase orders are released with full lead time.

There is a purchasing policy that states the set of criteria that defines "key" items, which are planned and scheduled through a supplier scheduling process. Typical considerations include factors such as 80 percent of purchase content, long lead times, critical items, and so on.

Accountability for supplier delivery performance has been established, and the method of measurement and the goal agreed upon. Supplier delivery performance is 95 to 100 percent of the plan.

The Mechanics of Manufacturing Resource Planning (MRP II)

SECTION 1
THE CLOSED LOOP SYSTEM

The basic logic of the closed-loop MRP II system is extremely simple. It's in every cookbook. The "bill of material" says, "Turkey stuffing takes one egg, seasoning, bread crumbs, etc." The routing says, "Put the egg and the seasoning in a blender." The blender is the work center. The master schedule is Thanksgiving.

But, in manufacturing, there is a lot more volume and a lot more change. There isn't just one product. There are many. The lead times aren't as short as going to the corner store. The work centers are busy rather than waiting for work—because some of them cost a third of a million dollars or more—and it simply is not wise economically to let them sit idle and to have excess capacity. In addition, the sales department will undoubtedly change the date of Thanksgiving several times before it actually arrives! And this isn't through perversity. This is because the customers want and need some things earlier or later.

The volume of activity in manufacturing is monumentally high; something is happening all the time. And change is the norm, not the exception.

243

But the point is that the *logic* of MRP II is very straightforward indeed. Figure D.1 shows the closed-loop system.

The production plan is the *rate* of production for a product family typically expressed in units like, "We want to produce 1,100 Model 30 pumps per week." The production plan is made by taking into account current inventory, deciding whether inventory needs to go up or down during the planning period, projecting the sales forecast, and determining the rate of production required to maintain, raise, or lower the inventory level. For a make-to-order product, as opposed to a make-to-stock product, the "order backlog" rather than the inventory is the starting point for the production plan.

Figure D.2 shows a typical production plan. Figure D.3 shows a business plan which is simply an extension of the production plan into dollars. The complete business plan in a manufacturing company will include research and development and other expenses not directly related to production and purchases. But the core of any business plan in a manufacturing enterprise is the production plan. With MRP II, the pro-

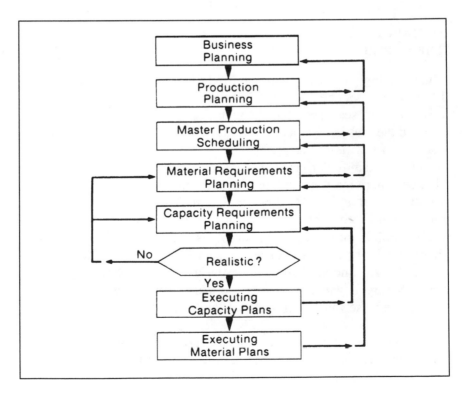

Figure D.1   MRP II.

Month Ending		Sales (thousands)	Production (thousands)	Inventory (thousands)
3/31	Plan			
	Actual			60
4/30	Plan	30	35	65
	Actual	25	36	71
6/30	Plan	30	35	75
	Actual			

Figure D.2 Production Plan.

duction plan and business plan are interdependent and, as the production plan is updated, it is extended into dollars to show it in the common denominator of business—money.

The MRP II system then takes a master schedule ("What are we going to make?"), "explodes" this through the bill of material ("What does it take to make it?"), and compares this with the inventory on hand and on order ("What do we have?") to determine material requirements ("What do we have to get?").

This fundamental material requirements planning (MRP) logic is shown in Figure D.4. Figure D.5 shows the bill of material. For this example, a small gasoline engine for a moped is the product being manufactured. The bill of material shown in Figure D.5 is what's known as an "indented bill of material." This simply means that the

Month Ending		Sales (thousands)	Production (thousands)	Inventory (thousands)
3/31	Plan			
	Actual			6,000
4/30	Plan	3,000	3,500	6,500
	Actual	2,500	3,600	7,100
5/31	Plan	3,000	3,500	7,000
	Actual	3,800	3,200	6,500
6/30	Plan	3,000	3,500	7,500
	Actual	3,200	3,700	7,000
12/31	Plan	3,000	3,500	10,500
	Actual			

Figure D.3 Business Plan.

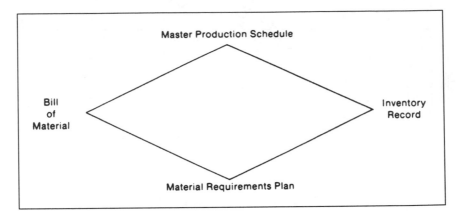

Figure D.4   MRP Logic.

Part Number	
87502	Cylinder Head
94411	Crankshaft
94097	Piston Assembly
91776	Piston
84340	Wristpin
81111	Connecting Rod—Top Half
27418	Connecting Rod—Bottom Half
81743	Piston Rings Compression (2)
96652	Piston Ring Oil
20418	Bearing Halves (2)
59263	Lock Bolts (2)
43304	Crankcase Half Right
28079	Crankcase Half Left
80021	Locater Pins (2)

Figure D.5   Moped Engine Bill of Material.

highest-level items in the bill of material are shown farthest left. For example, the piston assembly components are "indented" to the right to indicate that they go into that assembly. Therefore, in this example, they are at "level 2."

A bill of material "in reverse" is called a "where-used" list. It would say, for example, that the locating pins go into the crankcase half-left, which goes into the engine.

Figure D.6 shows a master schedule for engines. In a make-to-stock company, the master schedule would be very similar, but it would take into account the inventory on hand.

SECTION 2
MATERIAL REQUIREMENTS PLANNING (MRP)

Figure D.7 shows the material requirements plan for the crankcase half-left and also for the locator pin that goes into the crankcase half-left. The projected gross requirements come from the master schedule plus any service parts requirements. "Scheduled receipts" are the orders that are already in production or out with the vendors. The projected available balance takes the on-hand figure, subtracts requirements from it, and adds scheduled receipts to it. (In Figure D.7, the starting on-hand balance is 120 for the crankcase half-left.) This calculation projects future inventory balances to indicate when material needs to be ordered or rescheduled.

The material on hand and on order subtracted from the gross requirements yields "net requirements" (60 in Week 8 for the crankcase half-left in Figure D.8). This is the amount that is actually needed to cover requirements. When the net requirements are converted to lot sizes and backed off over the lead time, they are called "planned order releases."

The "planned order releases" at one level in the product structure—in this case 200 "crankcase half-left"—become the projected gross requirements at the lower level. The 200-unit planned order release in period four for the crankcase half-left becomes a projected gross requirement of 400 locater pins in period four since there are two locater pins per crankcase half-left.

Master Production Schedule
Engines

	Week							
	1	2	3	4	5	6	7	8
Master Schedule	80	0	100	0	0	120	0	120
Actual Demand	40	40	30	30	30	40	40	20
Available to Promise	0	0	10	0	0	40	0	100

Figure D.6   Master Production Schedule.

**Material Requirements Plan
Crankcase Half – Left**

LEAD TIME = 4 WEEKS ORDER QUANTITY = 200	Week							
	1	2	3	4	5	6	7	8
Projected Gross Requirements		80	0	100	0	0	120	0	120
Scheduled Receipts				240					
Proj. Avail. Bal.	120	40	40	180	180	180	60	60	-60
Planned Order Release					200				

**Material Requirements Plan
Locater Pin (2 per)**

LEAD TIME = 4 WEEKS ORDER QUANTITY = 500	Week							
	1	2	3	4	5	6	7	8
Projected Gross Requirements					400				400*
Scheduled Receipts									
Proj. Avail. Bal.	430	430	430	430	30	30	30	30	-370
Planned Order Release					500				

*Requirements from Another Crankcase

Figure D.7   Material Requirements Plan.

Most MRP systems also include what is called "pegged require-ments." This is simply a way to trace where the requirements came from. For example, the pegged requirements for the locater pins would indicate that the 400 in period four came from the crankcase half-left and that the 400 in period eight came from another product. Pegged re-quirements show the quantity, the time period, and the higher level item where the requirements are coming from.

Figure D.8 shows the same crankcase half as in Figure D.7. Note, however, that now the scheduled receipt is shown in period four. This means that the due date on the shop order or the purchase order is Week 4. An MRP system would generate a reschedule message for the planner to move the scheduled receipt from Week 4 into Week 3 to cover the re-quirements in Week 3.

Note, also, that the fact that the scheduled receipt for the crankcase half needs to be rescheduled does not affect the requirements for locater pins. The locater pins have already been released into production for the

MRP — Rescheduling
Crankcase Half — Left

LEAD TIME = 4 WEEKS ORDER QUANTITY = 200		Week							
		1	2	3	4	5	6	7	8
Projected Gross Requirements		80	0	100	0	0	120	0	120
Scheduled Receipts					240				
Proj. Avail. Bal.	120	40	40	-60	180	180	60	60	-60
Planned Order Release					200				

MRP — Locater Pin (2 Per)

LEAD TIME = 4 WEEKS ORDER QUANTITY = 500		Week							
		1	2	3	4	5	6	7	8
Projected Gross Requirements					400				400*
Scheduled Receipts									
Proj. Avail. Bal.	430	430	430	430	30	30	30	30	-370
Planned Order Release					500				

*Requirements from Another Crankcase

Figure D.8   MRP—Rescheduling.

crankcase halves that are on order. The "requirements" for locater pins are for planned orders that have *not* been released yet.

The bill of material is the instrument for converting planned order releases at one level into projected gross requirements at a lower level. The bill of material for the crankcase half-left, for example, would show that two locater pins per crankcase half were required.

SECTION 3
CAPACITY PLANNING AND SCHEDULING

Capacity planning for the manufacturing facility follows the same general logic as the material requirements planning shown in Figure D.4. Figure D.9 shows this capacity requirements planning logic. The remaining operations on released shop orders and all of the operations on planned order releases are "exploded" through the routings (like bills of material for operations) and posted against the work centers (like an in-

Figure D.9   CRP Logic.

ventory of capacities). The result is a capacity requirements plan in standard hours by work center showing the number of standard hours required to meet the material requirements plan. This capacity requirements plan shows the capacity that will be required to execute the master schedule, and consequently, the production plan.

It's important to note that everything in an MRP II system is in "lockstep." If the capacity to meet the material requirements plan can't be obtained either through a company's own manufacturing facilities, subcontracting, or purchasing material on the outside, obviously the master schedule will have to be changed. But that is the last resort. The objective is to make the master schedule happen.

Operations scheduling involves assigning individual schedule dates to the operations on a shop order using scheduling rules. Scheduling rules would typically be similar to these:

1. Allow two days for inspection. (This is a matter of judgment.)

2. Round the standard hours up to the nearest day.

3. Allow X days for queue time.

4. Release work to stockroom one week prior to first operation.

Scheduling with a regular calendar is extremely awkward. For example, if a job was to be completed on August 31 (see Figure D.10) and the last operation—inspection—was scheduled to take two days, the previous operation would have to be completed on August 27, not August 29

Calendar

AUGUST

S	M	T	W	T	F	S
1	2	3	4	5	6	7
8	9	10	11	12	13	14
15	16	17	18	19	20	21
22	23	24	25	26	27	28
29	30	31				

Figure D.10   Calendar.

(Sunday) or August 28 (Saturday). The scheduler would have to reference the calendar continuously to avoid scheduling work on weekends, holidays, during plant vacation shutdown week, etc. Figure D.11 shows a "shop calendar" where only the working days are numbered. This allows the scheduler to do simple arithmetic like "subtract two days from day 412"; thus the previous operation is to be completed on day 410.

Shop calendars are in very common use in manufacturing companies today, but they do have drawbacks. People don't relate to these calendars as easily as they do to a regular calendar. And, of course, they are awkward in dealing with customers who don't use the same shop calendar. Therefore, the shop calendar dates must, once again, be translated back to regular calendar dates. There is a simple solution to this problem with today's computers. A shop calendar can be put in the computer and the computer can do the scheduling using the shop calendar, but print the schedule dates out in regular calendar days. If a company has a shop calendar, there is no reason to discontinue using it if people are used to it. On the other hand, there is no need to introduce the shop calendar today when the computer can do the conversion.

Figure D.12 shows a shop order for the locater pin. This will be used as an example of operations scheduling and, in this example, a shop cal-

Figure D.11   Calendar.

endar *will* be used in order to make the arithmetic of scheduling clear. The due date is day 412 and that is determined, in the case of the locater pin that goes into the crankcase half-left, from the material requirements plan.

Operations scheduling works back from this need date to put scheduled finish dates on each operation using scheduling rules like those discussed above. Inspection will be allowed two days. Thus, finish turn must be completed on day 410. It is assumed that the work center file indicates that there are two shifts working in work center 1204 (two shifts at 8 hours apiece equals 16 hours); thus the 27.3 hours required for finish turn will take two days. Planned queue time in this example is assumed to be two days ahead of finish turn. Rough turn must be completed four days earlier than the finish turn must be completed, and its scheduled finish date, therefore, is day 406. The standard hours are calculated by multiplying the quantity by the time per piece and, in this case, adding in the setup time. Where machine operators do not set up their own machines, it might make sense to keep this separate.

It is important to recognize that Figure D.12 shows the information that would be in the computer. *The finish dates would not appear on the shop paperwork that was released to the factory.* The reason is that ma-

Shop Order NN. 18447
Part No. 80021 – Locater Pin
Quant. 500   Due: 412   Release 395

Oper.	Dept.	Work Center	Desc.	Setup	Per Piece	Std. Hrs.	Finish
10	08	1322	Cut Off	.5	.010	5.5	402
20	32	1600	Rough Turn	1.5	.030	16.5	406
30	32	1204	Finish Turn	3.3	.048	27.3	410
40	11		Inspect				412

Figure D.12   Shop Order NN. 18447.

terial requirements planning would be constantly reviewing the need date to see if it had changed. If, for example, the left crankcase halves are scrapped because of a problem with the castings, and the best possible date to have a new lot of castings for the crankcase halves is day 422, the master schedule would be changed to indicate that. The shop order for the locater pins in the computer would be given a new finish date of 422 and operation 30 would then become 420, operation 20 would become 416, and so on.

Capacity requirements will not be posted against the work centers using the routine shown in Figure D.9. A capacity plan, as shown in Figure D.13, will be the result.

Work Center   1600

Part No.	SO No.	Qty.	Week 396-400	Week 401-405	Week 406-410	Week 411-415	Week 416-420
91762	17621	50		3.5			
80021	18447	500			16.5		

Includes Planned Orders

Total Std. Hrs.			294	201	345	210	286

Figure D.13   Capacity Requirements Plan.

This capacity plan has, of course, been cut apart to show it in the figure. It would include many more shop orders, as well as the planned order releases from MRP, in reality. The locater pins are shown here as a released shop order. (Note: there is no released shop order for locater pins in Figure D.8. It would show as a "scheduled receipt" if there were.) One of the great values of MRP is the fact that it projects "planned order releases." These planned order releases are used to:

1. Generate lower level material requirements.

2. Generate capacity requirements.

3. Determine when lower-level material—both purchased and manufactured—must be rescheduled to earlier or later dates.

This ability to see capacity requirements ahead of time is especially important to good manpower planning. Seeing the capacity requirements coming rather than seeing the backlogs of work out on the factory floor enables factory supervision to do a far better job of leveling production, resulting in less overtime, and less need to hire and lay off people on a short-term basis.

Figure D.14 shows a summary of the capacity requirements over an eight-week period. In practice, this would typically be projected over a far longer period. The summary is drawn from the capacity requirements plan illustrated in Figure D.13 which would also extend much further into the future than the five weeks shown. A typical manpower plan would extend three to six months into the future and would be calculated weekly. A "facilities plan" that would be used for determining

Capacity Requirements Summary (in Standard Hours)

Week	4-Week Total	4-Week Average	Hours	Week	4-Week Total	4-Week Average	Hours
1	294			5	286		
2	201			6	250		
3	345			7	315		
4	210	1050	263	8	257	1108	277

Figure D.14   Capacity Requirements Summary (in Standard Hours).

what new machine tools were needed would be calculated typically once every two to three months and extended three to four years into the future because of the lead time for procuring machine tools.

The most important information for a manufacturing supervisor is the average hours that he must plan to turn out. This production rate is usually calculated as a four-week average because the individual weekly hours are not particularly significant. The variations between these hours are more random than real. Figure D.13 shows one reason why this happens. The 16.5 hours for part number 80021, the locator pin, are shown in the week bracketed by days 406 to 410. Referring back to Figure D.12, it can be seen that these 16.5 hours are *actually going to be in work center 1600 Tuesday of the previous week!*

Many people have tried to develop elaborate computer load leveling systems because they were alarmed by the weekly variation in the apparent "load" shown in the capacity requirements plan. These variations are random. They are exaggerated by the fact that capacity plans are usually done in weekly time periods, and any manufacturing supervisor can attest to the fact that the hours never materialize exactly the same way they are shown on the plan. The most important thing to know is the average rate of output required so that *manpower* can be planned accordingly.

In Figure D.14, the four-week averages are 263 standard hours for the first four weeks and 277 for the second four weeks, or an average of 270 standard hours per week. Now the capacity planner must determine whether that capacity requirement can be met. The first step is to find out what the output from the work center has been over the last few weeks. This is called "demonstrated capacity." (This term was coined by David Garwood and is very useful in describing the present capacity of a work center as opposed to its potential capacity when all shifts are manned, etc.)

It is the job of the capacity planner to then determine whether or not the current capacity is sufficient. Or, what needs to be done to get the capacity to meet the plan. Or—as a last resort—to feed back information that the plan cannot be met.

If the plan cannot be met, the master schedule and, perhaps, even the production plans will have to be changed. If, for example, a company has one broach and it is the only one of its type available because it was made specifically for this company, it could well become a bottleneck. If the capacity plan indicates that more hours were required at the broach than could possibly be produced, the master schedule would have to be changed to reflect this.

Once again, however, it's important to emphasize that this is the *last resort*. The job of the capacity planner is to get the capacity that is needed to meet the plan. And that is an important point to emphasize. If there is any problem that exists in practice with capacity planning, it is the fact that people expect the computer to do the capacity planning rather than recognizing that all it can do is generate numbers that will be given to an intelligent, experienced person—the capacity planner—to use in working with other people to fix capacity problems.

Once it is agreed that the capacity requirements can be met, an output control report as shown in Figure D.15 is set up. Three weeks have passed since the one in the figure was made, and the actual standard hours produced (shown in the second line of the figure) are falling far short of the required standard hours at work center 1600. The deviation in the first week was 20 hours. In the second week, it was 50 hours—for a cumulative deviation of 70 hours. In the third week, it was 80 hours, giving a total cumulative deviation of 150 hours. This is a true *control* report with a plan and feedback to show where actual output In standard hours compares with the plan. It shows the deviation from the plan. The 150-hour deviation in Week 3 indicates that 150 standard hours of work required to produce material to meet the master schedule has not been completed.

The amount of tolerance around the plan has to be established. If it were determined, for example, that the company could tolerate being one half week behind schedule, the tolerance in Figure D.15 would be 135 standard hours. When the deviation exceeds 135 standard hours,

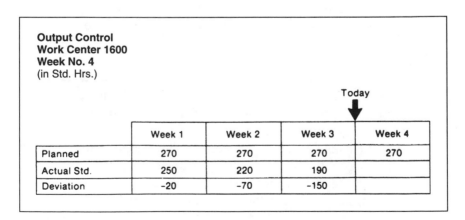

Figure D.15   Output Control.

that would require immediate attention to increase output through overtime, adding people, and so on. Whenever the planned rate in the output control report is changed, the deviation will be reset to 0.

It's a good idea to show input to a work center as well as output. That way, when a work center is behind on output because a feeding work center has not given them the work, it can be detected very quickly since the input report will show the actual input below the planned input. This is called an "input/output report."

The capacity planning and output control reports are concerned with capacity. The dispatch list shown in Figure D.16 is concerned with priority.

The dispatch list is generated daily—or as required—and goes out to the shop floor at the beginning of the day. It shows the sequence in which the jobs are to be run according to the scheduled date for the operation in that work center. The movement of jobs from work center to work center is put in to the computer so that each morning the foremen can have an up-to-date schedule that is driven by MRP. If part 80021 had been rescheduled to a new completion date of day 422 as discussed above, its priority would drop on the dispatch list because its scheduled date would now be 416. This would allow part number 44318 to be made earlier. The dispatch list gives the manufacturing supervisors the priority of jobs so that they can pick the proper job to start next. Since the dispatch list is driven by MRP, it tells the manufacturing supervisors the right sequence in which to run the jobs to do the best job of preventing predicted shortages.

Dispatch List **Work Center No. 1600**				**Day 405**
Shop Order No.	Part No.	Qty.	Scheduled Date	Std. Hours
17621	91762	50	401	3.5
18430	98340	500	405	19.2
18707	78212	1100	405	28.6
18447	80021	500	406	16.5
19712	44318	120	409	8.4
			Total Hours	**76.2**

Figure D.16 Dispatch List.

Section 4
The MRP II Output Reports

The figures thus far in this appendix represent the major operating reports that are used in an MRP II system. Referring back to Figure D.1, the functions of the production plan (Figure D.2), the master schedule (Figure D.6), the material requirements plan (Figures D.7 and D.8), and the capacity requirements plan (Figure D.13) are illustrated. The output control report (Figure D.15) is the means for monitoring output against the plan to be sure that capacity plans are being executed. The dispatch list (Figure D.16) is the report for the factory to use in executing the material plans. Supplier scheduling is the way the material requirements plans are executed with the "outside factories."

It is important to emphasize the feedback functions in a closed loop system. For example, if suppliers are not going to ship on time, they must send in an anticipated delay report as soon as they recognize that they have a problem. In the past, ship dates were not valid. The typical company had many past due purchase orders with the supplier. With MRP II—if it is properly managed—dates will represent real need dates, and, thus, it is important to feed back information as quickly as possible to indicate when these dates cannot be met. This, of course, is also true for the plant, where the anticipated delay report should be a regular part of their feedback to the closed-loop system.

The financial reports that can be a by-product of these operating reports in an MRP II system are shown in Figure D.17.

Operations	Finance
Production Plans	Business Plan
Master Schedules	Shipping budget (make-to-stock companies), transfers to inventory (make-to-stock companies)
Material Requirements Plans	Current inventories, projected consumption, purchase commitments, manufacturing schedules, and projected future inventory balances
Capacity Requirements Plans	Labor requirements by labor grade
Input/Output Reports	Standard hours of output by work center in units and dollars
Dispatch Lists	Work in process, labor reporting, efficiency reports
Supplier Schedules	Commitments by supplier

Figure D.17   Financial Reports.

We've already discussed the relationship of the production plan and business plan (see Figures D.1 and D.2). In a company where the production plans are kept current and costed out properly, they should be the basis for the business plan. Actual sales, production, and inventory can be recorded against the production plans and they can be used as *control reports*. The business plan can be kept up to date as production plans are changed. Management can see the financial impact of changes in the production plans on the business plan.

The master schedule, costed out, is the basis for *"transfers to inventory"* in a make-to-stock company or the *shipping budget* in a make-to-order company. This is, of course, the same as "production" in the production plan. Management can review the projected shipping budgets to make sure that the objectives of shipping to budget and shipping the *right* orders to the *right* customers are being properly reconciled.

Figure D.18 shows the inventory of components for a company making pumps. The inventory file is coded to show which components go into the pumps. The first column in the projected available balance shows the on-hand inventory in units extended by the cost. This is the current number of dollars of pump components in inventory. Projected gross requirements from MRP are costed out, as are scheduled receipts. The projected available balance shows the projected future stockroom inventory month by month based on the projected gross requirements derived from the master schedule which, in turn, is derived from the production plan and, in an MRP II system, represents the detailed execution of the business plan.

Costing out the material requirements plan and summarizing it by product group categories results in:

Pump Component Inventory — in $(000)

		Month			
		1	2	3	4
Projected Gross Requirements		250	250	300	300
Scheduled Receipts		250	250	270	290
Proj. Avail. Bal.	540	540	540	510	500

Figure D.18   Component Inventory.

1. On-hand inventory (in dollars) by product group.

2. How much material will be consumed (in dollars) to support the current production plans ("requirements").

3. What will have to be purchased to support the current production plans (in dollars).

4. What the projected stockroom inventory balances by product group in dollars should be for months into the future.

5. What will have to be made—this is the shop schedule that will become input to capacity planning and can be converted into labor dollars.

Comparing the actual withdrawals from stock against "requirements," the actual purchases against the plan, and the actual inventory dollars against the projected balances, tells management if the plans are really being executed—and if the *business plan* is actually being executed at the detail level.

From a manufacturing point of view, the output of material requirements planning is released shop orders and planned order releases—the shop schedule. When this is run through the capacity requirements planning section of an MRP II system, the result is the standard hours by work center, by time period, required to satisfy the master schedule and the production plans. This can be converted to labor dollars by labor grade, by time period, and by product group. From this information, management can see how many dollars of material and labor will have to be purchased by time period to support any given production plan with its particular product mix. Some companies, in order to project cash flow with greater accuracy, actually offset the due dates by the payable dates.

Costing out the open shop order file that is used to make the dispatch list yields current work in process in dollars. Labor reporting is usually tied in with dispatching and is the basis for labor efficiency reports. The supplier schedules costed out tell how much of the purchased material is due to be shipped *by supplier* by time period to support the plan.

Perhaps, the most important result of an operating system that can work is inventory valuation. When the inventory records are correct—as they have to be for an MRP system to operate—having accounting cost these records out to get the value of the inventory is a very straightforward matter.

When the operating system works, using it to drive the accounting system means that accounting has better numbers to work with than ever before. It also means that the operating system makes more sense to management than ever before because dollars are the language of business. And when the operating system and the financial system are saying the same things, the financial people and the operating people can talk the same language to management rather than presenting conflicting information.

(*Note:* Material in Appendix D is taken from *Manufacturing Resource Planning: MRP II—Unlocking America's Productivity Potential, Revised Edition,* by Oliver Wight, Copyright © 1984 by John Wiley & Sons, Inc.)

Index

263